D1563580

Cambridge Monographs on the History of Medicine

EDITORS: CHARLES WEBSTER AND CHARLES ROSENBERG

Joan Baptista Van Helmont
Reformer of science and medicine

Van Helmont's vision of the Sepulchre of Truth illustrated by Johann Jacob Sandrart (1655-98) as frontispiece to *Aufgang der Artzneykunst* (Sultzbach, 1683), the German translation of the *Works* by Christian Knorr von Rosenroth (see Bibliography). The vision is narrated in *Tumulus pestis*, 1 (*Opp.* II, p. 203; *Aufgang*, p. 530). It shows Van Helmont standing erect facing the tomb which hides the truth inside a cave filled with poisonous vapours and bats. He has come nearest to it, having superseded Galen, Avicenna, and even Paracelsus, who lie prostrate, overcome by the vapours.

Joan Baptista Van Helmont
Reformer of science and medicine

Walter Pagel

CAMBRIDGE UNIVERSITY PRESS

CAMBRIDGE

LONDON   NEW YORK   NEW ROCHELLE

MELBOURNE   SYDNEY

Edited for the series by Margaret Pelling,
Wellcome Unit for the History of Medicine,
University of Oxford

Published by the Press Syndicate of the University of Cambridge
The Pitt Building, Trumpington Street, Cambridge CB2 1RP
32 East 57th Street, New York, NY 10022, USA
296 Beaconsfield Parade, Middle Park, Melbourne 3206, Australia

First published 1982

Printed in the United States of America

Library of Congress Cataloging in Publication Data
Pagel, Walter, 1898–
Joan Baptista van Helmont: reformer of science and
medicine.
(Cambridge monographs on the history of medicine)
Bibliography: p.
Includes index.
1. Helmont, Jean Baptiste van, 1577–1644.   2. Phy-
sicians – Belgium – Biography.   3. Scientists – Belgium –
Biography.   4. Medicine – 15th–18th centuries.   I. Title.
II. Series.   [DNLM: 1. Science – Biography.   2. Medicine
– Biography. WZ 100 H4813Pj]
R524.H4P313   610'.92'4   [B]   81–24193
ISBN 0 521 24807 8   AACR2

In Memoriam
Magda Pagel-Koll (26.6.1894–22.8.1980)
Albert Pagel (3.12.1885–?1943 Auschwitz)
Charlotte Pagel (29.9.1894–?1943 Auschwitz)

CONTENTS

PREFACE

From the time of his death, almost three and a half centuries ago, Van Helmont continued to provide a living source of inspiration. It actively influenced medicine and chemistry, theory and practice, up to the early decades of the nineteenth century. Thereafter he emerged as a key figure in the history of science and medicine. Much attention has been paid to his biography and to those aspects of his work which have a modern ring. The present author has been engaged in Helmont-research for more than fifty years. Here he wishes to submit a synthesis of Van Helmont's scientific and medical discoveries and ideas with his cosmology and religious philosophy. An attempt has been made to re-situate the former in their original context and background, which were neither modern, nor scientific, nor medical. The savant is presented as an integrated whole in his own personal view of God, the world, and man – "idiocentrically" – by contrast with a selection of what strikes us as relevant and meaningful today – "nostricentrically". It demands an effort at converting oneself into a contemporary of the savant. However short this must fall of the target, it may at least help to illuminate the ways in which a discovery was made, or a concept meaningful in science and medicine today was arrived at in spite of its original religious or cosmological overtones. A similar endeavour has guided the author in research on Paracelsus and Harvey.

He records with pleasure his gratitude to the Trustees of the Wellcome Foundation; for some twenty-five years, under the original aegis of the late Sir Henry Dale, they have permanently supported his work, including the present book. At the Wellcome Institute for the History of Medicine in London much bibliographical help has been extended to him by members of the staff, notably Marianne Winder, Renate Burgess, and John Symons, as also by R. D. Gurney. Dr W. F. Bynum, continuing the tradition of the late F. N. L. Poynter, never failed in giving personal and literary advice and support. The author wishes to thank Dr Richard L. Ziemacki, History of Science Editor of Cambridge University Press, for his sustained active interest and attention. That he could carry out research at all the author owes to the late Dr Magda Pagel-Koll for her life-long and tireless dedication and cooperation.

London   WALTER PAGEL
February 1982

ABBREVIATIONS

Hirsch (ed.), *Biog. Lex. hervorr. Ärzte*:
      A. Hirsch (ed.), *Biographisches Lexikon der hervorragenden Ärzte aller Zeiten und Völker*, 6 vols. (Vienna and Leipzig, 1884–8)
Pagel, *Harvey*:
      W. Pagel, *William Harvey's Biological Ideas* (Basel and New York, 1967)
Pagel, *New Light on Harvey*:
      W. Pagel, *New Light on William Harvey* (Basel and New York, 1976)
Pagel, *Paracelsus*:
      W. Pagel, *Paracelsus. An Introduction to Philosophical Medicine in the Era of the Renaissance* (Basel and New York, 1958)
Pagel, *Van Helmont*:
      W. Pagel, *J. B. Van Helmont. Einführung in die philosophische Medizin des Barock* (Berlin, 1930)
Paracelsus. . . ed. Sudhoff:
      Theophrast von Hohenheim (Paracelsus), *Sämtliche Werke. Abteilung I: Medizinische, naturwissenschaftliche und philosophische Schriften*, ed. K. Sudhoff, 14 vols. (Munich and Berlin, 1922–33)
Partington, *History of Chemistry*:
      J. R. Partington, *A History of Chemistry*, 4 vols. (London, 1961–70)
Van Helmont, *Aufgang*:
      See Bibliography, p. 210
Van Helmont, *Opp*:
      See Bibliography, p. 210
Van Helmont, *Oriatrike*:
      See Bibliography, p. 211

1

The life of Van Helmont in the light of his endeavour

Pessimism, scepticism, and criticism are the outstanding key-notes of all of Van Helmont's works and researches. He rejected the world into which he was born because he felt rejected by it. The historical situation of his family and its social standing provide a ready explanation for this attitude. His country was in the throes of the Spanish occupation with all its attendant cultural and doctrinal convulsions. Among these could be included the presence of the Jesuits, whom Van Helmont regarded as pseudo-scientific doctrinaires who sold rhetoric and word-splitting in place of true knowledge. They had aggravated that obscuring of truth which original sin had enforced upon mankind. Complacent human reason had ousted the only true source of knowledge of the physical world: the spiritual union of man and nature. Man could now attain knowledge only by patiently knocking at nature's door, observing, weighing, and measuring, and by experimenting in a way that was informed by imagination and vision. This search had to be crowned by personal illumination through the divine mind that should inhabit the ground of the soul, untainted by dogma. The state to be desired was that "in the kiss", the *binshika* of the rabbis, through which Moses was united with God.[1] By contrast Van Helmont saw about him a world of appearances, flighty and fickle, an evil world of untruth, at best a fool's paradise. It was epitomised in university protocol, in the ornate gear on the empty heads of the professors. At the completion of his studies in all fields of academic instruction, Van Helmont "retreated into himself" in sheer disgust. He chose to take with him into his retreat the works of the great Christian mystics, Thomas à Kempis and

---

[1] Van Helmont, *Venatio scientiarum*, 51, *Opp.* p. 28. This expression is further explained below.

Johann Tauler, as guides to that "new devotion" which bore the stamp of a homeland yet free of the foreign yoke.[2]

Van Helmont was born in Brussels on 12 January 1579, the year in which Belgium lost its hope of independence. Shortly before, Don Juan, son of Charles V and victor of Lepanto, had died. He was replaced by Alexander Farnese, third duke of Parma who, unlike his predecessor, succeeded in subjugating the country. In Van Helmont's words, this year, 1580, was for all of Belgium the most calamitous in its history. It was also the year in which his father, Christian Van Helmont, state counsellor of Brabant, died. Christian's widow, Marie de Stassart, was left with a number of children, Joan Baptista being the youngest. The latter's association with the Flemish landed gentry into which he had been born was made even closer by his marriage to Margarita Van Ranst in 1609. This contract made him manorial lord (*toparcha*) of Merode, Royenborch, Oorschot, and Pellines.[3]

Fatherless, and left to his own devices, the young Van Helmont soon realised what counted for most in the corridors of academic power at Louvain University. It was as if gowns and college pro-

---

[2] *Studia authoris*, 7, *Opp.* p. 16.

[3] Van Helmont's autobiography is contained in *Studia authoris*, *Opp.* pp. 15–19. His juvenilia were edited for the first time by C. Broeckx, *Commentaire de J. B. Van Helmont sur le premier livre du Régime d'Hippocrate: Peri diaites* (Antwerp, 1849); idem, "Commentaire de J. B. Van Helmont sur un livre d'Hippocrate intitulé: peri trophes", *Annales de l'Académie archéol. belg.*, 8 (1851), 339–433, repr. Antwerp, 1851; idem, "Le premier ouvrage (Eisagoge in artem medicam a Paracelso restitutam, 1607) de J. B. Van Helmont", *Ann. Acad. archéol. belg.*, 10 (1853), 327–92 and 11 (1854), 119–91; repr. Antwerp, 1854. Broeckx also provided the main source material concerning the middle period of Van Helmont's life, particularly the proceedings taken against him by the Inquisition: "Notice sur le Manuscrit Causa J. B. Helmontii, déposé aux archives archiépiscopales de Malines", *Ann. Acad. archéol. belg.*, 9 (1852), 277–327 and 341–67, repr. Antwerp, 1852; idem, "Interrogatoires du docteur J. B. Van Helmont sur le magnétisme animal", *Ann. Acad. archéol. belg.*, 13 (1856), 306–50, repr. Antwerp, 1856; and idem, *Apologie du magnétisme animal* (Antwerp, 1869). For particulars on birth and family see G. des Marez, "L'état civil de J. B. Van Helmont", *Annales de la Société d'archéol. de Bruxelles*, 21 (1907), 107–23. Easy access to the dates and data of Van Helmont's life and the results of his scientific research is afforded by the small, but well-documented work of H. de Waele, *J. B. Van Helmont*, Collection nationale, series VII, no. 78 (Brussels, 1947). Chiefly bibliographical is A.J.J. Vandevelde, "Helmontiana", 5 parts in *Verslagen en Mededeelingen. K. Vlaamsche Academie voor Taal-en Letterkunde*, pt. 1 (1929), 453–76; pt. 2 (1929), 715–37; pt. 3 (1929), 857–79; pt. 4 (1932), 109–22; pt. 5 (1936), 339–87. See also W. Pagel, "Helmont, Johannes (Joan) Baptista Van", *Dictionary of Scientific Biography*, ed. C. C. Gillispie, Vol. VI (New York, 1972), pp. 253–9.

tocol in themselves were sufficient to confer scholarship and learning. Stunned by the low standards set, Van Helmont felt that their own naïveté and credulity had made the students a laughing-stock. Probing his own proficiency in philosophy and the attainment (*adeptus*) of truth and knowledge, he saw himself inflated by verbiage and stark naked as if he had partaken of "the apple", or clad only with skill in artificial wrangling (*artificiose altercari*). He knew nothing, and what he thought he knew was worth nothing (*nihil scirem et scirem quod nihili*). Nauseated by the general subjects taught, he turned to astronomy, logic, algebra, Euclid, and Copernicanism, but learnt from these only vain "eccentricities and yet another circumgyration of the heavens". He became bored and exasperated with astronomy, which promised but little certainty and truth.[4] It seemed hardly worth the time and labour which he had invested. On completion of the course he refused the title "Master of Arts", from a consciousness of his ignorance of anything substantial or true. On leaving the university he was promised a well-endowed canonry, but heeded St Bernard's warning against "living on the sins of the people". Instead he prayed to the Lord to make him worthy of his vocation as would please him. The Jesuits had then begun delivering lectures in philosophy, against the will of the king, the notables of the land, and the university, as well as an injunction issued by Clement VIII. Prominent among the Jesuits was Martin del Rio; the famous author of the *Disquisitionum*

---

[4] The terms in which Van Helmont's early brush with astronomy is epitomised (Van Helmont, *Studia authoris*, 4, *Opp.* p. 16) have obscured the fact that he was a Copernican. What he expresses in his autobiography is his definite disbelief in the Ptolemaic system of "eccentricities". There is also a note of general scepticism aroused by the necessity of substituting one cosmic system by one or even several new systems. Van Helmont speaks of the "vain eccentricities, or things not having one and the same Center . . . Astronomy promised . . . but very many vain things" (*Oriatrike*, p. 12). The rendering in *Aufgang* (par. 5, p. 15) is preferable: "dass es mit den Mittelpunkts-Änderungen (*Excentricitates*) ein eyteles Wesen sey; dass sich die Himmel gantz auf eine andere Art herumb wirbeln; und dass dasjenige nicht einmal der Mühe werth sey, was ich mir einbildete mit grosser Arbeit vom Himmel erlernt zu haben".

By contrast Van Helmont makes it quite clear in his *Astra necessitant* (47, see the section on "Stars as light signals" in Chapter 3 of this work) that all astrology will collapse when the Copernican view has met with general recognition, noting that so far not a few, including some great authorities, had subscribed to it, although they did not say much about it. In keeping with this, and even more explicitly, he states that the earth is *toto orbe mobilis* and has been subject to internal changes, as for example the penetration of water caused by burrowing moles (*Terra*, 17, *Opp.* p. 54).

magicarum lectured on this very subject. He had been judge to a Spanish military detachment and member of the Senate of Brabant, from which he retired to join the Society of Jesus.[5] Eagerly attending his courses, Van Helmont reaped but empty ideas and senseless prattle. Seneca, and more especially Epictetus, promised solace in his disappointment; he finally toyed with the idea of joining the Capuchin order as the way to true Christian stoicism. This was the point when, as he put it, the quest for eternity "smiled upon him". Frail health put paid to the project, however. Fatigued by devotional exercises aimed at perfection in Christian stoicism, Van Helmont saw himself as an empty bubble (*bulla*) and recognised that stoicism had made him arrogant whilst lending him an outward appearance of modesty. It was thus that stoicism became odious in his eyes.[6]

In this extremity Van Helmont turned to herbs and medicines. God's grace should, he reasoned, have ministered most admirably to the welfare of mankind through the virtues of the herbs which he had created. Hence, Van Helmont took to browsing through Matthioli and Dioscorides. Unhappily he found that the herbal art had made no progress since the classical period. There was no more than idle discussion as to the meaning of Dioscorides' descriptions, and nothing new about the real virtue, properties, and uses of herbs. Instead much ink was spilt debating the question of their fictitious "grades" and the "qualities" which were supposed to make up their "nature" and composition by mixture (*crasis*). And yet Van Helmont himself knew some two hundred herbs deemed identical in quality and grade, but quite different in virtue. The converse was also true, as was particularly evident in potions for sufferers from wounds. So not the herbs – the seals of divine love – but the herbalists forfeited his respect.[7] Where, then, were the axioms and rules of medicine by which certainty could be achieved, in place of the instability and obscurity displayed by the herbalist physicians; where was medicine taught and transmitted like any other of the arts and sciences? A professor had informed

---

[5] Martin Antoine del Rio (Delrio), a Jesuit, was born 1551 at Antwerp and died in 1608 at Louvain. He was famous for his *Disquisitionum magicarum libri sex* (Louvain, 1599–1600; Mainz, 1600; Venice, 1608), rather than his biblical commentaries: see Daniel Georg Morhof, *Polyhistor literarius, philosophicus et practicus*, 4th edn., 3 vols. (Lübeck, 1747), Vol. I, lib. I, cap. 21, 94, p. 253.

[6] Van Helmont, *Studia authoris*, 7, *Opp.* p. 16. Ibid., 8, *Opp.* p. 17.

[7] *Studia authoris*, 11, *Opp.* p. 17.

him that Galen and Avicenna had left nothing undiscovered concerning the gifts, properties, applications, and fitness of herbs, from hyssop to the cedar of Lebanon. But, then, why should he who created medicine not have continued dispensing it at all periods?

Distrustful, and failing to find any certainty in herbal medicine, anxious and uncertain as to what profession he should aim at, Van Helmont next studied customs, laws, and rescripts – all man-made and dependent upon the whim of man. Again he found his time wasted. There was nothing to be learned from judging and evading the "thousand thorns of obscurity" that stood in the way of good government and justice. Meditation on the afflictions of mankind drove him, with a singleness of purpose, to the study of natural objects. He read the textbooks or *Institutiones* of Fernel and Fuchs, only to find the whole story of natural phenomena and actions locked up in the fictitious systems of elemental qualities. He read all of Galen twice, Hippocrates once, all of Avicenna, the Greeks, Arabs, and their contemporaries; some six hundred works altogether. From these as well as from the leading surgeons of the time, Jacques Houllier, Tagault, Guy de Chauliac, Vigo, Paulus Aegineta, he extracted copious notes. He found all these authorities wanting, and felt their deficiencies most acutely when at the age of seventeen he was called upon to give courses in surgery in the Medical College at Louvain. In his later judgment, he had then presumed to teach from books what could only be learned through observation, manual labour, long experience, and sharp discernment.[8]

He soon realised that all these books sang the same song and that his thick note-books were so much rubbish, empty of all solid knowledge and truth. Neither the study of the appearances of the herbs and drugs which he had personally collected, nor attendance at the daily rounds of a medical practitioner, would teach him more than the insufficiency, uncertainty and guess-work of healing. He found great proficiency in theoretical argument (*problematice disputare*) about any disease, and yet ignorance as to how to cure toothache or itch. In place of a cure there was the verdict of incurability. In short, medicine was an invention full of deceit. The Romans had lived much more happily for the five hundred years before the Greeks brought medicine to Rome, than afterwards. As often as a cure was obtained empirically or, as it were,

---

[8] *Studia authoris*, 16–20, *Opp.* p. 18; *Aufgang*, p. 16. *Tumulus pestis*, *Opp.* II, p. 207; *Aufgang*, I, 28, p. 535.

experimentally, treatment based on medical theory led to failure. Good God, Van Helmont exclaimed, how long will you remain angry?

Having acquired a medical degree in 1599 at Louvain, frustrated and disgusted with the sham of academic life, Van Helmont embarked on the grand tour of Europe. He visited Switzerland and Italy between 1600 and 1602, and France and England between 1602 and 1605. He mentions a visit to London in 1604 as well as a previous occasion, possibly late in 1602, when he joined the Court at the Palace of Whitehall "in the presence of the Queen herself". Nothing he saw or learnt on his travels alleviated his frustration; he found only laziness, ignorance, and deceit. A period of practising medicine during a plague epidemic at Antwerp in 1605 made him even more conscious that useful knowledge and truth had eluded him. When offered a rich canonry he had refused to live on the sins of his fellow-men; he now declined to practise medicine, unwilling to grow rich on their misery. Nor would he accept such alluring calls as were extended to him by Ernest of Bavaria, Archbishop of Cologne, or the Emperor Rudolph II.[9]

What remained to him was a further retreat from any public or professional performance. He turned to a programme of research into natural philosophy, which consisted of private work to be carried out in his own laboratory, remote from university or court patronage. In a stillness undisturbed by the sermonising altercations of the scholastics he set out to "unhinge" the works of nature and to lay bare her instruments. The separation of components of complex bodies, the building-up of composites from simples, measuring and weighing – in short, chemical analysis and manipulation – were his deliberate choice, combined with meditation at the site of the still (the *athanar*), in a quest for intellectual union with the objects of his research and the divine power which had created them. Using this twofold approach he hoped to arrive at last at the truth, the invisible kernel of things. His endeavour was to make visible the invisible, which to him meant the real.[10]

In turning to chemistry Van Helmont felt that he was obeying a divine call. I praise, he said, the bounteous God who called me to

[9] *De lithiasi*, II, 13, *Opp.* II, p. 10; *Astra necessitant*, 48, *Opp.* p. 122. *Promissa authoris*, III, 5–7, *Opp.* p. 12; *Promissa authoris*, III, 7, *Opp.* p. 12. *Studia authoris*, 6, *Opp.* p. 16. *Tumulus pestis*, *Opp.* II, p. 208.

[10] *Tumulus pestis*, *Opp.* II, p. 208; ibid., p. 208. *Promissa authoris*, II, 9, *Opp.* p. 11.

the art of fire (*pyrotechnia*), away from the "dregs" – the so-called sciences and professions; for its principles do not rest with syllogism, but are made known by nature and manifest by fire. It enables the mind to penetrate to nature's secrets and thus to ultimate truth. It admits the worker to the first roots of things through separating and exarticulating nature's deeds, through all that art can achieve in developing the virtues of the semina to maturity and perfection.[11]

Concentrating on chemical research did not prevent Van Helmont from following his own principles by ceaselessly curing the sick and devising and dispensing his own medicines free of charge. From his earliest youth, he averred, he had preferred knowledge to riches and abhorred lucre. He was fortunate enough to be able to dedicate himself to natural philosophy and medicine in the auspicious atmosphere of happy and affluent family life, at Vilvorde near Brussels from 1609, the year of his marriage, until the family moved to Brussels in 1616. At Vilvorde his wife possessed land, and here were born four of his daughters and his well-known son and literary executor, Franciscus Mercurius Van Helmont (1614–99). Franciscus published and introduced the first edition of Van Helmont's collected works, the *Ortus medicinae* of 1648, and collaborated in both the exemplary German translation of the *Ortus* by Christian Knorr von Rosenroth, which appeared in 1683, and in the most comprehensive edition of the *Opera* in 1682.[12]

Van Helmont's blissful retirement into the solitude of private research lasted for some fifteen years. It was to end as a result of his outspoken criticism of his traditionalist contemporaries and in particular the Jesuits. His root-and-branch rejection of the aca-

---

[11] *Pharmacopolium et dispensatorium modernum*, 32, *Opp.* p. 441. *Promissa authoris*, III, 7, *Opp.*, p. 12; *Tumulus pestis*, *Opp.* II, pp. 208–9.

[12] Franciscus's life was marked by his many journeys from court to court, his friendship with Leibniz to whom he suggested the term "monad", his brushes with the Roman Inquisition and the Quakers, and his extensive discussions with Lady Conway against whose headaches he fought a losing battle. He continued spiritualist speculation on cosmos and man (*Paradoxical Discourses*, London, 1685), suggested teaching the deaf and dumb with the help of the supposedly archetypal Hebrew alphabet (1667), devised an orthopaedic stool for the deformed, and wrote cabbalistic and alchemical tracts. See Johann Christoph Adelung, *Geschichte der menschlichen Narrheit*, Vol. IV (Leipzig, 1787), pp. 294–323; H. Ritter, *Geschichte der christlichen Philosophie*, Vol. VIII (Hamburg, 1853), pp. 1–47. C. Merchant (Iltis), "The Vitalism of F. M. Van Helmont: Its Influence on Leibniz", *Ambix*, 26 (1979), 170–83, C. Broeckx, *Le Baron Francis Mercure Van Helmont* (Antwerp, 1870).

demic and medical establishment could not fail to become known and indeed to be publicised by his two first printed treatises. These were to initiate the storms of the 1620s and 1630s, which abated only a few years before his death. His work on Spa water (1624) was issued as a "Supplement" to the *Spadacrene* (1614) of the influential Henri de Heer (*c.* 1570–*c.* 1636). Van Helmont's criticism of traditional theories, notably those concerning the origin of water from air on the top of mountains and its use in medicine, was bound to arouse de Heer's indignation. De Heer answered Van Helmont immediately (1624) and six years later pilloried him as an empiric who had done no good in a certain case.[13] Unfortunately, the enemies Van Helmont had made among his medical colleagues found strong allies in Jesuit circles and, through them, among the ecclesiastical authorities. Already in 1621 his "magical" tract on the *Magnetic Cure of Wounds* had been published in Paris, without, as he asserted, his knowledge and with malicious intent. Religious prosecution followed, lasting for some twenty years, at the end of which time (1642) formal proceedings against him were officially discontinued, although his long house-arrest had been lifted six years before.

An adverse destiny involved Van Helmont in a controversy that agitated and divided the minds of religious natural philosophers and physicians in the early decades of the seventeenth century. The protagonists were Rudolphus Goclenius (1572–1628), Protestant Professor of Philosophy at Marburg, and Jean Roberti (1569–1651), a Jesuit casuist and Professor at Douai, Trier, Würzburg, and Mainz. Goclenius was a firm believer in natural magic as operating through sympathy and antipathy between natural objects; Roberti, a preacher warning and arguing against any form of magic as the deceitful work of the devil. A literary warfare from 1617 to 1625 produced seven attacks and counter-attacks between Goclenius

[13] Henri de Heer, *Spadacrene, hoc est Fons Spadanus; eius singularia, bibendi modus, medicamenta bibentibus necessaria* (Liège, 1614; 2nd edn., Leipzig, 1645). Idem, *Deplementum supplementi de Spadanis fontibus* (Louvain, 1624), replying to Van Helmont's *Supplementum de Spadanis fontibus* (Liège, 1624). De Heer, *Observationes medicae oppido rarae in Spa et Leodii animadversae* (Liège, 1630; 2nd edn., Leipzig, 1645), Observ. XXV, p. 287: "Euphorbium...ab empirico Helmontio Bruxellensi propinatum...extimam stomachi tunicam erosit" (and likely to have caused fatal perforation of a chronic gastric ulcer). Idem, *Spadacrene ultimis curis polita hoc est Fons Spadanus accuratissime descriptus* (Liège, 1635; 2nd edn., Leyden, 1645). On de Heer see Hirsch (ed.), *Biog. Lex. hervorr. Ärzte*, iii, 110, by Van den Corput. A.J.J. Vandevelde, "Helmontiana", pt. 2 (1929), pp. 722–4.

and Roberti. The first tract of the former had appeared in 1608.[14] When Van Helmont became party to the controversy in 1621, Roberti immediately contested the "pernicious disputation" of the "pyrotechnic physician of Brussels". Roberti had acquired Van Helmont's manuscript and probably procured its publication.[15]

The issue at stake was the pseudo-Paracelsian idea of a "weapon-salve".[16] This was to be applied not to the wound, but to the weapon which inflicted it. It was supposed to act by sympathy whatever the distance between the patient and the "doctor" treating the weapon. Van Helmont took the attitude of the unprejudiced observer who collects all available case-reports, and wanted to give the method every chance to be proven. He found fault with both contenders, criticising Goclenius's factual evidence and Roberti's appraisal of the phenomenon as a whole. The former had omitted the presence of inspissated blood on the weapon, which in Van Helmont's opinion was essential for the method to be effective. Moreover, Goclenius's contention that the moss which was an ingredient of the salve must come from the skull of a hanged criminal was not true; any skull would be suitable. Roberti, on the other hand, had looked for his arguments in a field that was most unproductive for the natural philosopher, namely theology in general and action of the devil in particular. He had treated a

[14] In Sylvester Rattray's collection, *Theatrum sympatheticum auctum...de pulvere sympathetico...de unguento vero armario* (Nürnberg, 1662), easy access is given to: R. Goclenius, *Tractatus de magnetica vulnerum curatione* of 1608, on p. 177; J. Roberti, *Tractatus novi de magnetica vulnerum curatione autore D. Rod. Goclenio...brevis anatome*, on p. 226; R. Goclenius, *Synarthrosis magnetica* of 1617 on p. 237; and J. Roberti, *Goclenius heautontimorumenos* (1618) on p. 309, Van Helmont's tract following thereafter on p. 457. See de Waele, *J. B. Van Helmont*, pp. 27–8 for further titles.
[15] Van Helmont's manuscript was submitted in 1618 by a publisher to P. Stevart at Liège for an *imprimatur*. This was first granted, but revoked later. On request Van Helmont sent a manuscript copy to Remacle Roberti, the brother of Jean. The latter is not unlikely to have published it without the author's knowledge and consent. For details of the ensuing prosecution and the medical opinions submitted to the courts, see Broeckx, "Notice sur le Manuscrit Causa J. B. Helmontii", pp. 277–327, 341–67; and idem, "Interrogatoires du...Van Helmont", pp. 306–50.
[16] For the ingredients of the weapon-salve see Knorr von Rosenroth in *Aufgang*, pp. 1008–9, "Anmerckung" with reference to the original source, the pseudo-Paracelsian *Archidoxis magica*, ed. Sudhoff, xiv, 448.

problem of natural science as a *quaestio juris* rather than a *quaestio facti* as it should be.[17]

In Van Helmont's view the reported effects were amenable to explanation in naturalistic terms. They were indeed attributable to "magnetic" forces, to attraction, that is, of particles; in the present instance, particles of the ointment mixed with blood sticking to the weapon were attracted to the wound. The miraculous power of blood, its "magic", was similarly open to our understanding. This power included the preventing and healing effects of the blood of convalescents, which could retard the spread of the poison of a rabid dog in the body of the person bitten; it could grant a "*supersedeas* [a writ staying proceedings] to prorogue the time of the Venom's energy, the poyson being charmed into inactivity". Similarly, "fatally destructive" shingles was safely and expeditiously cured by anointing the patient with the blood of someone who had already recovered from this condition. Conversely disease can be transmitted – "transplanted" – to an animal by the blood of the patient, who may thereby be rid of his own disease.[18] Although an aspect of the attraction of matter by matter, and achieved by matter, these effects are at the same time spiritual; they are product and expression of that sense and sympathy which dwell in each object of the created world. Indeed, spirit is the primary driving force to which all material change is subordinated. This, however, does not imply a dualistic view in which spirit is imposed on matter; the spiritual and the material are rather seen as the two convertible faces of the same coin, the individual unit, in which they are inseparably interwoven. The spirit is not additional but intrinsic to the body of the object; "the magnet is endowed with various senses and also with imagination, a certain *Naturall phansy*". In other words the spiritual impulse or "life" is inherent

---

[17] Machination of the devil was commonly adduced as the cause of what looked unnatural. Its deep roots are best revealed in del Rio's *Disquisitionum magicarum*, I, 3, quaest. 3, pp. 30 et seq., on the miraculous effects of imagination; ibid., II, quaest. 8, pp. 127 et seq. on how the devil works miracles and transmutations and how the magi do so through him. "Black magic" operating by virtue of the devil or by incantation (words), or amulets, which are also of the devil is invoked by Thomas Fienus (1567–1631) who denied the power of imagination in favour of humoralist theories (*De viribus imaginationis*, Louvain, 1608, p. 83). Del Rio as well as Fienus taught at Louvain when Van Helmont was a student there.

[18] Van Helmont, *De magnetica vulnerum curatione*, 49–50, *Opp.* p. 712; *Three Treatises*, trans. Walter Charleton (London, 1650), p. 12; *Oriatrike*, p. 763. *De magnetica vulnerum curatione*, 20, *Opp.* p. 707.

in all things, not only in those which appear to be animated. Like yearns to join like, and the sympathy that pervades the cosmos accounts for effects that are deemed "paradoxical" and hence are attributed to the devil. These effects belong, however, to natural magic, in which the agent is not the devil as "fiddler", but rather the world-soul or "mundane spirit", the "common Intelligencer" in which sympathy between all things is invested. No devilish trick or force can come between magic and nature, not even when it is practised by the witch who "kills a horse, in a stable removed at good distance, by a certain naturall power derived from her spirit".[19]

Magnetic effects, then, may be wrought in dead-looking metal or through the "will of nature" intrinsic in flesh and blood; they may act by touch as in the shock dealt by the electric fish, or at long distance as by the destructive stare of the basilisk. In all instances they are perfectly legitimate and natural, nature being the magician by virtue of universal sense and sympathy, rather than the devil who may seduce, corrupt, and deceive, but who is incapable of bringing about physical change. Reports of phenomena of natural magic, however hair-raising and unbelievable at first, must at least be given the benefit of investigation. Van Helmont was not alone in giving credit to such accounts; others such as Harvey and Boyle set great store by unorthodox "Helmontian" cures, leaving aside the multitude of contemporary Paracelsians and the "Chemical Philosophers".

Van Helmont presented his doctrine as "Christian philosophy", opposed to the delusions and otiose dreams of the heathens. This not only implied the aim of demolishing the whole traditional syllabus of ancient natural philosophy and medicine but also contained an insinuation of heresy against the established scholars, theologians, and physicians whose life and work stood and fell with this very syllabus. This was unfortunate enough. Even more fatal to Van Helmont's security were the open criticisms and ridicule which he levelled against the Jesuits. On the matter of the moss needed for the weapon-salve, Van Helmont wrote point-

---

[19] *De magnetica vulnerum curatione*, 142–4, *Opp.* p. 727; *Three Treatises*, trans. Charleton, pp. 76–7. *De magnetica vulnerum curatione*, 151, *Opp.* p. 728; *Three Treatises*, trans. Charleton, p. 80. *De magnetica vulnerum curatione*, 152–4, *Opp.* pp. 728–9. *De magnetica vulnerum curatione*, 108 et seq., *Opp.* p. 723, and 87, p. 720; *Three Treatises*, trans. Charleton, pp. 62, 56.

edly: "For, if a *Jesuite*, put to death by strangulation, or any other kinde of martyrdom, be left *sub die*, in an obedient position to receive the influence of the stars; yet his head will yeeld the same crop of Moss, equivalent in use, and equally ripe, with the head of a *Thief*". Why, the adversaries of the weapon-salve rhetorically demanded, had the world had to wait for Paracelsus, a "lewd, dissolute and ignorant fellow", to invent this remedy? Van Helmont pilloried this line of argument as insolence not only to the dead, but also to God:

As if he ought not to have infused the knowledge of so divine a secret into Paracelsus, but some other person (some *Jesuite* perhaps) nor to have manifested so great a consonancy and harmony of Nature, in the days of *Paracelsus*, but much earlier, in the infancy of the world. But I beseech you, why came *Ignatius Loyola* so late, and in the evening of the world, to be the founder and establisher of a *Society*, so useful and profitable to the whole world? Why did he not spring up, and appear many ages sooner? Alas, wretched man, whither doest thou hurry thy self by presumption?[20]

Ecclesiastical prosecution soon followed. In 1623 members of the Louvain Medical Faculty denounced Van Helmont's tract as a "monstrous pamphlet". In 1625 the General Inquisition of Spain declared twenty-seven of its propositions as suspect of heresy, as impudently arrogant, and as affiliated to Lutheran and Calvinist doctrine. A year later the tract was impounded by order of Sebastian Huerta at Madrid. In 1627 Van Helmont affirmed his innocence and submitted to ecclesiastical discipline before the curia of Malines, which referred the matter to the Louvain Theological Faculty. In 1630 the defendant admitted his guilt and revoked his "scandalous pronouncements", to be duly convicted by the Faculty for adhering to the monstrous superstitions of the school of Paracelsus, that is of the devil himself, for "perverting nature by ascribing to it all magic and diabolic art and for having spread more than Cimmerian darkness all over the world by his chemical philosophy [*pyrotechnice philosophando*]".[21]

In March 1634 Van Helmont spent four days in the archiepiscopal prison, but was transferred, against high securities, to the

---

[20] *De magnetica vulnerum curatione*, 174, *Opp.* p. 732; ibid., 41, *Opp.* p. 711; ibid., 52, *Opp.* p. 713; *Three Treatises*, trans. Charleton, pp. 92, 24, 30–1 (par. 51).

[21] Opinion of the Louvain Theological and Medical Faculties 1630–4, given in Broeckx, "Notice sur le Manuscrit Causa J. B. Helmontii", pp. 30–1. Van Helmont was here bracketed with the painter Otho Venius (Van Veen, 1556–1634), the teacher of Rubens.

Minorite Convent at Brussels, and after several interrogations released on house-arrest. As we have seen, formal proceedings continued until 1642, when he also obtained an ecclesiastical *imprimatur* for his treatise on fevers. Two years after his death, in 1646, his widow secured his official rehabilitation by the archbishop of Malines.[22] Prosecution had disrupted and embittered Van Helmont's life in many respects. Two of his children died while separated from him owing to the restrictions imposed upon his movements. For some twenty years, between 1624 and 1642, he published nothing. He suffered much anxiety, which he felt had fallen on him through no fault of his own and which at one time brought about one of his introspective visions. And yet he continued his research and prepared the bulk of his treatises which have come to us in the *Works* (*Ortus medicinae*, The Rise of Medicine). He still took part in contemporary discussions in which his opinion was sought by such authorities as Marin Mersenne.[23] The treatise which was the cause of all the misery, the erstwhile "monstrous pamphlet" on the magnetic cure of wounds, was finally reprinted in all editions of the *Works* between 1648 and 1707, again perhaps not with the will of the author, but at any rate under the aegis initially of the editor, his son Franciscus Mercurius. In 1661 Robert Boyle expressed his admiration for Van Helmont, with the pointed exception of just this treatise.

Our knowledge of Van Helmont, his life, his natural philosophy, and his medicine, derives from the *Ortus*, published four years after his death, and from the appended *Opuscula* which had first appeared in 1644.[24] It might be assumed that his son's task would have been to collect, arrange, and integrate into a whole a number of scattered and discontinuous manuscripts. This was not so. We know from the best possible source, namely Van Helmont himself, that the *Ortus* existed as such a long time before he died.

---

[22] Broeckx, ibid. Idem, "Interrogatoires du... Van Helmont". De Waele, *J. B. Van Helmont*, pp. 33–40. For some minor points see P. Nève de Mévergnies, *Jean-Baptiste Van Helmont, Philosophe par le Feu* (Paris, 1935), pp. 122–42.

[23] Van Helmont, *Imago mentis*, 13, *Opp.* p. 256; *Aufgang*, pp. 871–2. P. Tannery and C. de Waard (eds.), *Correspondence du Père Marin Mersenne*, Vols. I–III (Paris, 1932–46): 3 letters to Mersenne in Vol. II, and 11 in Vol. III (1630–1).

[24] Van Helmont, *Ortus medicinae, id est initia physicae inaudita. Progressus medicinae novus, in morborum ultionem, ad vitam longam* (Amsterdam, 1648). Idem, *Opuscula medica inaudita: I de lithiasi, II de febribus, III de humoribus Galeni, IV de peste*, 2nd edn. with *Ortus Medicinae*, 1648; 1st edn., Cologne, 1644.

In 1643 he wrote in a mood of renunciation and doubt in his own vocation:

I seriously begged of the Lord that He would vouchsafe to choose another more worthy than myself: wherefore the Lord being deservedly wroth suffered this Evil and unprofitable Servant to be sifted by Satan...I knew perfectly that the hand of the Lord had touched me: And therefore, *in a full tempest of Persecutions, I wrote a Volume*, whose Title is the *Rise or Original of Medicine; The unheard of Beginnings of natural Phylosophy*; wherein I have discovered the accustomed errours of the Schools in healing.[25]

Hence Van Helmont "found a rest in my Soul, such as I never found in the times of my Prosperity". He speaks of "great storms" (*tantae procellae*) and his suspicious surprise that they had failed to disturb the rest of his soul and the sleep of his body. It would seem that the "full tempest of persecutions" and the "sifting by Satan" which God had allowed as punishment for his doubt, were allusions to the Inquisition and his trial. His long house-arrest should have provided both ample leisure and the need for the distraction and satisfaction of giving a coherent account of his researches and indeed of his personal view of the world. That the work was of one piece is also evident from the not infrequent cross-references to be found in it.

The *Ortus* and the *Opuscula* present, in Latin, the complete and legitimate text of Van Helmont's work. In addition an account is extant in Flemish, the *Dageraad* (1659).[26] This is shorter, simpler, and more factual than the *Ortus*. That it was also written earlier is suggested by the wording of the title of the German translation of the *Ortus*. This exemplary work, the *Aufgang der Artzney-Kunst*, was composed by Christian Knorr von Rosenroth in cooperation with Franciscus Mercurius. Published in 1683, it offered in addition to extensive chemical and alchemical commentaries, supplementary passages from the *Dageraad* interpolated into the text of the *Ortus* in translation. The title informs us that this is: "The Rise of Medicine, that is Unheard-of Doctrine of the Principles of Nature...now in consultation with his Son, Franciscus Mercurius Baron Van Helmont, translated into High-German, properly ar-

---

[25] *Opuscula medica inaudita* (1644); trans. John Chandler in *Oriatrike* (London, 1662), sig. Nnnnn2 in *Unheard-of Little Works of Medicine...of the Stone.*

[26] *Dageraad, ofte nieuwe opkomst der geneeskonst, in verborgen grondtregulen der Natuere...Noit in't licht gesien, en van den Autheur zelve in't Nederduits beschreven* (Amsterdam, 1659; Rotterdam, 1660).

ranged and with the addition of what was more or different in the first edition printed in *Dutch* called The Dawn...".[27] In some parts, the earlier text, though much shorter and less mature, can claim as much attention as the *Ortus* by reason of its content and arrangement as well as the very fact of its seniority.

Franciscus Mercurius wrote a lengthy introduction to the *Ortus* expressed in theosophical terms. In the German translation, the *Aufgang* of 1683, we are told by the translator and commentator Knorr von Rosenroth that his friend did not wish it to stand. Franciscus Mercurius regarded his introduction as a juvenile product, now, after thirty years, obsolete. Knorr would, however, repeat from it the following information: the father had died on 30 December 1644 at six o'clock in the evening; he was in full possession of his mental faculties, and at his own wish fortified by the rites of the Roman church. For seven weeks his strength had failed, his breath become difficult, and his side painful following some exertion on a cold and foggy day. On his own showing he seems to have been subject to attacks of side-pain (*pleuresis*) which he treated with sympathetic nostrums. Though feeling better and even able to write to a friend in Paris, he intimated in this letter that the Lord should be praised, "for it has pleased him to call me away from this world within twenty-four hours from now". He was right. A few days before his death, he had enjoined the son to bring all his writings together, those still incomplete as well as those revised, and to deal with them as he should see fit.

Knorr went on to state that Van Helmont had intended to write his whole work in Dutch. Having accomplished much of it, including a preface, he discontinued it in view of the many terms alien to the vernacular which he would have had to employ. He gave the work, which he called *The Dawn (Dageraet)*, into the hands of his daughter, from whom it was borrowed by a friend who had it published. The preface was translated into Latin by the son and incorporated in the *Ortus* of 1648. It was also at Franciscus Mercurius's request that Knorr inserted the supplementary and variant Flemish sections in German translation into the appropri-

[27] *Aufgang der Artzney-Kunst, das ist noch nie erhörte Grund-Lehren von der Natur, zu einer neuen Beförderung der Artzney-Sachen, sowohl die Kranckheiten zu vertreiben als ein langes Leben zu erlangen* (Sultzbach, 1683). For full title see Bibliography. Repr., ed. by W. Pagel and F. Kemp (Munich, 1971); see pp. xxi–xxxviii for Kemp on Knorr's life and writings. K. Salecker, *Christian Knorr von Rosenroth (1636–1689)*, Palaestra, no. 178 (Leipzig, 1931).

ate places in the *Aufgang*. This juxtaposition was to reveal what and where modifications had been introduced, as well as clarifying some points and adding remedies not found in the *Ortus*.

In his preface to the *Dageraad* Van Helmont revealed the deeper motives by which he was actuated in writing in the vernacular. He was convinced that the first conception that comes to the mind of an author is obscured and alienated from its original meaning when he presents it in a foreign language. For the mind deciphers it first "by Words in the Mother Tongue". For instance, the origins of a man who normally spoke nothing but Spanish and was called "the Spaniard", became manifest when after severe brain injury he failed to understand Spanish, but talked a lot in Italian.[28] It is, then, only by means of language that ideas dimly coming to the mind are clarified and made distinct. This function belongs first and foremost to the mother-tongue and only derivatively so to any other language. If, as Van Helmont believed, such ideas and images are divine and decoded first by the mother-tongue, this must be closer to deity than other tongues. Hence the expression of such ideas in the mother-tongue will contribute to the sanctification of God's name, comparable to the sanctifying, ceaseless song of the angels.

A further incentive to write in the vernacular was to "help my neighbour". This had been the main motive of Paracelsus in abandoning the academic Latin.[29] Like Paracelsus, Van Helmont had no use for outlandish drugs, from "the ends of the East", for he knew that the Almighty gave healing to all nations. He did not reserve special virtues for products from the banks of the Indus, nor had he failed in kindness to mortals prior to the discovery of the In-

---

[28] Preface to the *Ortus*: IHWH Verbo Ineffabili..., sigs. *2–*3. The rendering is improved in *Aufgang*, sig. x4v.: "der nichts als Spanisch zu reden pflag, so dass man ihn auch den Spanier hiess". Also preferable is the variant reading of *in commodum* – "zu Nutz maines Nächsten" – as against *incommodum* in the *Ortus* and "dammage of my neighbour" in *Oriatrike*.

[29] Paracelsus specifically addressed himself to the barber-surgeons who were excluded from the academic curriculum. Moreover, he believed that, since therapy like disease was regionalised, medicine was language-conditioned. Greek and Arabic medicine were of no use in his own country. "What use is Rases for Vienna, Savonarola for Freiburg, Arnaldus for Suebia?": Paracelsus, *De gradibus*, Begleitbrief an Clauser, ed. Sudhoff, iv, 71–3; *Das ander Buch der Grossen Wundarznei*, 3. tract. von den offenen Schäden, cap. 6, ed. Sudhoff, x, 365. Pagel, *Paracelsus*, pp. 243–4. G. A. Wehrli, *Der Zürcher Stadtarzt Dr Christoph Clauser und seine Stellung zur Reformation der Heilkunde im XVI. Jahrhundert* (Zürich, 1924), pp. 22–7.

dies. Divine loving kindness had thus taught Van Helmont that illness at home finds its remedy there.[30] All these were truly pragmatic motives alien to any chauvinist parochialism, however much Paracelsus for his part had stigmatised Galenic pharmacy as "foreign arrogance" and from a "mistaken fatherland".

Moreover, use of the vernacular is natural and so is truth itself. It is no more so than when divested of all ornaments. Were I to write for scholars, Van Helmont stated in a second preface to the *Dageraad* addressed to practitioners, my work would go the way of all controversies. To be learned is tantamount to being fatuous and heedless of essentials. The scholar admires the products of his own mind, but misses great arcana and wisdom that are necessary for the common weal. The diseases that form the subject of Van Helmont's book are largely those that befall common man and should therefore be presented in a language which can be understood. Furthermore, what Van Helmont has to offer is unique and unknown. It is a gift of grace lavished upon him personally. He had found traditional lore about diseases to be itself diseased and miserable:

Thus I write new things. For the Art grows every day. If it has pleased the Father of Lights to increase the number and severity of diseases in our own and our fathers' time, it may be hoped that His goodness has opened the treasure whereby can be relieved what He as Father has inflicted. At all times the physician was the intermediary between God and the patient. The physician gifted and chosen will please and reconcile Him.[31]

[30] Van Helmont, *Pharmacopolium et dispensatorium modernum*, 33, *Opp.* p. 442.
[31] *Dageraad*, sigs. **3–**4. *Aufgang*, sig. xxxxx6: Dritte Vorrede vor sein Niederländisches Wercklein.

The only life-size portrait of Van Helmont, from: *Aufgang der Artzneykunst*, the German translation of the *Ortus* (1648) of 1683. It is a derivative of the vignette frontispiece to all editions of the *Ortus* (with one exception, that of 1651). It is the work of Johan Alexander Baener (1647-1720). The verses play on the name *Helmont* – "Helle Mond" (bright moon) – "Helle Mund" (bright speech); "for the knowledge of medicines, for long life, the riddance of disease he opens Nature to her deepest ground, come hear what says truth bright sound".

2

New aims: the hunt for perfect knowledge

Van Helmont's earliest experience of academic studies had left him almost obsessed with the defects of traditional Galenic medicine. "I shall renounce the errors of the schools concerning what they rashly regarded as the groundwork of medicine". Van Helmont's promise applied equally to natural philosophy in general. The "heathen nonsense and invention of an evil spirit" is the target of his frontal attack. His intention was the demolition of the whole ancient system of the elements, the humours and their qualities, their mutual conflict and contrariety in mixture, their excess or deficiency. None of these, according to Van Helmont, has a role in disease or a service to render in therapy. A blatant example of error is the universal use of laxatives. Meant to diminish faulty humours, they really attract and then convert mesenteric blood into putrid material; they are poison in themselves. The rest of the traditional humoralist expedients such as venesection, cauterizing, and diaphoretics are equally fraught with danger and shorten life. Nor can the madness of catarrh be tolerated or reliance placed on any of the Paracelsian devices such as tartar and his three principles, salt, sulphur, and mercury.[1] Neither Galen's opposites (*contraria*) nor Paracelsus's similars (*similia*) will cure stroke, leprosy, dropsy, asthma, gout, stone, hysteria, poisoning, or plague. These have never been understood. To uncover their true roots, their true anatomy is an urgent concern of religious charity. For only when their causes are known can effective therapy follow in the form of a cure that is specifically adapted to the nature of each. Indeed, a radical re-examination was required of what constituted the operations of life itself, since no answer existed for this question.

[1] Van Helmont, *Promissa authoris*, Proem, *Opp.* p. 6; ibid., 2, *Opp.* p. 6; ibid., Proem and I, 9; ibid., Proem.

The root of the evil that had befallen medicine was the replacement of the Hippocratic art by Galenic theory. Thus, the "prattle of the Greeks" had given rise to literary physicians who practised medicine not "through the work of healing", but through "speaking whereby they hoped to be spoken of as healers". Hence the ever-swelling list of incurable diseases and the reliance on palliatives.[2] Medicine, however, has to do with man and not literature. To restore the ancient art a clean sweep must be made and the physician's mind must become again a "planed and naked table". Medicine must be purged of all the logical and mathematical devices that had been fabricated by "enforced reason". Scholastic physicians had allowed rash prejudice to overrule cautious investigation. Premature "plucking of buds and flowers" had left the "wasters of the promised fruit" ignorant of truth and useless to mankind. For nature knows nothing of schemes dictated by reasoning, the products of impatient ambition and vanity. Grace from above will leave the "flowers of nature fresh, fragrant and of most pleasing and lightsome colour" in the hands of the patient observer. This was the frame of mind in which, in 1609, Van Helmont retired to Vilvorde, away from the bustle of metropolitan vanities, to embark on personal research and the search for truth. Instead of syllogism, the traditional method believed to illuminate the relationship between things, his aim was the things themselves. These he searched after for full seven years "by a curious analysis or unfolding, by opening bodies, and by separating all things".[3]

It was through perfect knowledge (*scientia adepta*) that the "bolts" behind which truth "had hidden itself from him" were removed, by virtue of the "art of fire", that is, chemistry. This study is concerned with analysis, the dismantling of composite bodies down to the invisible semina of things; and with the knowledge of how the semina mature and how the complex is formed from the simple (synthesis). Such semina are, for example, those which cause clear and limpid water to engender stone. It is through this chemical analysis that the idle Aristotelian speculations on prime matter, on privation, chance, infinity, and the vacuum will be superseded.[4]

[2] *Promissa authoris*, I, 3, *Opp.* p. 8; ibid., I, 5, *Opp.* p. 8.

[3] *Confessio authoris*, 13–14, *Opp.* p. 15; *Oriatrike*, p. 10; *Confessio authoris*, 7 and 12, *Opp.* pp. 14–15; *Promissa authoris*, III, 7, *Opp.* p. 12; *Oriatrike*, p. 7.

[4] *Promissa authoris*, III, 5, *Opp.* p. 12; ibid., III, 8, p. 12; ibid., III, 7, p. 12; *Pharmacopolium et dispensatorium modernum*, 32, *Opp.* p. 441.

The seeker of truth should therefore purchase coal and phials. For the price set on the arts by the gods is the sweat of manual labour, not reading and learning. This echoes the admonition of Petrus Severinus (1542–1602), the Paracelsian expositor: "Go, ye sons, sell fields, house and garments, burn books, buy boots, climb mountains, search the deepest bottom of the earth, the properties of every thing, then buy coal, construct furnaces, watch and cook with patience".[5]

Reason endeavours to persuade the higher intellect (*mens*) that it is its guide, guardian, and nurse, the steering rudder, the prow and poop of the mind and thereby the inventor of knowledge and science. However, the intellect challenges the claim of reason. It recognises that, through reasoning, faith has been perverted into a welter of sophist dissensions and schisms. In the place of belief and grace there is opinion and fickle craftiness; instead of singleness of truth there is multiplicity of error. Reason, not unlike disease, is a "foreign guest"; it takes possession like a parasite.[6] It is the useless logical discourse that concerns itself with premises and conclusions – it always "savours of the arse". For reason dwells in the lower part of the soul and hence is encumbered, being tied to body. It follows that reason is radically different from truth. A child of opinion, reason is nothing real, whereas truth stands for being that is real. Reason conjures up a concordance between logical categories and the nature of objects, a harmony that is fabricated by human fancy and thus "confused, obscure, mobile and unstable in itself". The only field in which it can convey certainty is mathematics. This, however, is given to measuring measurables and hence is foreign to nature. Simple Christian life, not any amount of reasoned discourse, will convert the heretic.[7]

The inferiority of reason is shown in the degree to which animals may possess it. The adult fox remembers by experience and acts by rational discourse wherein he surpasses the cub. The bee counts: in a row of hives it recognizes its personal home by counting. This can be put to experimental test:

For if the fifth or sixth hive, be removed into the seventh. . .and the number being turned in and out, the Bees which return laden with

[5] *Supplementum de Spadanis fontibus*, VII, 22, *Opp.* p. 660; ibid., VII, 55, p. 663; Petrus Severinus, *Idea medicinae philosophicae* (Basel, 1571), cap. VII, p. 73.

[6] Van Helmont, *Venatio scientiarum*, 9, *Opp.* p. 21; *Ignotus hospes morbus*, pp. 462–82.

[7] *Venatio scientiarum*, 26, *Opp.* p. 23; ibid., 27, *Opp.* p. 23; ibid., 29, *Opp.* p. 23.

Honey and Wax...do reckon again, upon the fifth or sixth numbred Hive: the Citizens whereof, seeing they are strangers to that little Bee, coming unto them, do kill the same.

Thus, by transposing hives thieves can ruin a whole community of bees in one night. The wolf outwits the watch-dog: it cunningly waits until a second wolf has taken possession of an "oven" that it knows to be the dog's habitual dwelling and refuge, and then drives the dog towards it. Hence man should never have been defined as a "rational animal". This was a heathen idea, negating man's creation in the image of God and his possession of a divine immortal soul. Man owes his excellence not to animal reason, but to the archetype whom he resembles as an image reflects the original. Fauns, satyrs, and human-like monsters are thus neither man nor demon, but animals endowed with reason; they are supposed to exist in Scotland and Zeyland.[8]

The ancients had begun by observing the multiplicity of material things and their parts, in the belief that these are easier to grasp than the invisible, in particular the mind and its capability of understanding the objects of the outside world. Van Helmont wanted this order of priorities reversed. Cognition of nature has to begin at the highest level, its "apex and perfection" which is the human mind.[9] Nor is observation real knowledge, knowledge that is of those "anterior causes" that are operative inside objects; these are understood according to the lights of the person who is trying to understand: the means and ways of the recipient, rather than as the objects are in themselves and in reality.[10]

It is surfaces, then, which we observe; we do not penetrate to the true essence, the reality of things. Moreover, there is the personal make-up of the observer which cannot fail to influence the result of his observing. He is liable to change the object, to alienate it from itself and thus to pass off a "foreign mask", surface appearances, as essential and real truth. All study of nature therefore has to begin with a study of the student, the capacity and specific qualities and faculties of his mind. Knowledge of the ego has to precede the hunt for knowledge, a point on which Van Helmont

---

[8] *Venatio scientiarum*, 34–35, *Opp.* p. 24; *Oriatrike*, p. 20.

[9] *Tractatus de anima*, 1, *Opp.* p. 330; *Aufgang*, p. 858.

[10] Van Helmont, *Tractatus de anima*, 10, *Opp.* p. 332; *Tumulus pestis*, *Opp.* II, p. 234 (imaginantur mineralia); *Aufgang*, par. 12, p. 599; *Oriatrike*, p. 1116 (recte 1107), an allusion to St Thomas Aquinas, *Summa theologica*, I, quaest. 84, art. 1.

agreed with Pico, although without the latter's emphasis on microcosmic analogy.[11]

Yet there is good reason why we should have access to reality and truth. The reason lies in the kinship between all objects of nature in that they are products of a single act, that is creation; hence their kinship with the human soul. It is this relationship between souls whereby the investigator can achieve true union with his object.[12] Man, being created last, contains the essences of all fellow-creatures, and knowledge of himself can thus lead to knowledge of the world and nature. Such knowledge will be obscured by all the products of reasoning, by the snares of logic and mathematical devices, and by surface appearances, but powerfully assisted by that probing in depth which chemical analysis can achieve.

The sensitive and reasoning soul obscures the glimpses of divine intellect which our higher mental faculties are capable of receiving. It is these that enable us to penetrate to the kernel of things, to what is essential, real, and true in them and through them. It is through the mind that our reasoning and what we believe we have observed are criticised and corrected. To partake of this higher light our soul must first be totally "emptied" of all earthly vanity and ambition. This is achieved through meditation and contemplation, which indeed must precede all investigation. For it is thus that the naturalist can receive the intuitions by which his research must be directed; it is thus that he will find access to a problem which before his act of meditation had seemed unsolvable.

Objects and phenomena of nature are, then, "given" to the human intellect through an illumination which is comparable to prophetic vision; it is the true light that shows the way to the "naked" being of things, by contrast with the deceitful advice derived from reason. Illumination prepares the mind for legitimate scientific analysis; the latter is legitimate in that through it truth and reality will coincide with truth of cognition.[13] Van Helmont describes on several occasions the meditations which he engaged in as preliminary

---

[11] See Giovanni Pico della Mirandola (1463–94), *Apologia adversus eos*, in *Opera* (Basel, 1557), p. 235; idem, *Heptaplus*, IV, 2, in *Opera*, p. 31; idem, *In astrologiam*, III in *Opera* (1601), p. 347.

[12] For a perceptive discussion see D. Goltz, "Naturmystik und Naturwissenschaft in der Medizin um 1600", *Arch. f. Gesch. d. Med.*, 60 (1976), 45–65 (at pp. 58–9).

[13] Van Helmont, *Venatio scientiarum*, 54, *Opp.* p. 28, with ref. to Aristotle, *Metaphysics*, IV, 1, 1003a et seq.

to scientific investigation.[14] He appraised such spiritual exercises as a "stepping out" by the mind, an *ecstasis* through which the mind unites with the intellectual light that emanates from divinity. This was the "Kiss of God", the *binshika* of the rabbis, in which Moses died "through the mouth" (*al-pi*) of the Lord.[15] Traditionally, to be "transported" in this way had been regarded as fatal for ordinary human beings, being the punishment for arrogant enquiry into divine mysteries, a "spiritual adultery". Van Helmont in all humility begs to differ. There is no danger to our intellectual faculties as the rabbis had feared, for in this condition those faculties are at rest as if they had never existed.[16] Being an act of clemency, it is played out on a level far above organic life, sensation, and suffering. Indeed, how could the divine light which illuminates the soul interfere with that life that depends upon it? He who has partaken of the light can remain without food and drink for three days and be unaware of hunger or thirst.[17]

All things have their origin in images; images are their architects.[18] "All necessity of nature I have consigned to the semina".[19] In these basic statements Van Helmont expresses the hegemony of the spirit and its activity in the semina, those primordia from which all things created were to develop. Generation and development are consequently not the work of seminal matter, but of the operative and formative "images that are struck, impressed and sealed in the semina".[20] Images are the blue-prints that pre-

[14] Van Helmont, *Venatio scientiarum*, 41–43, *Opp.* p. 26; *Studia authoris*, 20, *Opp.* p. 18; *Confessio authoris*, 4, *Opp.* p. 13; *Imago mentis*, 13, *Opp.* p. 256.

[15] *Venatio scientiarum*, 51, *Opp.* p. 28; *Tumulus pestis*, *Opp.* II, p. 236, in *Aufgang*, XI, 12, p. 594 with ref. to Paracelsus and Pico. Deut. XXXIV, 5. For commentary see *Venatio scientiarum*, 51, *Opp.* p. 27; *Aufgang*, p. 27.

[16] On the rabbinical view, see H. Graetz, *Gnostizimus und Judenthum* (Krotoschin, 1840), pp. 57 et seq.; M. Joel, *Blicke in die Religionsgeschichte am Anfang des zweiten christlichen Jahrhunderts*, Vol. I (Breslau, 1880), pp. 163–6. Closer to Van Helmont are the renaissance sources for *binshika*, in particular the *morte di bacio* as referred to by Pico: see *Opera* (1557), pp. 108–9 and pp. 916–17. See also E. Wind, *Pagan Mysteries of the Renaissance* (London, 1958), p. 131; F. A. Yates, *Giordano Bruno and the Hermetic Tradition* (London, 1964), p. 99; O. Hannaway, *The Chemists and the Word* (Baltimore, 1975), p. 20. Pico alone was cited by Van Helmont: *Tumulus pestis*, *Opp.* II, p. 236; *Aufgang*, XI, 12, p. 594, but Oswald Croll (1560–1609) and Georgius Venetus (i.e., Zorzi: 1460–1540) are also relevant.

[17] Van Helmont, *Venatio scientiarum*, 51, *Opp.* p. 28.

[18] "Bilder sind der Ursprung der Dinge" as the Index to the *Aufgang* has it: i.f. a3r. *De febribus* XVI, 11, *Opp.* II, p. 148.

[19] *Imago ferm.impraeg.mass.sem.*, 8, *Opp.* p. 108.

[20] *Ortus imaginis morbosae*, 2, *Opp.* pp. 523–4.

figure ideally what is to happen actually; indeed it is images that "make the semina fertile".[21] Images and ideas, then, come first. It is in the course of the process initiated by them, that they are "clad with body".[22] Where there are images, there must be "imagination" through which they are translated into empirical reality. This imagination is afforded by the archei, the vital principles which "conceive" generative ideas and images.

Imagination is bound up with sense (*sensus*); both must be operative in all objects of nature. The latter include such "dead-looking" objects as minerals and metals,[23] subject as they are to sympathy and antipathy which pervade the cosmos and are indeed binding for all that was created. Cosmic sympathy and antipathy, the instinctive (not reasoned) knowledge of what to seek and what to avoid, are only possible through the omnipresence of *sensus* in all individual parts and members of the cosmos.

Van Helmont's hunt for knowledge can be traced back to the revival during the renaissance of Neo-Platonic tradition from Plotinus onwards. These ideas on the investigation of nature find expression in mediaeval alchemy, in Nicolaus Cusanus (1401–64) and Paracelsus, in Paracelsians such as Severinus, Valentin Weigel (1533–88), Alexander von Suchten (fl. 1560), Israel Harvetus (fl. 1604) and in Bernadino Telesio (1509–88) and Tomaso Campanella (1568–1639). The mechanical skill (*nostra mechanica scientia*) of the Lullist alchemists, for example, implied chemical manipulation for them as it did for Van Helmont; similarly, the simple skilled workman (*mechanicus idiota*) of Cusanus corresponds to Van Helmont's *pyrotechnicus* who works a *posteriori* on the mechanical process of generation and transmutation, *per ignem*, that is through the mechanical art of fire. The *pyrotechnicus* arrives at that knowledge which is the basis of assimilation and union with natural objects in the framework of cosmic sympathy, in the same way that it had been propounded in Plotinian terms by Pico della Mirandola or by Weigel, or by Campanella; it was given new impetus by Van Helmont who was himself following closely the lead of Paracelsus.

Mediaeval Christian mystics had strongly criticised complacent human reason and its claims to achieve the knowledge and con-

---

[21] *De febribus*, XVI, 14, *Opp.* II, p. 148.
[22] *De febribus*, XVI, 10, *Opp.* II, p. 148.
[23] *Tumulus pestis*, *Opp.* II, p. 236a; *Aufgang*, XI, p. 594.

quest of nature.[24] This critique implied a religiously inspired scepticism towards scholastic learning, in favour of simple observation
and a search for the divine spark in God's creatures. It was the
trend promoting natural magic (*magia naturalis*), which in the era
of the renaissance further developed scientific thinking and discovery.[25] It is best illustrated by the alchemist's striving for divine
illumination and union with the objects of his meditation in a
laboratory that is no less *oratory*. And yet Lullist alchemists operated
on the basis of Aristotelian principles; those, that is, which underpinned transmutation. Moreover, all Lullists relied upon tables of
"grades" and the alphabetical commutations and permutations of
Lullian universal *scientia* presented in the strait-jacket of arboreal
diagrams. These were the very views of the Aristotelian scholastics, their "mathematical" devices which Van Helmont vociferously rejected. Surprisingly, therefore, he incorporated a long excerpt
from the Lullist *Testamentum* in *On the Stone*, a treatise from the
last period of his life. Less surprisingly, the passage quoted supports his view of logic as useless and as demanding replacement by
observation and chemical experiment. The piece was aptly chosen
indeed; it is congenial to the reforming ideas which he cherished,
and at the same time reveals the kinship of these ideas and motives
with traditional alchemy, however much Van Helmont may have
opposed the Aristotelian principles on which it was based.[26]

A further Lullist point that is relevant in the Helmontian (and
Paracelsian) context is the introduction of the *Idiota* motif. The
simple rustic unencumbered by theory and learning achieves more
and better knowledge than the learned. He promotes the virtues
of heaven, fattening and cultivating the soil. Similarly, the alchemist loosens and subtilizes gross matter. What he achieves is the
"exaltation" and purification of essences, their liberation from "unnatural" cold moisture through fire that is generative rather than
destructive. This is obvious and in no need of logical proof (*logicali
probatione*). The logician, however proficient in argument, of necessity remains at the surface of things, remote from the internal
nature, virtue, and strength by which seed is made fruitful and

[24] W. Pagel, "Religious Motives in the Medical Biology of the XVIIth Century",
    Bull. Hist. Med., 3 (1935), 107, 110–11.
[25] Ramon Lull, *Testamentum* (Cologne, 1573), Theorica, cap. XXII, fol. 40; fol. 48
    (cap. XXVI) in the 2nd edn.
[26] Van Helmont, *De lithiasi*, cap. III, 1 (contentum urinae), *Opp.* II, p. 12.

growing. His are the "fantastic presumptions" of "logical sophistication" – the opposite pole to masterly instruction, the *magisteria*. The latter are the fruit of true natural philosophy; they provide "the delicious banquet to which nature will invite those who through industrious probing and uncovering [of] evidence" have attained to the understanding of the internal "knowledge" possessed by the *semina*. It is, then, experience and practical work, notably with minerals, that illuminates the intellect through truth. Experimentation leads the way to understanding and thereby to the mastery of nature (*magisterii naturalis*). Eventually there will be revealed the secret of how the "tincture", the philosophers' stone, brings about transmutation by multiplying and impressing its own likeness. It is in this revelation that nature manifests her ultimate and radical truth.[27]

Experience is thus gained *per nostram mechanicam scientiam*, which emends the intellect. This juxtaposition of the *Idiota* motif and the superior wisdom of the *mechanicus* strikes a distinct Cusanian note. The three dialogues of Cusanus contrast the *Idiota* or *Mechanicus* with the *Orator* or *Philosophus*. The former derives knowledge, wisdom, and truth from unprejudiced observation of nature including experiments with the employment of the balance; the latter, from book-learning and academic tradition.[28] Paracelsus speaks of the activities of man and of cosmic forces (*astra*) as those of *mechanici* and of the "*kraft astri mechanici*". His close follower Severinus quite commonly refers to the innumerable *scientiae et mechanici processus* in nature. Van Helmont identifies *mechanica* with chemical fact as opposed to the quest for final causes.[29]

Alchemical and Paracelsian tracts of Van Helmont's own time abound with warnings against logic and dialectic rules. Such rules bear the mark (*symbolum*) of devilish imperfection and corruption; they are the "withered and mutilated invention of curious men". By contrast there is a perfection which comes to us through divine

---

[27] Lull, *Testamentum*, Theorica, cap. XXVI, fols. 50r to 51v.

[28] For *idiota* versus *orator*: Nicolaus Cusanus, *Idiota de sapientia*, I–IV with *De mente*, incorporating *De staticis experimentis*, in *Opera Omnia* (Paris, 1514), fols. xciv verso–xcviii. For *mechanicus* versus *philosophus*, see the editions edited by Walther Ryff appended to Vitruvius, *De architectura* (Strasburg, 1543 and 1550).

[29] Paracelsus, *Von hin fallenden Siechtagen der Mutter*, lib. II, de caduco matris, par. II, ed. Sudhoff, viii, 333, 335, 349; *Opus Paramirum*, III, tract. 3, ed. Sudhoff, ix, 140 and tract. I, p. 127. Severinus, *Idea medicinae philosophicae*, cap. VI, p. 59, and VII, p. 63. Van Helmont, *De febribus*, IX, 26, *Opp*. II, p. 131.

rays, not through books written or dialectic axioms postulated, for the "book" of the rays is too vast to be squeezed into the "dungeons of logic".[30]

The consensus between Cusanus and Van Helmont is not limited to the two essential Cusanian topics of *Idiota* motif and *Orator*. Van Helmont's *Venatio scientiarum* obviously recalls the *Venatio sapientiae* of Cusanus. Moreover, there is the "sweet taste of perfect knowledge", the *dulcedo sapientiae adeptae* of Van Helmont, which echoes the "sweetness of savour", the *praegustata dulcedo* which Cusanus promises to him whose striving for wisdom transports the intellect to what lies beyond the confines of the body.[31] These are not mere borrowings of terms, but indicate deepseated indebtedness to the substance of Cusanian doctrine. Van Helmont praises that condition of the mind which Cusanus had deemed the most desirable – the *raptus* and "stupor" of admiration. For Cusanus this was the ecstasy in which the self relinquishes the world of the senses that otherwise drags the soul away from the royal road leading to its union with divine wisdom and truth. Books and *traditio* will never lead to the sweetness of that truth which emanates from the essential kernel of an object. Here the student will find the "thingliness" (*quidditas*) which any object can claim as part of divine creation, a "book" sealed and closed to human reason; for it was written with God's own fingers.[32] Nor can logic approach it, based as this is on sensuous perception and the predications derived from it. Indeed, logic and truth are diverse in root and power of penetration,[33] as Van Helmont expressed it: "logica et veritas sunt in radicibus disparatae." On the same level Van Helmont follows Cusanus in ascribing the highest dignity to the divine mind in man, his *mens*. It is the godly semen that encompasses the images, the archetypes of all things that through the semen are given to man.[34]

---

[30] *Commentarii in septem tractatus Hermetis de Lapidis Physici secreto* (1610) in *Theatrum Chemicum* (Strasburg, 1613), iv, 680 et seq.: "Scholia" to a text originally in the *Ars chemica* of 1566, of Arabic-mediaeval date. The probable author of the Commentary is Israel Harvetus; its editor, "Gnosius Belga" (Gerhard Dorn?). See C. Gilly, "Zwischen Erfahrung und Spekulation. Theodor Zwinger und die religiöse Krise seiner Zeit", *Basler Zeitschrift für Geschichte und Altertumskunde*, 77 (1977), 57–137 (at p. 75). ·

[31] Cusanus, *De sapientia*, I, in *Opera*, fol. 78r; *De ludo globi*, II, in *Opera*, fol. 161v.

[32] Cusanus, *De sapientia*, in *Opera*, fols. 75r, 78r.

[33] Cusanus, *De mente*, cap. 2, in *Opera*, fol. 82v; F. J. Clemens, *Giordano Bruno und Nicolaus von Cusa* (Bonn, 1847), pp. 138–9.

[34] *De mente*, cap. 4, in *Opera*, fol. 83v; ibid., cap. 5, fol. 84v.

True knowledge or knowledge of truth, then, is not on, of, or about things, in Van Helmont's terms, but of things as they are in themselves. It is concerned with insights (*scientiae intellectus*) that are immediate and not demonstrable, with the object as a truly real being (*ens reale verum*) as against the non-entity (*non-ens*) of human reason.[35] It follows that penetration to the truth implies penetration of the mind into the essential kernel of an object, away from the *extera consideratio* of logic that remains at the surface, towards assimilation and unification of the intellect with the object. It is in this very act that the intellect is defined, as the power which can adapt to everything, can conform to everything by making itself similar to everything by assimilation.[36] The striking epistemological parallels between Van Helmont and Cusanus are further borne out in the context of Van Helmont's experiments in vitro and in vivo.

As we shall see, Campanella has to be considered in relation to Van Helmont in more than one respect. Here the former's definite statement concerning union with the object must find its place. In this as in his natural philosophy in general Campanella acknowledged a debt to Telesio. Campanella insisted on the passive, or receptive, character of perception. We perceive when we suffer something (*patimur*). It is, then, not by means of outside information that we perceive objects (as Aristotle believed), but through a specific alteration and transmutation of our perceiving "substance". The nature of this alteration depends upon the specific properties of the object.[37] Our *sensus* responds with a transmutation that is specifically attuned to the properties of the object and is thereby united with it through perception. That we can have any knowledge of the world's denizens is due to the universal kinship through which we are linked with them as the products of divine creation. From this union and identification with the object it also follows that knowledge of and about the object presupposes knowledge of ourselves.[38]

---

[35] Van Helmont, *Logica inutilis*, 18, *Opp.* p. 42; *Venatio scientiarum*, 27, *Opp.* p. 23.

[36] Cusanus, *De ludo globi*, in *Opera*, fol. 155v; trans. F. A. Scharpff, *Des Nicolaus von Cusa wichtigste Schriften in deutscher Übersetzung* (Freiburg, 1862), p. 224. *De mente*, cap. 7, in *Opera*, fols. 86 et seq.

[37] Bernardino Telesio, *De rerum natura juxta propria principia libri novem* (Naples, 1586), viii, 3, p. 314 and 10–11, pp. 324–6. Tomaso Campanella, *De sensu rerum et magia* (Frankfurt, 1620), i, 4, p. 11.

[38] Campanella, *Universalis philosophiae seu metaphysicarum rerum juxta propria dogmata partes tres*, in *Operum* (Paris, 1638), pt. II, lib. VI, cap. 8, pp. 60 et seq.; idem, *Realis philosophiae epilogisticae partes quattuor, hoc est de rerum natura, hominum . . . cum annotationibus physiologicis a Tobia Adami nunc primum editae* (Frankfurt, 1623),

The worthlessness of reason and the necessity of union with the object were prominent points in Paracelsus's natural philosophy. For him spirit is not born from reason, but from will alone. What lives according to will lives in the spirit; what lives by reason lives against the spirit.[39] Experience is true knowledge. By contrast experiment is fallacious and accidental. To acquire experience the investigator must meet and unite with the internal "knowledge" possessed by the individual thing investigated. To know, then, is to "learn of", to "listen to", to be "taught by" the object (*ablernen, ablauschen*), the knowledge, for example, that enables a pear tree to grow pears and not apples. If you learn (*ablernst*) from scammony its *scientia* so that there is in you that which is in scammony, then you have experience *cum scientia*.[40] This unification with the internal *scientia* of the object is a matter of imagination and not in the grasp of reason. By conceiving images the physician forces a herb to reveal its occult nature – to release it, as it were.[41] A specific spirit is thus born inside the physician that communicates with the plant.[42] Reason, therefore, does not teach medicine, but imagination does. The more "wit", the more impenetrable the "labyrinth", for man's reason does not beget the art of medicine.[43] The spirit engendered *in* the physician by imagination *is* the physician. Man has a mind that flies out and does not remain in him; for mind is spirit. If he intends to experience heaven, his spirit is in heaven, if herbs, his spirit is in herbs, also in air, also in water. Their several spirits and his spirit come together.[44]

Image, similitude, and identification are key concepts in the world of Paracelsus. This is evident in the homoeopathic principle which he espouses. Identification (*gleichheit*) with nature is the physician's aim. He should strive for what is "adequate to nature and proves itself as uniform with the light of nature". Likeness of

lib. I, physiologicor. cap. 12, p. 131; idem, *De sensu rerum et magia*, p. 12. See M. Carriere, *Die philosophische Weltanschauung der Reformationszeit* (Stuttgart and Tübingen, 1847), p. 563; E. Cassirer, *Individuum und Kosmos in der Philosophie der Renaissance* (Leipzig and Berlin, 1927), pp. 57, 370.

[39] Paracelsus, *Volumen medicinae paramirum*, lib. IV, de ente spirituali, cap. 3, ed. Sudhoff, i, 217–18.

[40] *Labyrinthus medicorum errantium*, VI, ed. Sudhoff, xi, 191.

[41] *Weiteres zur Astronomia Magna*, ed. Sudhoff, xii, 484 (probatio in scient. incertar. artium).

[42] *Philosophiae tractatus quinque*, tract. V, ed. Sudhoff, xiii, 354.

[43] *Labyrinthus medicorum errantium*, 2nd preface, ed. Sudhoff, xi, 168.

[44] *Weiteres zur Astronomia Magna*, ed. Sudhoff, xii, 484. *Liber de lunaticis*, I, ed. Sudhoff, xiv, 58.

form (*gleichförmiges Bildnus der Natur*) is the reward promised by "astronomy", that is, the study of the parallels between the greater and the lesser world. The "language of nature" is thus disclosed through signatures. *Euphragia* (eyebright) bears a resemblance to the eye; this, its signature, indicates its usefulness in diseases of the eye. It reveals that eye and plant are "friend and blood-brother". The same cosmic seed has begotten them. Microcosmic anatomy delineates the image in which the parts stand in the macrocosm; this is no text-book illustration, no atlas, but an understanding of the exemplar through a likeness achieved by means of a process of identification or union with nature. Images, signatures, and anat-omy thus document the consanguinity of man with the objects of creation, as well as the means that enable him to acquire true knowl-edge of them. Possession of the image of the enemy that caused disease immediately gives the key to the appropriate therapy. It is through images that magic operates. "All things stand in the image".[45]

Van Helmont's quest for knowledge through unification with its object finds its ultimate historical basis in Stoicism and in Plotinus. Here the cosmos was seen as a coherent commonwealth whose members were bound to each other by a common sensuality and affinity, that is, by cosmic sympathy. Moreover, each individual object of the outside world was thought to be represented in our mind, the bearer of stamp-copies of all things. A "sensual image" emanating from the object was thus "united" with a "spiritual image" on the higher, illuminated level of contemplation.[46] An even closer relationship between Stoic and Plotinian tradition on the one hand, and Van Helmont on the other derives from the Stoic concept of formative ideas which direct and actuate the semina, the invisible germinal prologues of all things. These ideal seminal agents are the so-called *logoi spermatikoi*,[47] in Van Helmont's parlance the *Idea formatrix seminalis*. It is this which according to Van Helmont "disposes" and lends form to matter. In Plotinian terms, it "blows" life and movement into all objects of the physical world.[48]

---

[45] *Das ander Buch der Grossen Wundarznei*, lib. II, tract. I, cap. 12, ed. Sudhoff, x, 260–1; ed. Huser, 70–1; *Opus Paramirum*, I, 5, ed. Sudhoff, ix, 62.

[46] Plotinus, *Enneades*, bk. IV, 3, 10, ed. H. F. Müller, 2 vols. (Berlin, 1878–80), ii, 20; ibid, IV, 6, 3, ed. Müller, ii, 101–2; ibid., I, 2, 4, ed. Müller, i, 16; E. Zeller, *Die Philosophie der Griechen*, III, 2, 5th edn. (Leipzig, 1923), pp. 638, 610; K. Keiling, "Über die Sympathie bei Plotin" (dissertation, Jena, 1916), pp. 28, 33–35, 39.

[47] Zeller, *Philosophie der Griechen*, III, 2, p. 610.

[48] Plotinus, *Enneades*, V, 1, 2, ed. Müller, ii, 142.

There is a further point from Plotinus which is relevant in the present context. Plotinus, by contrast with Stoic materialism, denied any physical basis for transmission of sympathetic effects.[49] To Plotinus remoteness and nearness do not affect the action of one part of a whole on another such part – the whole thing being the cosmos as well as the individual. No part lies so far from another in a unified organism that it would not be near enough to be subject to sympathetic action. Any part of the cosmos viewed as an animated whole influences in some way any other part, and that by immediate spiritual, rather than even the most subtle material contact.[50] This applies above all to the semina; what is important in them is not moisture or breath (*pneuma*), but what is invisible, namely number and reason (*logos*).[51]

Magnetic attraction or sympathy between objects in a unified cosmos was the keynote of the treatise on the *Magnetic Cure of Wounds*, which as we have seen so badly affected Van Helmont's life. The same theme was taken up on a grand scale in his work on the plague, *Tumulus pestis* (1644).[52] Both these treatises clearly reflect Stoic and Plotinian views on cosmic sympathy. The absence of material transmitters, and of pre-formed anatomical channels by which distances between bodies could be bridged in order to enable them to act sympathetically on each other, is consistently emphasized. Instead it is an occult virtue exercised by one whole – one *tota substantia* – upon another whole within the cosmic whole, that must be held responsible for such sympathetic or magic effects. One outstanding example is the central regulating force in the organism, the *actio regiminis*, which stems from a "power-nod" or "power-word". The spiritual and imperceptible nature of all "beginnings" of bodies, the primacy of idea, image, and imagination, was emphatically and persistently propounded by Van Helmont. This he linked to the invisible driving and fertilising forces in the omnipresent semina. It is by their being endowed with images that they are developed and directed to specific destinations. In the semen the spiritual type-plan is transmuted into body. All generation, then,

---

[49] Zeller, *Philosophie der Griechen*, III, 1, pp. 198 and 172, note 2.
[50] Plotinus, *Enneades*, IV, 32, ed. Müller, ii, 73. For the application of this to magic see *Enneades*, IV, 4, 40–1, ed. Müller, ii, 82–3. Zeller, *Philosophie der Griechen*, III, 2, pp. 610–13.
[51] *Enneades* V, 1, ed. Müller, ii, 146.
[52] Van Helmont, *Tumulus pestis*, *Opp.* II, pp. 232–4, under: imaginantur mineralia et herbae suo modo anomalo; *Aufgang*, cap. X, 1–19, pp. 587–91.

presupposes an image according to which specific dispositions are brought to fruition.[53] All sympathy occurs by choice of an image, by some obscure sensation, imagination, and selection.[54] It requires some instinctive awareness of what to follow and what to avoid; in other words, the self-love (*philautia*), that is a gift of the creator, nature's "first-born daughter made for Nature's protection".[55]

Nothing ever happens in nature without motion that is proper to an individual object (*motu proprio*). Hence the wide, indeed cosmic, range of sympathetic attraction. It holds good for animals, plants, and minerals alike. It embraces sympathetic effects arising from such "dead" objects as the animal skin lining a drum: if wolf-skin had been used, another drum lined with ass- or sheep-skin will not emit "sympathetic" resonance when the former is beaten. A blanket made from the skin of a voracious animal such as the Swedish *gulo* induces dreams of hunting and rich meals in the abstemious who have never hunted.[56] It applies to precious stones; for example, the red coral pales when worn by a hysterical woman as if it "sensed" her infirmity. By virtue of its proper motion the magnet verges north as if it were endowed with life (*quasi vitalis esset*). Indeed it moves by active motion rather than by obedience to attraction, or rather by a single act of sympathetic cooperation of attractive and inclining forces, and not a "skirmish between one pulling and the other struggling to resist". On the contrary, it is desire and the activity following from it that precedes attraction, which is the effect of the former. Desire thus appertains to minerals depending upon the presence and nature of its object. There are, of course, differences and as it were "grades" of desire between the animate and the inanimate, from obtuse urges via lust, self-love, and wilful pleasure to selection through deliberate discernment.[57] No wonder, then, that sympathetic effects emerge in much grander scale from flesh, blood, and in particular from semen. These in-

---

[53] *Tumulus pestis*, under: animal phantasticum, *Opp.* II, p. 236a–b; *Aufgang*, cap. XI, 13, p. 594; trans. J. H. Seyfried (Sulzbach, 1681), cap. XI, p. 197.

[54] *Tumulus pestis*, *Opp.* II, p. 232a; *Aufgang*, X, 3, p. 588.

[55] *Tumulus pestis*, *Opp.* II, p. 232a; *Aufgang*, X, 7, p. 588.

[56] *Tumulus pestis*, *Opp.* II, p. 233a; *Aufgang*, X, 8, p. 589. *Gulo*: gulosus, gastrimargus, glutton, "Vielfrass", also the name of a voracious animal known in Sweden. Quoted in the same context of dreaming in *De magnetica vulnerum curatione*, 165, *Opp.* p. 731.

[57] *Tumulus pestis*, *Opp.* II, p. 233b; *Aufgang*, X, 10, p. 589. *Tumulus pestis*, *Opp.* II, p. 234a; *Aufgang*, X, 11–12, p. 590.

Table 1. *Van Helmont's hunt for knowledge: motifs and conceptual background*

ENTIA RATIONIS–Fallacy, fiction	*ENTIA ENTITATA*–Reality, truth
Products of complacent *Human Reason*	Products of *Divine Thought*
Dogma, Doctrine, Schools	*Logoi, Ideae* activating *Semina*
Formal Logic	Observables – *Naturalism* –
	— as such
	— as signatures and seals
Geometrical patterns applied to	Experimentalism
nature	— "knocking", probing, praying;
	—visionary immediacy of knowledge
	Art *per ignem* – *Chemistry*
	Use of *Balance*
"*Mathematics*" as underlying	*Quantification*
Astrology	*Invisibilia et Volatilia* – *Gas*
	— the invisible agent conferring
	specific "disposition" on matter–
	the Individual
Graded Medicine based on	*Reform of Medicine*
— qualities, mixture and	— new disease concept (ontology
transmission of humours	— versus dyscrasia) – *Entia*
and vapours (dyscrasia)	— new Hermetic and chemical
— herbal medicines – their	medicines–virtue of
"grades" worked out rationally	words, herbs, stones
from Lullian tables	

clude awareness, discernment, imagination, love, fitness, similitudes – and, equally, fear, depression and repugnance, the anticipation of advantage and disadvantage, of well-being and ill-faring, of prevailing and failure, of acting and being acted upon in general.

Generally speaking, things inanimate or lifeless-looking are interconnected by sympathy through a deaf perception, a deaf cognition, and an adumbration of sense. In inanimate objects these take the place of vision and intellect, enabling them to form images of choice and thus to satisfy an indwelling feeling, desire, and imagination.[58]

Although dependent upon his predecessors, Van Helmont proposed a new initiative in the reform of natural philosophy and medicine, which may be laid out diagrammatically, as in Table 1. Later chapters will give particular examples of the consequences of his reformed view of nature.

[58] *Imago mentis*, 36, *Opp.* p. 260. *Tumulus pestis*, X, 3, *Opp.* II, p. 232; *Aufgang*, p. 587. *De magnetica vulnerum curatione*, 32, *Opp.* p. 708.

3

The nature of nature

Criticism of Aristotle and the Galenic "schools", widespread throughout Van Helmont's works, provides the key-note in the two treatises: *Beginnings and Causes of Natural Things* and *The Natural Philosophy of Aristotle and Galen Ignorant*. The gap which in the author's eyes divided him from Aristotle, may in some respects impress the present-day observer as exaggerated and indeed as non-essential. If Aristotle's realisation of perfection (*entelecheia*) stood for the driving force that is intrinsic and specific to an individual object, this likewise epitomises Van Helmont's main tenet, namely that the object is not composed of "form" superadded to "matter", but that "form" is the force intrinsic to and inseparable from "matter".[1] Neither has any precedence: primacy is instead attributed to the individual unit, in Van Helmont's terms matter specifically "disposed". This he found empirically confirmed by his attempt at making visible the essential kernel of an object. It appeared to be demonstrable in the test-tube, *per ignem*, by burning away the object's coarse material "husks". What remained was a smoke with particular object-specific properties. This was the *gas* of the object or, rather, the object itself divested of deceptive shapes and coverings and reduced to its pure essence. Van Helmont believed he had by chemical manipulation penetrated to the prime *ens* of the object, its seminal essence; that is, its *entelecheia*.[2] This had to be "spiritual" and yet not entirely uncorporeal; it had to be volatile, but different from those *volatilia* of which all things par-

---

[1] Zeller, *Philosophie der Griechen*, II, 2, 3rd edn. (Leipzig, 1879), pp. 479 et seq.

[2] Van Helmont's letter to Mersenne of 6 Feb. 1631 in C. de Waard (ed.), *Correspondence du Père Marin Mersenne*, Vol. III, 2nd edn. (Paris, 1969), p. 81, letter no. 192.

take, namely air and water-vapour. By contrast with the latter, *gas* had to be object-specific, and to vary in accordance with the different properties of the objects examined. Van Helmont again used *entelecheia* to denote the form by which each thing is what it is. The term was applied to the most subtle and excellent kernel whereby a substance is epitomised in its *entelecheia*.[3]

A monist view of immanence of form in matter, and their inseparable union, was one of the Aristotelian aspects of Van Helmont's chemical discovery. At the same time he was led to a pluralist view of the world as the sum total of individual units. Each of these he saw as endowed with natural perception; some also possessed its higher grades of *sensus* and *intellectus*. In other words the world consisted of enmattered psychoid impulses that were intrinsic, rather than superadded to matter. They accounted for its function and "life". These monist and pluralist concepts reveal the close conceptual kinship of Van Helmont with such staunch Aristotelian biologists as William Harvey (1578–1657) and Francis Glisson (1597–1677) and which emerges in the concept of tissue-irritability and omnipresent "natural perception" which is common to all three thinkers.[4] It is true, however, that in traditional usage *entelecheia* meant an intellectual concept rather than something that could be empirically apprehended, let alone made visible in the test-tube. Thus, Van Helmont's interpretation could well be seen as alien or even opposed to Aristotle.

Van Helmont's anti-Aristotelian arguments may be summarised under the following headings: the rejection of *entia rationis* and of logic and mathematical patterns in the investigation of nature; Aristotle's faulty definition of nature; his recourse to causes and stimuli that act on objects from outside, comparable to the work of the artist in shaping raw material; his elemental and humoral doctrines; his preoccupation with heat as the driving force in nature; his correlation of soul with conditions of matter; and his concept of *pneuma*, "fifth element" and astral body.

Logica inutilis is the title of one of Van Helmont's treatises, adapted from Bacon's verdict that logic is useless in scientific invention. Syllogism, Van Helmont says, negates and detracts rather than adds. It brings nothing new, but will prove anything, even

---

[3] Van Helmont, *Tria prima chymicorum principia*, 76–9, *Opp.* pp. 396–7.
[4] See also the "deaf perception" in *Imago mentis*, 36, *Opp.* p. 260 and "shadow of sensation" in *De magnetica vulnerum curatione*, 32, *Opp.* p. 708.

the impossible, if it is begun on wrong premises. On the other hand, syllogistic reasoning manages to come to correct conclusions from wrong premises, or even to pass from correct premises to faulty conclusions, as already noted by St Augustine. Where logical *demonstratio* can be helpful is in making matters already known more distinct and in supporting the memory of the pupil in recalling what he knew already. Knowledge, however, is not gained by memory, as it would be if in us all knowledge were pre-formed.

Syllogism thus does not lead to invention in science, but serves for the demonstration to others of opinions already invented. Moreover, all true and new intellectual knowledge is immediate, and as such, on Aristotle's own showing, not demonstrable by logic. Demonstration is based on reason which, again according to Aristotle, cannot furnish the knowledge of principles. Van Helmont issues this challenge: Let the scholastics who are so addicted to logic say what branches of knowledge and science are indebted to it – geometry, music, glass-making, printing, agriculture, medicine, hydraulics, mining, strategy, arithmetic, manufacturing, or anything indeed that is useful to anybody! By contrast do I not gain new and useful knowledge, when I am told for instance how to prepare calamine, what it contains, how it mixes with copper, and to what use brass can be put. Therefore to recommend logic as true philosophy smacks of deceit. Nor finally is there any need of logic for answering the heretic, when all depends upon pious belief, exemplary life, incorrupt behaviour, and abstinence from lust and pride. Good actions and not dialectical quibbles make the word of God fruitful.[5]

Van Helmont's position is similar with regard to geometrical constructs. The example adduced is that circular wounds and ulcers are less amenable to cure than others. This had been postulated because of the circle being the most capacious of the figures in a single plane. It is proved false by anal and lacrymal, that is longitudinal, fistulae which are much more recalcitrant than large circular wounds in the leg. An immense syphilitic ulcer with round contours was healed by Van Helmont within twenty-eight days by administering mercury – the "Corrolate" of Paracelsus – on

5 Francis Bacon, *Novum organum scientiarum*, aphor. 54 (Amsterdam, 1694), p. 43. Van Helmont, *Logica inutilis*, 14, *Opp.* p. 42. *Logica inutilis*, 22, *Opp.* p. 43. *Logica inutilis*, 25, *Opp.* p. 43.

eight occasions only.[6] It did not weigh with Van Helmont that the Hippocratic experience with circular wounds was used by Aristotle in a purely epistemological and not in a scientific or medical context. Aristotle's aim was to illustrate what happens when observer and theoretician meet in considering a single fact. The theoretical basis for the observation is provided in geometrical terms; the surgeon observes that round wounds are less tractable than others, the geometer gives the reason why.[7] Van Helmont's approach has at least the merit of showing how far Aristotle was prepared to go in attaching significance to *entia rationis* in the explanation of natural phenomena.

In his *Physics*, Aristotle defined nature as the origin of motion and rest in bodies in which this nature is of itself and not by accident. All natural bodies have in themselves the beginning of motion and rest (*arche tes kineseos*) with reference to place, increase, diminution, and alteration. A chair or a garment, for example, has no inborn tendency to alteration (*horme metaboles*); such a body is not "natural" since it contains nothing that is natural of itself, but only by accident. All that is natural consists of bodies, but only those bodies are natural that are moved and, unlike artifacts, harbour the cause of motion in themselves.[8]

Van Helmont's main objection is that priority is thereby given to motion rather than to being and existence. In his view, bodies must exist before the question of motion and rest arises. Had the creator failed to command motion and rest there would have been creatures but no nature. Motion is largely induced from outside, such as the growth of seed through the heat of the sun; windmills and watermills are moved by artful contrivance. No such effects

---

[6] *Causae et initia naturalium*, 40, *Opp.* p. 37.

[7] Hippocrates, *On Wounds in the Head*, XIII, prescribing with the aim of converting circular wounds into longitudinal ones by a double incision. See *Hippocrates, III*, ed. and trans. by E. T. Withington (Loeb edn. no. 149, London, 1928), pp. 30–1. Ger. trans. by R. Fuchs, *Hippokrates, Sämtliche Werke*, Vol. III (Munich, 1900), p. 271. *Peri helkon*, VIIIa, ed. C. G. Kühn, Vol. III (Leipzig, 1827), p. 312; trans. F. Adams, *The Genuine Works of Hippocrates*, 2 vols. (London, 1849), ii, 797; Fuchs, *Hippokrates*, Vol. III, p. 285. Briefly mentioned by G. Falloppio, *De ulceribus*, cap. 4, in *Opera Omnia*, 3 vols. (Venice, 1606), ii, 8, repeating Galen, *De methodo medendi*, IV, 5, ed. Kühn, Vol. X (1825), p. 284. Aristotle, *Analytica posteriora*, I, 13, 79a15; trans. G.R.G. Mure (Oxford, 1925). Aristotle, *Mechanica*, 847a20; trans. E. S. Forster (Oxford, 1913).

[8] Aristotle, *Physica*, II, 1, 192b13, ed. and trans. C. Prantl (Leipzig, 1854), p. 54. Zeller, *Philosophie der Griechen*, 3rd edn., pp. 384 et seq.

could on Aristotle's definition be called natural. And yet Aristotle emphasised the immanence of efficient causes in natural objects, even in his definition of nature.

Against Aristotle's definition Van Helmont poses his own: nature is the "command of God whereby a thing is that which it is and doth that which it is commanded to do or act". In this there is no materialist trend; this he condemns in Aristotle, who remained concerned with body and heat, though he shifted and wavered, sometimes considering instead the power of the soul, the "fifth element of the firmament of the stars", and what makes seeds fertile. In the last resort it would appear that Aristotle had decided for heat as the basis for the whole action of nature. With this he excludes from nature metals which he elsewhere presented as the products of condensation by cold. If it were heat that fertilises seed, objects Van Helmont, what about the fertility of fishes and other "cold" animals that exceeds by far the fertility of "warm" animals? Heat warms by itself and essentially so, but it fertilises by "accident", initiating motion in the semina. It would thus be "natural" *qua* "beginning of motion", but "non-natural" *qua* "accidental". Heat does not admit of specific differences, only of quantity or grade. It can therefore be only an accidental factor in generation, which is initiated by an intrinsic life force.[9] Furthermore, linking "natural" fertility with the frothy part of semen, which for Aristotle possessed the most noble grade of vital heat, would exclude plants in which this froth is missing. Nor could a Christian admit any astral power in the generation of plants since they were created earlier than the stars, *secundum scripturam*.[10]

In sum, heat is a factor that enters a thing from outside, but has nothing to do with the thing in itself; and it is to individual units, to things, that Van Helmont's thought and investigation were directed. By contrast, Aristotle was ignorant of the "thingliness of nature" and concentrated on figments of reason. This, according to Van Helmont, led him to accord monopoly to such a non-specific, non-seminal, and accidental agent as heat.[11]

---

[9] Van Helmont, *Physica Aristotelis et Galeni ignara*, 3, 4, par. 19 and 8–10, *Opp.* pp. 45 and 46; *Oriatrike*, pp. 42 and 43.

[10] *Physica Aristotelis et Galeni ignara*, 4, par. 24, *Opp.* p. 46.

[11] Ibid., 7, *Opp.* p. 47. The rendering in *Oriatrike*, p. 44, of *quidditas* as "thingliness" is preferable to the somewhat insipid *Wesen der Natur* in *Aufgang*, p. 51.

What, then, does make and form the object? What is its internal efficient? Van Helmont's answer is, the archeus; that is, matter specifically "disposed", the psychosomatic unit, in which the psychoid part is merely one aspect of an object in which it is inseparably bound up with its matter, that is, its material aspect. Whatever happens in and to this object is from inside. Aristotle, however, had "externalised" the efficient, as if the object were a work of art. Indeed, his whole speculation was concerned with artifices, or matters external to nature. Admittedly the father in engendering the offspring enters from without; yet the true efficient force in generation is not the father, but the archeus inside the semen, whilst the father merely provides an external or "occasional" cause. Equally what grows from seed is indebted to the mother-plant for no more than a remote and "occasional", accidental cause. For it is the seed which, when properly stimulated and brought to the surface, by its own effort fabricates and "effects" the new plant. Accessory and external factors have their part to play, but it is the internal seminal efficient that determines all that is essential to a given object: its time of appearance, tendencies, capabilities, potential, shape, motions, and deficiencies.[12]

The issue that prompted Van Helmont's sharpest criticism of Aristotle was the correlation which the latter proposed between body and soul. First, Aristotle had postulated that active forces require matter that is already "disposed" in a certain way ("quod actus activorum tantum esset in materiam dispositam"). Van Helmont by contrast refused to grant matter – in his view "empty" water – a share in any forming and individualising activity. There could be no "natural correspondence of the active and passive" whereby, according to Aristotle, action and response would be speedy and simultaneous. Nor could matter be endowed with any potentiality of acquiring a soul. In other words there is no such thing as Aristotle's *oikeia hyle*: matter, that is, of a specific kind, appropriate for realisation and actualisation.[13] Instead total and exclusive power should be accorded to the non-material force, in transmuting matter (water) into the specific object.

[12] *Causae et initia naturalium*, 9, *Opp.* p. 32; ibid., 10–13, *Opp.* p. 33.
[13] *Causae et initia naturalium*, 39, *Opp.* p. 37. Aristotle, *De motu animalium*, 8, 702a13; trans. A.S.L. Farquharson (Oxford, 1912). Aristotle, *De anima*, II, 2, 414a20; trans. J. A. Smith (Oxford, 1931).

More important still, Van Helmont vehemently objected to "grades" of soul and matter which had been supposed to correspond to each other. The immediate target here is the famous passage from the third chapter of the second book of *Generation of Animals*, on vital heat as the productive force in semen. Matter different from and more divine than the elements is here said to be specifically connected with the "faculty of all kinds of soul". Though not "elemental", this *soma* is still matter. Moreover, *soma* has in common (*kekoinonekenai*) with soul certain proportions according to "honour and dishonour" (*timoteti kai atimia*). The correspondence here is one of quality. The most noble grade of *soma* is that vital heat which is neither fire nor anything like it, but is contained in the frothy part of the semen, making it fertile. This is *pneuma* or spirit, being analogous to the element of the stars. All beings have this vital heat in their semen.[14]

Van Helmont's response was categorical: "This precept praised by the Schooles, containeth almost as many Errours as Syllables . . . It is absolutely false, and an ignorant thing, that any power of the Soul is partaker of the Body, although it be tied to the body".[15] On the contrary, it is the body that partakes of the soul. Accusing Aristotle of having made covert concessions to materialist concepts, Van Helmont may well have had in mind the Aristotelian principle of contraries (*enantia*), which in the latter's system underpins all action in nature, in particular the change from hot to cold.[16] Van Helmont devoted a whole tract to this subject: *Nature Ignorant of Contraries*. Nor did he agree with Aristotle that generation presupposes corruption – that, for example, through mixing of two substances these are "corrupted" and a third substance is created de novo through introduction of a new form. Van Helmont's experiments had enabled him to recover quantitatively a metal from an acid solution. This had not been subject to "corruption" when the new body – the metal solution – had been produced. When "foreign" agents enter, they are not either entirely assimilated or discharged, but remain in a state of low vitality, namely, Van Helmont's "middle-life" and *magnum oportet*. In this he does

---

[14] Aristotle, *De generatione animalium*, II, 3, 736b; ed. H. Aubert and F. Wimmer (Leipzig, 1860), p. 150; trans. A. Platt (Oxford, 1910).

[15] Van Helmont, *Physica Aristotelis et Galeni ignara*, 4, *Opp.* p. 45; *Oriatrike*, p. 42.

[16] Aristotle, *Metaphysica*, I, 5, 986b. Idem, *Physica*, III, 5, 205a. Idem, *De generatione et corruptione*, I, 7, 324a. See also Pagel, *New Light on Harvey*, p. 75.

not seem to do justice to Aristotle's stipulation that "residua of animal nature harbour vital principles in them" and can be fertile like semen. The concept of spontaneous generation, which was also embraced by Van Helmont and his contemporaries, was a corollary of this view. Like Aristotle, Van Helmont discussed this question in connection with semen.[17]

The "astral body" that Van Helmont so angrily rejected is none-theless easily recognisable in his ideas on the traffic between archei which meet and teach at night (an echo also of Paracelsus).[18] Con-sequently, the Paracelsian and Helmontian semina and their intrin-sic dynamic, specific, and spiritual forces are related to the Aristotelian *pneuma* and its conveyance to the body as a *magnale* by the air. Finally, Van Helmont found a rewarding area for criticism in Aristotle's theory of time, thus joining a line of illustrious critics from Plotinus via Crescas to Bergson. Van Helmont's contribu-tion to this debate is discussed in Chapter 4.[19]

It may be concluded that none of the distinctly monist and pluralist aspects of Aristotle's theoretical biology should have in-vited Van Helmont's criticism. Indeed, Aristotle's *entelecheia* was given a new meaning and lease of life through Van Helmont's natural philosophy. It is meaningful and alive as a concept even in his scientific *inventio* and the chemical discoveries of the "philoso-pher through fire". The most incisive result of his investigations, the concept of *gas*, could pass for an attempt at demonstrating *entelecheia*, that is, immanent object-specific driving forces, in vitro. The kinship between his philosophy and Aristotelian vitalism emerges in the concept of natural perception, which he had in common with such staunch Aristotelians as William Harvey and Francis Glisson.

Where Van Helmont differs from Aristotle lies in what he calls Aristotle's "externalisation" of nature: the emphasis laid by the latter on *entia rationis* and above all on such non-specific factors as motion and heat. Heat in particular Van Helmont found wanting. It cannot, he thought, contribute to man's knowledge of the true "thingliness" of nature; heat knows nothing of species, or of any-

---

[17] Aristotle, *De generatione animalium*, II, 3, 737a1–5; trans. Platt, with note refer-ence to the generation of worms in manure heaps. Van Helmont, *Imago ferm. impraeg. mass. sem.*, 9, *Opp.* p. 108.

[18] Paracelsus, *Philosophiae tractatus quinque*, tract. IV, cap. 5, ed. Sudhoff, xiii, 352. Van Helmont, *Magnum oportet*, 50, *Opp.* p. 153.

[19] Section "On time, duration, and lastingness".

thing that makes one object specifically different from another object. It always remains the same by quality, varying merely by degree. Heat consequently acts *on* things, but not *in* things. It enters from outside. It promotes; it does not cause or initiate. Neither does it maintain anything by its own initiative. Preoccupied as he was with material causes such as elements and humours, Aristotle belied in Van Helmont's eyes his own vitalist principles. Indeed, he attributed in the last resort nature's whole action to heat, which betrays his "ignorance of nature".

Aristotelian natural philosophy was dominated by the contraries and their role as primary cause of all change, motion, and progress. They were regarded as first principles (*archai*).[20] Only those things were thought to act or to be acted upon, which either were contraries or involved contrariety.[21] This, as we are assured by Aristotle himself, was agreed upon by all philosophers and rightly so.[22]

In Van Helmont's opinion this whole structure had to be rejected as patently materialistic, based as it was on the "love and hatred" of material elements and qualities. These are but ancillary to what really actuates the world and its denizens: the semina and the spiritual forces, the archei, by which they are made to operate. It is by spiritual responses of sympathy and antipathy, imagination and spiritual (magnetic) attraction that action and interaction between individual units are determined. Ancient materialism had its worst repercussions in medicine where everything was judged in terms of contraries. Disease was deemed contrary to health. It had to be overcome by means of contrary measures: hot by cold, moist by dry, fire by water, in short by warfare and strife which seemed nowhere as obvious and definitive as in the crises, the turning point towards victory and cure. Attempts had been made at working out numerical proportions of elements and qualities which should ensure harmony by suppression of any claim of one of them to hegemony; time-scales had been set up for crises, as if medicine was governed not by nature, but by mathematics.[23]

---

[20] Aristotle, *Metaphysica*, I, 5, 986b; *Physica*, III, 5, 205a. Zeller, *Philosophie der Griechen* (1879), II, 2, 215–16.

[21] Aristotle, *De generatione et corruptione*, I, 7, 324a5 and II, 1, 329a; *De generatione animalium*, IV, 1, 766a15; *Physica*, V, 3, 226b.

[22] *Physica*, I, 5, 188a.

[23] Van Helmont, *Natura contrariorum nescia*, 12, *Opp*. p. 159.

A "graded" pharmacy had been the linchpin of ancient and traditional therapy. In this a grade of quality had been attached to each species or "simple". Pepper, for example, carried the highest (fourth) grade of heat, opium a high grade of bitterness and cold. A compound was intended to present a harmonious balance of simples with opposed qualities. Secular discussions were devoted to the proportions in which hot simples should be mixed with cold simples, how far the components of a mixture were still active in that state, whether a completely new form was achieved in the mixture, how far a rational or logico-arithmetical quantification of pharmacy was possible at all, how far drugs acted as such and as a whole (*tota substantia*) and to what extent they ought to be used on a purely empirical basis.[24]

Van Helmont denies in the first place that grades apply to elements.[25] These latter have no claim to primacy in natural processes; they are merely instrumental "relics" at the disposal of the true vital units, the semina, each of which follows its own schedule and destination. Consequently, it is to the seeds of simple bodies, and not to an element, that grades can be attached. Nor could dead material such as an element bring about a conversion of one thing into another, such as the production from simples of a compound with new properties. This requires "working spirits" and components that contain them. The elements, however, are bodies and not spirits and do not act on each other.[26] Nor, finally, do they enter as such into mixed bodies. Hence:

vain is the doctrine of the Schooles, touching the number, composition, temperaments, concerning the contrariety, proportion, strife and degree of elements...They are also vain trifles, whether the forms of the Elements do remain in the thing mixt? because they are those things which are not in it as an Element...vain therefore is their fight, interchangeable course, victory: and that hence, every disease, dissolution, ruine, healing and restoring doth depend. Vain also is the method which is framed by contraries fetched from hence.

All this is, of course, based on Van Helmont's idea that all bodies are, in the last resort, water, and so therefore are those that enter

---

[24] M. R. McVaugh (ed.), in *Arnaldus de Villanova, Opera Medica Omnia, II: Aphorismi de Gradibus* (Granada and Barcelona, 1975), Introduction, pp. 1–136 (reviewed by W. Pagel, *Annals of Science*, 34 [1977], 217–20).

[25] Van Helmont, *Aër*, 12, *Opp.* p. 61.

[26] *Progymnasma meteori*, 11, *Opp.* p. 66; *Oriatrike*, p. 66. *Natura contrariorum nescia*, 25–6, *Opp.* p. 162; ibid., 34, *Opp.* p. 163 and 16–17, pp. 158–60.

into a mixture. What does decide a mixture's nature, then, is not the material of the components as such, but their object-specific spirits or forms. The element that is "married" to the semina and is used by them in producing bodies is therefore single and so is the body produced. It is not mixed, that is, not the product of elemental qualities brought together in tempered harmonious proportions. This point alone "destroyeth the compact, temperature of the Elements, and the intestine, and uncessant Warr of qualities in us".[27]

If therapy requires contraries, Van Helmont asks, what about natural healing, the mainstay of all therapy? This occurs without crises, the supposed battle between contraries fought in the body. Indeed, all nature works singlemindedly, in a single direction, resolving the solid and solidifying the dissolved. It apportions what is needed to everything individually and specifically, in the same way as the "gold-making powder" (*pulvis chrysoplycius*) which hardens lead, makes mercury and tin difficult to melt, and takes these properties away from iron.[28] Where is the cold in the body that quenches fever?[29] Nor can Paracelsus be allowed to go unscathed, since he admits in his therapy the "storms" wrought by contraries and places his faith in the similia. The latter may be helpful occasionally, by promoting the entry of other medicines in the body, but can never be key agents in the cure.[30] Food may "cure" exaggerated activity of gastric acid in hunger, not as a contrary or a simile to the acid, but because it is just the appropriate "medicine". Poison acts not as an opponent, but in accordance with its natural properties. Administered by magicians or witches, it works as naturally as ever and without contrariety; this is even true of Satan – the supernatural fiend – when he employs natural powers.[31]

God is peace and wanted peace for those he created, for them to follow their own destinations equipped with their own specifically created properties.[32] Vicissitudes occur and "seminal dispositions"

[27] *Aër*, 12, *Opp.* p. 61. *Natura contrariorum nescia*, 31, *Opp.* pp. 162–3.

[28] *Natura contrariorum nescia*, 40, *Opp.* p. 167.

[29] Ibid.

[30] Ibid., 41, *Opp.* p. 167. Ibid., 14–15, p. 159 and 45, p. 168 on Paracelsus. Van Helmont allows that, his quest for similia apart, Paracelsus did regard a "dying down" of medicines to their basic components by chemical manipulation as prerequisite, although he administered amulets and arcana as such, without any chemical "dismembering".

[31] Ibid., 43, *Opp.* p. 167; ibid., 46, p. 169; ibid., 37, pp. 164–5; ibid., 48, p. 170.

[32] Ibid., 37, p. 164. As examples Van Helmont instanced the coexistence of cold air and burning solar radiation on high altitudes: ibid., 24, p. 161; the disappearance

of some may be harmful to others as in the case of hypersensitivity, for example to cheese. This, however, does not "argue a contrariety".[33] In short, contraries do not really exist; they are unknown to the objects themselves, they are fabrications with which we "bespatter the face of Nature", appraising natural properties as vices. Each thing does instead what it is commanded to do, as nature by definition is the sum total of such commands.

STARS AS LIGHT SIGNALS: THE REJECTION OF MICROCOSMIC ANALOGY

God alone is the "prince of life and death", averred Van Helmont, not the stars. He sends victory, war, famine, and pestilence, essentials as well as accidentals. The stars merely indicate and accompany the events that take place of necessity. Being comparable to an illuminated dial, they signify the regularity and continuity of courses in the framework of cosmic order; they are for "Signes, Times or Seasons, dayes and years".[34] They have no power of causing or of forecasting anything, they do not influence ("incline") anything or anybody.[35] Nor is there any evil attached to them. Instead, all inclination, all weakness and strength, and all properties linked with sex, age, and occupation derive from the *semina* as created and ordained by God.[36] The Copernican revolution in astronomy is bound to win general recognition, however cautious the terms used by its followers: "once breaking forth it will ruine all apparitions in the Heaven and Predictions".[37] Indeed, even the astrological determination of the hour of birth – the basis of all horoscopic prediction – is false. No credence can be lent to astral and elemental and humoral correspondencies, for example:

of heat from boiling water *sponte* on addition of cold water, not *expulsive*: ibid., 25, pp. 161–2; the mutual activity between partners in magnetic attraction: *De lithiasi*, I, 4, *Opp.* II, p. 3.

[33] *Natura contrariorum nescia*, 37, *Opp.* p. 164.

[34] *Astra necessitant*, 5–7 and 30, *Opp.* pp. 114–15 and pp. 118–19; *Oriatrike*, p. 119.

[35] *Astra necessitant*, 14, *Opp.* p. 116.

[36] Ibid., 41, *Opp.* p. 120. See ibid., 45, *Opp.* p. 121 for a denial of astral influence in disease, such as miners' "asthma" or the gilder's tremor and the gout of the glutton (given as *putator*, in *Ortus medicinae*, 1648, 1652, 1655, and as the "pruner of trees", *Oriatrike*, p. 126. The correct reading is probably *potator*, as in *Ortus*, 1651, p. 79, and *Opp.* 1682 and 1707, p. 121).

[37] *Astra necessitant*, 47, *Opp.* p. 122: the newly invented telescope (*tubus opticus*) has disproved the Ptolemaic tradition; the spots in the sun "refell all the Aphorisms of the Ancients". Mercury and Venus rotate in equal circles (*parius in Ortus*,

that Saturn is cold, earthy, and dry like black bile and hence promotes envy, theft, and treachery; that Jupiter and Venus are "airy",
merry, sanguine and good; that Mars is dry, hot, and evil-bilious,
and so forth.[38] Nor, finally and consequently, is there any justification for the adage "The wise will rule the stars". This implies that
the stars are capable of action which man can overcome by his free
will.[39]

Of Van Helmont's views as summarised above, his point that
the stars are luminous dials that indicate, but do not influence, is
Plotinian. Plotinus regarded the stars as letters written by their
continual movement in heaven. They are just one more of the
many signs of cosmic order, of universal sympathy and harmony.
It is within this framework of cosmic sympathy that auguries can
be read in many sources other than the stars, as for example from
observing birds and other animals.[40] Nearer and conceptually closer
to Van Helmont is Pico. The latter radically denied any astral
activity other than the emission of heat and light. Nor were there
for him any "celestial" (astral) causes of "critical days", as assumed
by Galen, or of man's infirmities and failures. Above all, nothing
could be learnt from the stars about properties that are specific to
an individual object (causae proximae). Instead they are concerned
with generalities, causes common to many or all (causae communes),
such as weather and seasons. Being born under the same constella-
tion as Aristotle never produced a perfect naturalist and philosopher. Disbelief in astrology should promote the contemplation
and exploration of cosmic harmony and the quest for the divine
arcana and miracles revealed in nature and the magic of nature.[41]

The stars occupied a position of high dignity in Paracelsus's
system of cosmology and natural philosophy, as a corollary of its
major principle, the close correspondence of the world at large,
the macrocosm, with the microcosm of man. Thus, each metal,
and each organ of the body had its star-patron and symbol which
determined its place, virtue, and function. Van Helmont rejected

1648, 1652, 1655; parvis, in Ortus, 1651, 1682, 1707. Oriatrike, p. 126 and Aufgang,
p. 169, have "equal" and "gleich" respectively).

[38] Astra necessitant, 49, Opp. p. 122; ibid., 50–1, Opp. p. 123.

[39] Cf. Paracelsus on plague as related to the influence of man's actions on the stars
(see Pagel, Paracelsus, p. 179). Van Helmont, Tumulus pestis, Opp. II, p. 215.

[40] Plotinus, Enneades, II, 3, 7–8, ed. and trans. Müller, i, 93–4; ii, 90 et seq.

[41] Pico, In astrologiam, III, 24, in Opera, p. 510. Ibid., III, 16, in Opera, pp. 492–9 and
III, 27, p. 518. Ibid., IV, 12, in Opera, p. 542; V, 8, p. 564 and 9, p. 566. Ibid., III,

the Paracelsian correspondencies and consequently the significance attributed to the stars. Paracelsus, moreover, believed in the mischievous arrows "shot" down by the stars to bring us plague and insanity as punishment for our sins, whilst "wisdom" and goodwill enable man to break loose from an evil star and choose a better tutor.[42] It is just this point which aroused Van Helmont's anger. However, Paracelsus was ambiguous; passages from his works in which the influence and power of the stars are severely curtailed or denied are not difficult to collect.[43]

Van Helmont's rejection of microcosmic analogies was based as much on naturalistic as on theosophic considerations. Of the former, one reason was connected with Paracelsus's ignorance of gas, and the gaseous nature of "wind" in man, which he saw as an equivalent of the macrocosmic "whirl of winds". Paracelsus located all four winds and their special "torments" in various places of the human anatomy. Equally "hieroglyphic" in Van Helmont's eyes were the remedies prescribed by Paracelsus for each of them. Juxtaposed to this we find Van Helmont's main theosophic argument. This reveals his kabbalistic expertise: microcosmic analogies between this or that divide the world and thus tend to come between man, the image of God, and his creator. Man should not mirror "parts of the world", as kabbalists had it; this partition is just as sacrilegious as the comparison of man as a whole with the world outside. The same applies to Paracelsus's identification of individual diseases with supposedly corresponding meteorological phenomena.[44]

Severinus, the outstanding Paracelsian expositor, transferred the power granted to the stars to the semina. It is these and not the stars that link invisibles with visibles, corruptibles with noncorruptibles, the upper with the nether world, the temporal with

---

27, in *Opera*, pp. 517 et seq. Ibid., III, 19, in *Opera*, p. 502 and *De hominis dignitate* in *Opera*, pp. 327–8.

[42] Paracelsus, *Weiteres zur Astronomia Magna*, ed. Sudhoff, xii, 467. *Das ander Buch der Grossen Wundarznei*, II, tract. 1, cap. 15, ed. Sudhoff, x, 266 et seq. *De natura rerum neun Bücher*, IX, ed. Sudhoff, xi, 378. *Astronomia Magna*, I, 2, ed. Sudhoff, xii, 41.

[43] *Das Buch der empfindlichen Dinge*, ed. Sudhoff, i, 282. *De vera influentia rerum liber*, ed. Sudhoff, xiv, 219. *Volumen medicinae Paramirum*, I, 4, ed. Sudhoff, i, 179. *Opus Paramirum*, II, 7, ed. Sudhoff, ix, 115.

[44] Van Helmont, *De flatibus*, 8, *Opp.* p. 400. Van Helmont's refutation of microcosmic analogy excludes him from membership of the Rosicrucian circle in which this mode of thought enjoyed the same prerogative as in Paracelsus.

the eternal. Indeed, all alteration, consumption, restoration, size and shape, duration and life-rhythm flow from the "inner law" that prevails in the semina, their intrinsic ideas and *scientiae*.[45] Obviously, Severinus had thus anticipated much of Van Helmont's own position in which all traces of astrological materialism, of influential astral rays and emissions are explicitly abandoned, and the "monarchy" of the semina is established.

Oswald Croll, a more mystical and religious Paracelsist than Severinus, rejected all astral influence and infusion of virtues outright. There are no arcana in us, the lower firmament, that stem from the upper firmament. The stars are "glowing coals" exhibited on the latter, but each being has its own astrum in itself. Through dew, rain, and seasonal changes the upper stars and the zodiac awaken and promote life and growth, but do not influence them. No form, colour, or flavour is attributable to the stars. Neither ascendant single nor constellate stars "incline or necessitate man", nor do they account for any of his conditions, properties or character; these are the gift of God through the divine breath of life. Hence it is for the mind of man to dominate the external astra, the stars on high. Almost identical are some of the anti-astrological themes of *Astrology Theologised*, attributed to the Paracelsian heretical pastor of Zschoppau, Valentin Weigel, and published in 1618.[46]

THE ELEMENTS: WATER AND AIR

Van Helmont criticised drastically the ancient doctrine of the four elements, their qualities and complexions. He reduced their number to two, namely water and air. These he called "original" (*elementa primigenia*). Fire to him was no element.[47] It is destructive, yet it helps the artisan to achieve grandiose effects in separating and composing, that is, in chemical manipulation. By itself it does not generate anything; just as heat promotes, but does not bring about, digestion. Nor is fire connected with star or firmament, as Paracelsus

---

[45] Severinus, *Idea medicinae philosophicae*, p. 81.

[46] Oswald Croll, *Basilica Chymica continens philosophicam propria laborum experientia confirmatam descriptionem et usum remediorum* (Frankfurt, 1609; citations from [1611] edn.), Praef. admonitoria, I, "de vera medicina", pp. 17–18. Valentin Weigel, *Astrology Theologised* (London, 1649), cap. 5, pp. 21–5.

[47] Van Helmont, *Elementa*, 7, *Opp*. pp. 50–1 and 10, p. 51. See below for criticism of the Paracelsian "Three Firsts" – salt, sulphur, mercury – as "elements".

believed. Water, on the other hand, is a component of heaven which also contains air and vital "ether" (*aura*). Earth, by far inferior to water in purity and simplicity, is convertible into water.[48]

For this as for almost all his arguments Van Helmont finds a scriptural basis. In creation water emerges before the first day; it constitutes heaven, the very object of creation. The Hebrew heaven (*schamajim*) stands for "there is water" (*schom-majim*).[49] Elemental matter – water – was before light, and the stars were created only on the fourth day. Because of its primacy water was not enumerated among the objects catalogued in the account of creation. The elements of the ancients, however, are fictitious: a "heathen doctrine" of no use to anybody.[50]

As far as its material basis is concerned, "body" is nothing but water. Heavy and solid bodies – such as rock, gems, stones, flint, sand, fire-stone, clay, earth, glass, lime, and sulphur – Van Helmont found to be convertible into salt equal in weight with the original body and finally into water of the same weight. Naturally plants, flesh, bones, fish, and similar organic matter convert to water more easily.[51] This is due to the inequality of the parts that compose their "seed", by contrast with metal and sand.[52]

Water circulates between the sea and the deepest layers of earth. The latter is earth at its most pure, its "live and vital ground", a uniform white sand (*quellem*) deep down under the surface, by contrast with the multi-coloured mineral gravel that is visible to us as "earth". Here lies the source from which the sea and all the rivers, brooks, and fountains come and to which they eventually return. Water dwelling here does not obey the laws of hydrodynamics; it does not "know of above and below", just as blood does

---

[48] *Complex. atque mist. elem. fig.*, 2, *Opp.* p. 100; ibid., 34, p. 105; *Calor non effic. dig.*, *Opp.* pp. 192–8; *Elementa*, 9, *Opp.* p. 51 with ref. to Paracelsus, *Liber meteororum*, 1, ed. Sudhoff, xiii, 133. Van Helmont, *Elementa*, 6, *Opp.* p. 50.

[49] *Elementa*, 4, *Opp.* p. 50. A complementary version sees in "heaven" a mixture of fire and water. Hence to Pico, heaven is a *natura media* between the fiery world above and the dark sublunary world of water: *In Heptaplum praefatio*, in *Opera*, p. 5. J. H. Alsted, *Lexicon theologicum* (Hanover, 1620), p. 108, "de caelo".

[50] Van Helmont, *Elementa*, 1, *Opp.* pp. 49–50; *Oriatrike*, p. 47.

[51] *Elementa*, 11, *Opp.* p. 51. For reproduction of these natural processes, see Knorr von Rosenroth in *Aufgang*, pp. 55–66 on the Paracelsian *sal circulatum* or *solvens* and the related mysterious liquor alkahest, the universal solvent.

[52] At the end of *Elementa*, 11, the extremely difficult conversion of metal into water is attributed to the *anatica comistio* of the metal-semen. *Aufgang*, p. 66, has "die Teile des samens in *gleichem Gewichte und Menge* vermischt". *Oriatrike*, p. 49, gives "undissolvable co-mixture of its own seed"; the former version is preferable.

not, as long as it courses through the vessels: once it has left their confines, blood will "obey the laws of places", and so does water surging up from the depths of sand (*quellem*).[53]

Water moving in a "circle" between sea and earth and back to sea serves to distribute the semina. These are stored in the entrails of the earth. They include in particular the semina of minerals and metals, and are appreciated as "reasons and gifts", spiritual directives, that is, which are to receive bodily garments. The movement of these seed-bearing waters is therefore not fortuitous or an "idle sliding down". It is rather subject to direction, as it were by a planning intelligence – "as if they were strong in understanding...the testimony of infinite Goodness and Providence".[54]

Water, then, plays the part of base (*matrix*) and carrier to minerals and metals. It is the bearer of their semina; these are the units that contain "Nature, Essence, Existence, Gift, Knowledge, Duration, Appointment", concentrated into a small space, still united and undispersed.[55] Hence semen is of a nature more noble than the object developed from it; for the objects, by the "unfolding of their Gifts, and necessity of their Functions are by degrees drawn asunder into a plurality", and become subject to disorder. Waters rich in semina are therefore of outstanding interest, especially for their curative properties. There are those that contain an acid ("hungry") salt (*sal esurinum*), that is akin to the digesting agent in the stomach. In his book on tartaric disease, Van Helmont notes, Paracelsus mentions one such mineral water spring in a valley of the Veltin, but more should be detectable emanating from the sources of great rivers at the summit of rocks.[56]

[53] *Terra*, 7, *Opp.* pp. 52–3. *Supplementum de Spadanis fontibus*, I, 5–8, *Opp.* p. 645. *Aqua*, 10, *Opp.* p. 56.

[54] *Supplementum de Spadanis fontibus*, I, 4, *Opp.* p. 645 and I, 20, p. 646. Ibid., I, 21, p. 646; *Oriatrike*, I, 20, p. 690, with ref. to *Ecclesiastes*, I, 7. *Aqua*, 11, *Opp.* p. 56 and *Supplementum de Spadanis fontibus*, I, 17, p. 646.

[55] *Supplementum de Spadanis fontibus*, III, 1, *Opp.* p. 649; *Oriatrike*, p. 693. *Terra*, 11, *Opp.* p. 52. For Paracelsus on *matrix* see Pagel, *Paracelsus*, pp. 95, 115, 129, 208, 215, 238, 321, 337, and idem, "Das Rätsel der Acht Mütter im Paracelsischen Corpus", *Sudhoffs Archiv*, 54 (1975), 254–66.

[56] *Supplementum de Spadanis fontibus*, III, 1, *Opp.* p. 649. Ibid., III, 4, *Opp.* p. 649. Paracelsus, *Das Buch von den Tartarischen Krankheiten*, cap. XVI, ed. Sudhoff, xi, 88. W. Pagel, "Van Helmont's Reformation of the Galenic Doctrine of Digestion – and Paracelsus", *Bull. Hist. Med.*, 29 (1955), 563–8, and idem, "Van Helmont's Ideas on Gastric Digestion and the Gastric Acid", ibid., 30 (1956), 524–36.

It is in this context of acid spring-water that Van Helmont introduces his important contribution to a problem that had occupied natural philosophers for decades: the apparent conversion of iron added to a solution of copper sulphate, into copper. In 1600 Andreas Libavius (*c.* 1540–1616) and as late as 1629 Daniel Sennert (1572–1637) believed that transmutation of iron into copper took place in these circumstances. Van Helmont rejected this. Copper, as he saw it, was merely attracted by the iron and was thereby deposited; what had been in solution and thus invisible had merely been made manifest, whilst the iron was taken up in solution by exchange. This he found evident from a depletion of the supernatant vitriol fluid of copper. He collated this with his parallel observation of the deposition of silver from a nitric-acid solution on addition of copper. There was as much silver deposited as had been dissolved originally. These Helmontian conclusions were some time later finalised by Joachim Jungius (1587–1657), who proved that the iron goes into solution by exchange at a volume-ratio equivalent to the copper deposited, with a colour change of the fluid from blue to green.[57] It had been the "hungry" acid and salt which led Van Helmont to this particular problem. His special interest in these substances was to assist his assiduous efforts to find the solvent of stone, which started from his insight into the acid agent in gastric digestion.[58]

A lengthy classical and gnostic tradition preceded Van Helmont's attribution of primacy to water.[59] In gnosticism's descendant, alchemy, water symbolised prime matter, the origin of all body, a chaotic abyss of darkness, the residence of Behemot or Dragon, the prince of evil, the antagonist of light.[60] It was in water that all transmutation and changes were brought about through the offices of the soul. Thus, George Ripley (?1415–90), the "great En-

---

[57] *Supplementum de Spadanis fontibus*, III, 10–15, *Opp.* p. 650 and ibid., III, 16. Before Jungius, then, Van Helmont had recognised that the iron went into solution by exchange with the copper. See the exhaustive and fundamental H. Kangro, *Joachim Jungius' Experimente und Gedanken zur Begründung der Chemie als Wissenschaft* (Wiesbaden, 1968), with reference also to Nicolas Guibert (1603, 1614) and Angelo Sala (1617; d. 1637) as objectors to transmutation.

[58] Pagel, "Van Helmont's Ideas on Gastric Digestion", p. 532, with ref. to *De lithiasi*, VII, 28, *Opp.* II, p. 52.

[59] See H. M. Howe, "A Root of Van Helmont's Tree", *Isis*, 56 (1965), 408–19.

[60] Isidorus, *Etymologiae*, VIII, 11 (Venice, 1483), "de diis gentium", fol. 41v. On water, devil, and desire versus the holy spirit see Konrad von Megenberg, *Buch der Natur*, II, 9, ed. F. Pfeifer (Stuttgart, 1861), p. 70.

glish philosopher" and alchemist, sings in his *Book of Gates* (1477) of water that it is the universal mother, the radical moisture; everything is finally converted into it, by nature or by the artisan. "Water...mevying causyth both Deth and Lyfe..ys the secret and lyfe of every thing...for of the Water eche thyng hath begynning...."[61] The outstanding position of water in alchemy was endorsed by Paracelsus. He regarded it as the matrix in which there were created heaven and earth. Water is the receptacle of the seed from which man grows; *elementum aquae* is seed-bed.[62]

Precedents have also been suggested for Van Helmont's attempt to prove the primacy of water experimentally. Van Helmont described the "willow-tree experiment" as follows:

That all plants immediately and substantially stem from the element water alone I have learnt from the following experiment [mechanica]. I took an earthen vessel in which I placed two hundred pounds of earth dried in an oven, and watered with rain water. I planted in it the stem of a willow tree weighing five pounds. Five years later it had developed a tree weighing one hundred and sixty-nine pounds and about three ounces. Nothing but rain (or distilled water) had been added. The large vessel was placed in earth and covered by an iron lid with tin-surface that was pierced with many holes. I have not weighed the leaves that came off in the four autumn seasons. Finally I dried the earth in the vessel again and found the same two hundred pounds of it diminished by about two ounces. Hence one hundred and sixty-four pounds of wood, bark and roots had come up from water alone.[63]

Attempts at repeating this experiment as it is described may run into technical difficulties and, if exactly repeatable in Helmontian terms, may lead to different results. That it was never performed by Van Helmont, but merely suggested, is unlikely, however, in view of the kind of quantification applied by him in this as well as throughout his chemical procedures. In the latter we have no doubt

---

[61] George Ripley, *Liber duodecim portarum*, VI, "de congelatione" in *Theatrum Chemicum*, iii, 859–60. Ibid., porta VIII, p. 862. Idem, *The Compound of Alchymye*, in Elias Ashmole, *Theatrum chemicum Britannicum* (London, 1652), pp. 164, 172.

[62] Paracelsus, *Opus Paramirum*, lib. IV, "dc matrice", ed. Sudhoff, ix, 191; ibid., p. 194. *Das Buch de Mineralibus*, ed. Sudhoff, iii, 34. See also spurious treatises such as *Liber Azoth*, ed. Sudhoff, xiv, 593, 571, 589; *De pestilitate*, ed. Sudhoff, xiv, 601, for the word "fiat" as first-created water. Fiat is prime matter according to Paracelsus, *Opus Paramirum*, I, 2, ed. Sudhoff, ix, 48.

[63] Van Helmont, *Complex. atque mist. elem. fig.*, 30, *Opp.* pp. 104–5; *Aufgang*, p. 148.

as to their actual performance. Whether Van Helmont was original in devising the willow-tree experiment is another question. As
already noted, the principle underlying the experiment, namely
the primacy of water and the emergence from it of all natural
objects, was of some antiquity. In addition, the experiment itself
had been envisaged long before Van Helmont and although it had
remained a thought-experiment until his attempt it suggests that
he was aware of his predecessors in this regard. This applies in the
first place to Cusanus. In the autumn of 1450 the latter finished the
fourth and last part of his "dialogues with the layman" (*idiota*) on
wisdom and the mind.[64] This last part was on experiments with
the balance.[65] Here the sound empiric (*idiota, mechanicus*) suggests
to the theoretician (*orator, philosophus*): If somebody places 100
pounds of earth in an earthenware vessel and collects 100 pounds
of herbs and seeds, weighed before their setting into the earth, and
weighs the earth again, he will find the latter only a little diminished in weight. He would conclude that the herbs collected have
their weight largely from the water. Water, then, condensed in the
earth has attracted earthliness and through solar action has solidi-
fied into plants. If the latter were incinerated, could one not con-
jecture from the difference of all weights how much earth one
would find exceeding 100 pounds, and also that this obviously
derives from water? For elements are converted one into another
by degrees. This we experience when a glass is put up in snow and
the air is converted into water therein. Also we find that certain
waters turn to stone: a solidifying and stone-forming virtue enables certain springs to harden to stone objects thrown into them.
A certain Hungarian water is said to exist which turns iron into
copper by virtue of its vitriol content. From such virtues it fol-

---

[64] Nicolaus Cusanus, *Idiota*: lib. I–II, *De sapientia*; lib. III, *De mente*; lib. IV, *De
staticis experimentis*, in *Opera*, fols. 75r–98v; trans. as *The Idiot in Four Books*
(London, 1650).

[65] Cusanus, *Opera*, fols. 94v–98v (for the experiment see fol. 96r–v). Appended to
Vitruvius, *De architectura* (1543), pp. [263–78]. On the earlier German translations
(e.g., Ryff, 1547; Bramer, 1617) and other editions of the tract, as well as a
modern translation, see H. Menzel-Rogner, *Der Laie über die Versuche mit der
Waage*, Vol. V of *Schriften des Nicolaus von Cues*, ed. E. Hoffmann (Leipzig,
1944), esp. pp. 30–1. That Cusanus had anticipated Van Helmont was first
pointed out by F. Prescott, "Van Helmont on Fermentation", *Arch. Gesch. Math.
Natwiss.*, 12 (1929), 70. See more recently H. E. Hoff, "Nicolaus of Cusa, Van
Helmont and Boyle. The First Experiment of the Renaissance in Quantitative
Biology and Medicine", *Jour. Hist. Med.*, 19 (1964), 99–117.

lows that waters are not purely elemental, but composed of elements. Indeed, it would be desirable to have the weights of all such waters with their various virtues; we could thus attempt an estimate of their virtues from the difference of their several weights in oil on the one hand, and in water on the other.

The experiment suggested by Cusanus was to demonstrate in the first place that all vegetable matter is a product of water. It does not necessarily follow that all solid material derives from water. Rather it is implied that water itself is not elemental, but composite, or at least that there is a spectrum of waters that varies in contents visible and invisible as well as in intrinsic virtues. Even when vegetable substance is generated from water, this has to attract "earthliness" (*terrestreitas*) from the ground.[66] In other words, neither the experiment suggested nor its conceptual basis was designed to present water as the prime and all-embracing element, however central the position granted to it in the transformation of one element and material into another.

Nevertheless it is just this point, namely the primacy of water as matter in general, which Van Helmont wishes to demonstrate using this Cusanian model. There is reason to believe that he was familiar with *De staticis experimentis*. The experiment with the willow-tree is not an isolated topic from this work, which happens to recur in his deliberations. On the contrary, Van Helmont's interest extended to a systematic examination of the specific gravity of fluids – such as urine for diagnostic purposes – and it was this feature which had earned the balance a specific recommendation in Cusanus. Moreover, as we have already seen, allusions to specifically Cusanian terms and concerns are not difficult to trace in Van Helmont's works.[67]

However, the story of the willow-tree experiment does not end here. As H. M. Howe has pointed out, Cusanus in his turn had an early Gnostic-theological predecessor in *Recognitions*, a work dating from somewhere between 200 and 400 A.D. Here it is suggested that the occult ways in which God makes vegetable seeds by the action of his spirit in water should be examined through "facts and models" (*rebus ipsis et exemplis probemus*). One of these is an experiment similar to that of the willow tree but involving very large quantities (for example, a great number of seeds and "three

---

[66] Cusanus, *De staticis experimentis*, in *Opera*, fol. 96r and v.
[67] Ibid., fols. 94v, 96v, 78r, 86r, 155v, 201r.

tons of earth"), and several years of observation. The conclusion is
that since the earth will show its original weight unaltered, all the
vegetable material must have sprung from the water used for the
moistening of the earth throughout the period of the experiment.
One single species, namely water, is thus credited with producing
a multitude of live beings, reflecting the single divine power in
forming, multiplying, and preserving species and genera.[68] Howe
has adduced evidence for Cusanus's acquaintance with *Recognitions*, and found ideological parallels with Van Helmont in the
older source. Certainly, in *Recognitions* the primacy of water is
much more definitely asserted than in Cusanus.[69]

It was through the willow-tree experiment that Van Helmont
had some influence upon his contemporaries and successors, notably the young Robert Boyle (1627–91). Boyle caused the experiment to be repeated, and found it satisfactory; he also devised
water-cultures of vegetable matter in the absence of soil. He was
critical, however, of the notion of water as "matter" in general and
in particular as the source of minerals and metals.[70]

Important functions were attributed to earth by Van Helmont,
but he denied that it was an element. Earth is a "sand" that was
made from the primogenial element, that is, water, and can be
wholly converted into water. It is productive of plants and of
minerals, the former through conversion into *leffas* and the latter,
through conversion to *bur*. These are both juices generated by
water entering putrifying earth under the direction of god-sent
semina and ferments. Earth, however, is not a "parent"; nothing

[68] See *Recognitions*, as cited in Howe, "Root of Van Helmont's Tree".

[69] Howe, "Root of Van Helmont's Tree", p. 411.

[70] Robert Boyle, *Sceptical Chymist* (1661), pt. II, p. 68 and in his earlier *Reflexions*
(of about 1657). See the fundamental analysis by C. Webster, "Water as the
Ultimate Principle of Nature: the Background to Boyle's Sceptical Chymist",
Ambix, 13 (1966), 96–107, which relates the willow-tree experiment to the water-
culture of plants as performed by Bacon (*Sylva sylvarum*, 1627), Sir Thomas
Browne (*Garden of Cyrus*, 1658) and in particular to the systematic work of
Robert Sharrock (1630–84) in *Propagation and Improvement of Vegetables* (1660),
probably in cooperation with Boyle. Isaak Walton (1593–1683) described Van
Helmont's experiment and subscribed to the view of water as primogenital
matter and element in his *Compleat Angler* (1653). On water as the matrix of
minerals and metals see R. Oldroyd, "Neo-Platonic and Stoic Influences on
Mineralogy in the 16th and 17th Centuries", *Ambix*, 21 (1974), 128–56; idem,
"Mechanical Mineralogy", *Ambix*, 21 (1974), pp. 157–78 and idem, "Phlogistic
Mineralogical Schemes", *Annals of Science*, 31 (1974), 269–305.

of it enters individual objects as one of their components. It is a receptacle, a womb for the semina, it is matrix rather than *mater*.[71] Van Helmont entirely denied the idea of elemental mixture. Glass, for example, is not a mixture of various components, but is entirely sandy matter. This can be recovered unchanged and in full weight from the product which it forms with alkali, that is, from glass. Indeed, sand is highly constant and resistant: only when extremely intense heat is applied will it be convertible into salt and finally into water.[72] It is in vain that we look for an earthy residue when solid objects are dissolved or destroyed, for instance when wood is burnt and becomes ash. This demonstrates that earth which is mere sand cannot play the part of an elemental component. It cannot enter into the seminal generations of nature.

However strong the resistance of earth-substance to change, the earth as a whole, its globe, is moved.[73] Moreover, there are gross internal changes that affect the earth as a whole. A small animal such as a mole can cause inundation of large tracts of land by eroding a dam. In the depths of the earth the remains are found of trees which normally grow at high altitudes, or animal bones may be uncovered, such as the whole maxilla with an elephant-tooth that came into Van Helmont's possession. Large lakes may spring up at short intervals of time and lands like Greenland may disappear temporarily. Fossilised, petrified, or mummified fish may be encountered in deep strata of the earth, remote from any water, much to the surprise of geologists, including Agricola.[74] At the same time such petrifactions demonstrate that minerals develop from water in the depths of the earth, the latter as well as water providing their matrices. Salty sea-water percolating into the earth loses its salt, being acted upon by the active principle, the archeus,

---

[71] Van Helmont, *Elementa*, 12, *Opp.* p. 51; *Terra*, 9, *Opp.* p. 53; *Terra*, 11, *Opp.* p. 53. The matrix-concept of the ancient elements is Paracelsian: see *Opus paramirum*, IV, "de matrice", ed. Sudhoff, ix, 183; *Astronomia magna*, I, 2, ed. Sudhoff, xii, 49. Pagel, *Paracelsus*, pp. 238–40; idem, "Das Rätsel der Acht Mütter".

[72] Van Helmont, *Terra*, 10, *Opp.* p. 53; ibid., 14, *Opp.* p. 54; ibid., 15, *Opp.* p. 54.

[73] Ibid., 17, *Opp.* p. 54; *Aufgang*, p. 70. This statement provides further evidence of Van Helmont's inclination to Copernicanism.

[74] *Terra*, 17, *Opp.* p. 54. In *Aqua*, 9, *Opp.* p. 56, sucking of sea-water into the original sand of the earth is made responsible for mummified and petrified fish. Van Helmont misrepresents the beliefs of Georg Agricola (1490–1550) and others on this subject. See Agricola, "De animantibus subterraneis" in *De re metallica* (1556; Basel, 1621), p. 501; also "de natura fossilium" in *De ortu et causis subterraneorum* (1546; ed. J. Sigfrid, Wittenberg, 1612), I, 13, p. 319.

of the earth, whereby earth is shown to be "alive". The water then assumes at appropriate places the semina of indigenous salt, mineral, or metal. Thus, out of water grow saltpetre, alum, vitriol, and sea-salt, the "first-born of water". These form a primitive mineral juice, the *bur*, which is the germ-cell of individual metals and minerals. The latter grow to maturity when there is no further influx of water.

Van Helmont was not original in also denying fire its position among the "elements". Paracelsus had regarded fire not as an element, but as a celestial agent superior to the common elements of the ancients. He had identified it with "firmament", as an *elementum coeli*.[75] However, he was not consistent in this, sometimes placing fire on the same level as the other elemental matrices. Crystals, beryls, ice, and thunderbolts he interpreted as "descending from the element fire".[76] Moreover, fire is accorded a place among the elements, where Paracelsus presents creation as a process of separation of one element after another from prime matter.[77]

Girolamo Cardano (1501–76) was much more definite in removing flame and fire from the list of elements. In Cardano's universe fire moves, unlike an element, and is in need of nutriment. It lives on air, which it burns up. Indeed, flame is nothing but air inflamed (*aer accensus*). Its uppermost part is continually converted into smoke. The latter is neither air nor flame, but an intermediate product of both.[78] Cardano's basis here is Aristotle.[79] Cardano would, then, appear to have connected flame with air rather than with smoke and earth, a view which was held by others, for example Jean Bodin (1530–96).[80] Van Helmont was basically in agreement with these ideas concerning the nature of fire and flame. He concedes that flame is smoke of a fatty exhalation set alight. Additionally he insists that flame and fire are identical in nature and that ignited material is no different from the

[75] Paracelsus, *Liber meteororum*, 2, ed. Sudhoff, xiii, 133, 138.

[76] Paracelsus, *Aus Kollegienheften De gradibus*, 4, ed. Sudhoff, iv, 94. W. Pagel and M. Winder, "The Higher Elements and Prime Matter in Renaissance Naturalism and in Paracelsus", *Ambix*, 21 (1974), 93–127 (p. 123).

[77] Paracelsus, *Philosophia de generationibus et fructibus quatuor elementorum*, 6, ed. Sudhoff, xiii, 12–13.

[78] Girolamo Cardano, *De subtilitate* (1550; Lyons, 1559), II ("de elementis"), pp. 50, 51. See F. Hoefer, *Histoire de la Chimie*, 2 vols. (Paris, 1842–3), ii, 99–100.

[79] Aristotle, *Meteorologica*, IV, 9, 388a2; endorsed by Albertus Magnus: see Partington, *History of Chemistry*, i, 104.

[80] Jean Bodin, *Universae naturae theatrum* (Frankfurt, 1597), lib. II, p. 148.

same material before ignition. Ignition is no more than the addition of light. This is demonstrated by two lighted candles, one of which stands slightly inclined above the other. When the lower light is snuffed the smoke ascending from it will catch fire immediately it reaches the light above, where it will burn as smoky gas whilst the flame descends to the wick.[81]

As is by now clear, in all fields of his endeavour Van Helmont is palpably indebted to Paracelsus. Yet he lashes out at Paracelsus hardly less frequently than at his legitimate targets, that is, Aristotle, Galen, and their scholastic commentators. First, he finds Paracelsus wanting in having retained materialistic concepts, first in relation to the four elements of the ancients. These still formed the conceptual basis of important chemical works of the master such as the *Archidoxis*: here they were regarded in traditional terms as the components of natural bodies. Second, Paracelsus visualised them elsewhere as matrices, each of the four forming a material receptacle that was productive of "fruit" such as herbs or minerals with characteristics that were determined by matter. Third, there was his other system, that of the "Three Firsts" (*Tria prima*), consisting of sulphur that indicated inflammable fattiness, mercury standing for the fluid, and salt for the solid state. These, too, had been regarded not only as states or workmen that acted upon the elements but also as actual components of each individual body. In other words, in common with the elements of the ancients, they were general media and principles, of which all things participated indiscriminately.

It was in Van Helmont's eyes a materialistic tendency in Paracelsus which riveted the latter's attention to these general principles instead of to the individual created units, the semina, and their intrinsic spiritual and object-specific virtues. Van Helmont not only denied the real existence of the three principles but also (and wrongly) accused Paracelsus of plagiarism in this respect.[82] Were they real

---

[81] Van Helmont, *Formarum ortus*, 28–9, *Opp.* pp. 131–2; *Aufgang*, p. 178.

[82] *Tria prima chymicorum principia*, 3, *Opp.* p. 385, and 6, p. 386 with reference to Basil Valentine, a supposedly late-mediaeval friar under whose name a number of alchemical tracts circulated, the probable author being Johann Thölde, a Paracelsian alchemist of the early seventeenth century. Van Helmont's accusation of plagiarism was rejected by Hermann Conring, *De Hermetica Aegyptiorum vetere et Paracelsicorum nova medicina* (Helmstädt, 1648), cap. X, p. 89, and by eighteenth-century authors, before H. Kopp's final assessment in favour of Paracelsus, *Beiträge zur Geschichte der Chemie*, 3 pts. (Brunswick, 1869–75), iii, 110–29.

components of objects, Van Helmont argued, they would be traceable in any given substance. However, where by chemical analysis they can be isolated, they emerge not as components of bodies, but as products of the interaction between other material components. They never appear together in the same basic substance. In other words they had not existed therein as "elements", but were formed de novo.[83] Paracelsus had thus used them on the same level as the elements of the ancients, replacing one set of material building-stones by another. Van Helmont however claims it is not by such material that the state of substances is determined – the fatty-inflammable, the fluid, and the solid – but through the restraining and adaptation to which matter is subjected by the higher authority of the spiritual or seminal forces. The multiplicity of building-materials is subject to the "unity of the vital principle", the archeus. Far from being primary, sulphur and salt, oil and ash are gradually increased in the growing plant, and with the plant-substance as a whole can easily be reduced to their true element, namely water. Unlike Paracelsus's first principles, water is not subject to any conversion; hence it is final and elemental, by contrast with products which may "slide into each other by any whirling of successive changes".[84] Besides water, the material element, there is only the seminal principle which is responsible for the specific properties of a natural body.

THE DISCOVERY OF GAS

In the annals of chemistry as a science Van Helmont is largely remembered as the discoverer of *gas* or perhaps more significantly of the gases.[85] His claim to this title is incontestable, and attempts

[83] Van Helmont, *Tria prima chymicorum principia*, 28 et seq, *Opp.* pp. 388–9. *Imago ferm. impraeg. mass. sem.*, 7, *Opp.* p. 108. On the rare occasions when Van Helmont uses the *tria prima* he immediately points out that these are used supposititiously, to "meet the weakness of our understanding": *Gas aquae*, 8, *Opp.* p. 71, for example, to explain the disintegration of water-gas at high altitudes in terms of a breaking of the link between its salt, sulphur, and mercury. For similar examples see *Magnum oportet*, 2, *Opp.* p. 140 and 40, p. 151; volatile salt kept solid, in *Blas humanum*, 38, *Opp.* p. 179. For the condemnation of metaphor and symbol in natural philosophy in general terms: *Tria prima chymicorum principia*, 28, *Opp.* p. 388.

[84] *Tria prima chymicorum principia*, 51, *Opp.* p. 392. Ibid., 60, p. 394, on the nature of mercury.

[85] For a comprehensive account of Van Helmont's achievement in chemistry from the modern chemist's point of view see Partington, *History of Chemistry*, ii, 209–43 (an extended version of idem, "Joan Baptista Van Helmont", *Annals of Science*, 1 (1936), 359–84).

at limiting his priority in favour of Paracelsus cannot be upheld.[86]
Van Helmont himself was aware of the novelty and importance of
his concept for the knowledge of matter and the essentials of
natural objects and phenomena. Indeed *gas* is central in his exploration of nature, which assures him an enduring place in the chain
of scientific chemists to the present day, as constructed by historians of science. *Gas* is also central to his naturalist philosophy and
cosmosophy, and this conception can expect but little, if any,
welcome or encouragement from the exponent of scientific chemistry – past, present or future. It is of great interest to identify the
fifteen various gases which Van Helmont described and to examine his experiments, and to show how these contributed to progress in chemical science. Yet an understanding of what led Van
Helmont to his discovery, and what *gas* meant to him in the
framework of his general philosophy and cosmology will not be
helped by an analysis of the role of gas in the history of modern
chemistry. What is important in the present context is first to
recognise Van Helmont's fundamentalist religious faith, since this
explains the position of high priority and dignity which he accorded to water. Water was the first matter to exist; the spirit of
the Lord hovered on the waters, and from water every object takes
its origin. As we have seen, for Van Helmont all things consist in
the last resort of water, even the strongest minerals and rocks as
well as earth and sand. The second indispensable point for an
understanding of Van Helmont's approach to *gas* is also religious:
God endowed every individual being with an object- and species-
specific plan of "life", of form, function, nutrition, reproduction,
and perfection at its destined end. This specific plan is an idea of the
creator and as such is enshrined in the semen of each being. Water
as such is "empty"; it is a general medium which precedes all
differentiation. On the other hand "all bodies are the fruit of water".
It is the semina that beget them on and in water. This, however, is
not enough. The third and last point is again religious: the "water"
that is productive of beings and of life cannot be ordinary water. It
must somehow conform to the spirituality of the creator. It must
be visualised as in a condition of neither solidity nor fluidity. It
must be volatile. Nonetheless, volatility as such is not sufficient.
Water vapour, though volatile, is still a general medium; it is not

---

[86] On etymological forerunners of *gas* (*chaos, geesen, gest*), see below.

specific, it is devoid of semina, of the stamps or "masks" (*larvae*) which the semina emboss upon water. By contrast *gas* is just that water which has been so embossed and "signed" by a semen, and presents itself in a volatile condition. It is water, but not water-vapour; it is exhalation specifically charged, and hence of the nature of smoke. *Gas* becomes manifest when a solid body is made to relinquish its "vestments", the husk or shell that conceals its essential (spiritual) centre. This is accomplished by burning the vestments away, *per ignem*, an "undressing" performed by the chemist or by nature, as for example in grapes that start fermenting on removal of their skins.

Van Helmont believed he had demonstrated this in vitro when heating coal in a closed vessel. Of sixty-two pounds of coal he found one pound deposited as ash and sixty-one pounds gone to form a subtle smoke. This was neither air nor water vapour, but a volatile substance sui generis, previously unknown and calling for a new term: *gas*.[87] Van Helmont also spoke of a "wild spirit" (*spiritus sylvestris*), because the substance tended forcibly to break out of the vessel and could not be reconverted into a solid unless deprived of its seminal aura.[88] Solid bodies may thus be seen to change into *gas* in their entirety. Their components have become volatile and confluent, forming a "con-crete" and "coagulate" spirit. *Gas*, therefore, is not as such or actually *in* the body; rather it is *the* body in a condition different from its original solid state. It has lost its cover but it has lost nothing that is essential. On the contrary, it is here in its purest form. It still has its material base, namely water, but this is not empty, elemental water, it is water charged by a specific "seed".[89] The latter is lost when, in the extreme cold of very high altitudes, *gas* reverts to non-specific ele-

---

[87] Van Helmont, *Complex. atque mist. elem. fig.*, 13, *Opp.* p. 102.

[88] Ibid., 14, *Opp.* p. 102. Was, then, Van Helmont unsuccessful in collecting gases? It does not seem so. For he assures us: the gas from coal was produced in a "vessel shut and heated" and "the wild spirit cannot depart, the vessel being shut", even if heated until doomsday: ibid., 13, p. 102; *Oriatrike*, p. 106. *Gas sulphuris (sal acidum)* – sulphur dioxide – from burning sulphur is said to have formed in a vessel filled with air and to be amenable to condensation in a bell-jar, *Magnum oportet*, 59, *Opp.* p. 155; *De flatibus*, 4, *Opp.* p. 399; *Complex. atque mist. elem. fig.*, 34, *Opp.* p. 105; *Tumulus pestis*, "Hippocr. rediviv.", *Opp.* II, p. 270. See Partington, *History of Chemistry*, ii, 231. Perhaps Van Helmont had found collecting gases easier with "heavy", "fatty", "sulphuric" gases that were less "wild and eructant" than others.

[89] *Complex. atque mist. elem. fig.*, 14, *Opp.* p. 102. Ibid., 12, p. 102; 38, p. 105.

mental water. *Gas*, then, under those conditions has ceased to exist, having lost itself.

Hence, *gas* may be defined as the material or watery vector of object-specificity, the spiritual carrier of the specific life-plan of an object. Air and water are general media shared by all objects; *gas* is a privilege reserved for the individual. It expresses the close inter-locking of matter with seminal spirit. It is the latter that confers on its partner "life", that is, a specific direction and schedule of form and function to a destined end. That *gas* is the object itself is shown in the case of gunpowder, the action of which stands or falls by its wholesale conversion into *gas*, brought about by its smallest par-ticles which burst asunder or become *gas*. Thus, the constituents of gunpowder, saltpetre, sulphur, and coal, convert each other into the effective *gas*, as it were by mutual destruction under the influence of intense heat. However, Van Helmont stresses that there is no question of air participating in the process, let alone of being set free through fire and heat. This is one of the common errors which even Paracelsus failed to avoid; he believed that air was hidden in all objects. In this he belied his own sti-pulation that all objects consist of salt, sulphur, and mercury and that the elements – including air – are not the constituents of things, but their "mothers", receptacles from which they emerge.[90]

The development of *gas* indicates the "beginning of transmuta-tion" of the whole object. Grapes with their skin intact dry out; deprived of their skins they soon "conceive the ferment of ebulli-tion", the "cause of fermenting", and so do fruit and vegetables of all sorts once they are crushed. Again this is not the liberation of something *from* the object; rather, the *gas* that develops is the object itself, whole and transmuted. *Gas* from grapes when in-gested with wine from vats in which it has been kept under pres-sure, as well as the consumption of too many grapes, can cause disease: the *gas* being indigestible can associate with the spirit of life, coagulating its carrier through its acid and impeding its venti-lation through perspiration. Indeed, the spirit of life in the blood-vessels is *gas*. As such it may be driven out and replaced by another (poisonous) *gas*, as for example in caves, wine-cellars, and mines, and may thus cause unconsciousness and death. Van Helmont

---

[90] Ibid., 21 et seq., *Opp.* p. 103; ibid., 19, p. 103.

himself once nearly died from *gas* developing from a charcoal heater.[91]

The vital *gas* in the blood is also called archeus. It is of the nature of light and a "balm of salt" – a preservative from corruption. It kindles the *archei insiti*, the vital principles that are resident in the organs and responsible for their several specific functions. In this connection the archei are visualised as smoke which is set alight by the central "influent" archeus, according to the ancient idea that a flame is lighted smoke. The *archei insiti* therefore are as much of the nature of *gas* as their "influent" principle.[92] Again, then, and on a much higher level, *gas* emerges not as a part or secretion of the object, but as the object itself in its purest essence, divested of its husk and revealing the closest possible interlocking between matter and seminal agent.

Van Helmont's "new term of Gas" is not unlikely to have been derived from "chaos". He himself indicated as much, saying of *gas* that it was not far removed from the "chaos of the ancients".[93] Being at a loss for a new name to indicate the difference between water that is volatile though not boiled, and water vapourised by heat (water vapour), he took the liberty in an unusual situation to call the former *gas* as there was no great difference between it and the "principal being that the ancients called *chaos*". At all events it was necessary to point out that it was *Wasser-geist* (water charged with an object-specific spirit) as against *Wasser-dampf* (non-specific water-vapour) – *gas* being much more subtle than vapour.[94]

"Chaos" was persistently used and favoured by Paracelsus as a term, but covered a number of quite disparate concepts. Nevertheless, it was said to have lent to Van Helmont's idea of *gas* not only the term but also its substance; consequently the laurels accorded to Van Helmont by historians of chemistry have on occasion been transferred to the older master.[95] However, there is no justification for this even on a generous interpretation of the meaning of the

[91] Ibid., 15, *Opp.* p. 102; ibid., 16, p. 102; ibid., 17, pp. 102–3; ibid., 41, p. 106. Ibid., 43, p. 106. For Van Helmont's own experience of *suffocatio a carbonibus*, see *Jus duumviratus*, 19, *Opp.* p. 289 (wrongly indexed as "289, 16", and again wrongly in 1707 edn. as "189, 16").

[92] *Complex. atque mist. elem. fig.*, 42, *Opp.* p. 106.

[93] Van Helmont, *Progymnasma meteori*, 29, *Opp.* p. 69.

[94] Knorr's translation in *Aufgang*, p. 108, is as usual very helpful.

[95] K. Sudhoff in J. Pagel, *Einführung in die Geschichte der Medizin*, 2nd edn. (Berlin, 1915), p. 239.

Paracelsian chaos. The common denominator of its various uses seems to be the designation of any medium or habitation, the ambit, from which an object derives its subsistence.[96]

Evidently, then, the Paracelsian chaos has little to do with Helmontian *gas*. Admittedly the former is object-bound and bears a connotation of specificity; it is from its chaos that the object derives its specific "food". Chaos is not restricted to organisms and their parts such as the lungs, but appertains to minerals, stone, and urine, in other words to all possible objects. This is of particular interest when applied to the Paracelsian arcana. The arcanum, Paracelsus says, is the "chaos and can be directed by the astra like a feather by the wind". Arcana are "virtue and power and hence are volatilia and have no bodies and are chaos and are clear and transparent and are subject to the star".[97] In such passages three features of the arcana are stressed which are responsible for their outstanding effectiveness as medicines. These are: their volatility (bodilessness), their close connection with astral forces and, following from this, their specificity. All three fall under the wider term of chaos and could be said to share these features with *gas*, in a very general and vague way of speaking. However, the Paracelsian chaos embraces air and water-vapour, that is, general non-specific media that are common to all objects and excluded from *gas* by definition. Even the arcana hardly compare with *gas* as the material vector of the specific life-plan of the individual, and in the multiplicity of individual gases thereby envisaged.

[96] Chaos mineralis, as "feeding stone": Paracelsus, *De modo pharmacandi*, I, 2, ed. Sudhoff, iv, 448; also *Bruchstücke zu Buch 1–3 des Modus Pharmacandi*, I, 1, ed. Sudhoff, iv, 473. Chaos urinae, giving urine its colour: *Deutsches zur Harnlehre aus dem Auto-gramm*, ed. Sudhoff, iv, 623. *Phil. de gen. et fruct. quat. elem.*, I, "de elemento aeris", cap. 10, ed. Sudhoff, xiii, 16, for air feeding fire, with earth, fire, and water being suspended in it like yolk in an egg. Chaos in the earth, as "feeding" the miner with mineral vapour: *Von der Bergsucht*, lib. I, tract. 1, cap. 2, ed. Sudhoff, ix, 465. Chaos dispersed in body, as violent internal wind causing epilepsy and fever: *Kolleghefte zu den Büchern der Paragraphen*, "De caducis", commentary in cap. 2, ed. Sudhoff, v, 290. Chaos and fever: *Theoricae figurae universalium morborum*, tab. IX, "de febribus", ed. Sudhoff, iii, 453. Chaos producing paralysis: *Entwürfe zur Syphilis*, tract. II, ed. Sudhoff, vii, 448. Chaos imparting "food": *Von Ursprung und Herkommen der franzosen*, II, 2, ed. Sudhoff, vii, 211. Chaos as elemental "food": *Von der Bergsucht*, lib. I, tract. I, cap. 2, ed. Sudhoff, ix, 465. Chaos changing with season: *Von Blattern, Lähme und Beulen...der Franzosen*, III, 8, ed. Sudhoff, vi, 364. Chaos as internal air causing a creeping eruption: *Von allen offenen Schäden*, cap. 9, ed. Sudhoff, vi, 187.

[97] Arcanum: *Das Buch Paragranum*, III, "von der alchimia", ed. Sudhoff, viii, 185. Ibid., ed. Sudhoff, viii, 182–6. See Pagel, *Paracelsus*, pp. 70, 95, 269.

Each object contains its own spirit and there are as many spirits as there are bodies and objects: there are spirits celestial, infernal, human, metal, mineral and salt, spirits in germs, marcasites, arsenicals, potables, aromatica, herbs, roots and wood, in flesh, blood, bones, and so on. It is these spirits that, as Paracelsus sees it, give life to all things – life that is a "spiritual, invisible and incomprehensible thing, a spirit and a spiritual thing". Hence, everything is alive and "what is life other than a spiritual thing?".[98] The "essential spirit" immanent in each individual object is closer to *gas* than chaos, but again no more than a vague approximation, the emphasis laid on the spirituality of all function and life being the most notable feature in this connection.

Gas developing from heated coal was called "wild spirit" (*spiritus sylvestris*) by Van Helmont because of its expansive and explosive nature. Generally however, other bodies so treated also of necessity "belch forth a wild spirit". The Paracelsian equivalent term for such behaviour is "male" (*mennisch*). The activity here acquired by an initially inert and quiescent body, Paracelsus saw as being demonstrated when sulphur was "ignited", when salt was dissolved, and when mercury was sublimated. When spirit of vitriol, tartar, and alum are dissolved together, male activity manifests itself "with all impetuosity".[99] Van Helmont may have been echoing Paracelsus in coining the term *spiritus sylvestris*, although the expression "wild" had not been used either by Paracelsus or by his Latin translator, who used *tumultuose*. Indeed, Van Helmont used *sylvestres* elsewhere, for exhalations of spirit of nitre, acetic acid, and so on, "in the process of resolution". From "being quiet they are stirred up and, as of a wild nature [*sylvestres*], they cannot

---

[98] *De natura rerum*, IV, "de vita rerum naturalium", ed. Sudhoff, xi, 329–30. In the *Philosophia ad Athenienses* (regarded as spurious), III, 3, 4, ed. Sudhoff, xiii, 420, 421, each individual tangible thing (including man) is visualised as a "curdled fume" whence we may conclude that there is a manifold coagulation. "One of wood, another of stones, a third of mettalls. But the body is nothing but a fume, smoking out of the matter or matrix in which it is . . . Man is a coagulated fume": H. Pinnell, trans., *Philosophy Reformed & Improved in Four Profound Tractates, III, Three Books of Philosophy written to the Athenians by that famous. . .Philosopher and Phisitian. . .Paracelsus* (London, 1657), pp. 57–8. The passage was prominently quoted by the Paracelsian protestant theologian Weigel in *Vom Ort der Welt*, cap. XIII, ed. W-E. Peuckert and W. Zeller (Stuttgart, 1962), p. 47.

[99] Van Helmont, *Complex. atque mist. elem. fig.*, 13, *Opp.* p. 102. Paracelsus, *Opus Paramirum*, I, 3, ed. Sudhoff, ix, 52; *Operum Medico-Chimicorum*, ed. Z. Palthenius, 11 vols. (Frankfurt, 1603–5), i, 65.

be re-composed and of necessity fly away or when repressed break the vessel". This usage occurs in Van Helmont's early treatise on the waters of Spa (1624) when he was even more under the banner of Paracelsus than later, when he developed his own idea of *gas*. His *sylvestris* is here, in 1624, used to describe the result of the same process as that called by Paracelsus male, namely the dissolution of certain mineral acids and salts. The products thus obtained were subsequently identified with *gas* by Van Helmont. It may also be recalled that chaos – the presumed origin of the term *gas* – was synonymous with *silva* in such mediaeval sources as the *De mundi universitate*, by Bernardus, who was correspondingly called Sylvestris.[100]

As indicated above, Paracelsus did not use the term *spiritus sylvestris*, despite assertions or inferences to the contrary. It has not been possible to confirm either that Paracelsus was, as alleged, very familiar with *gas* – "the effluvium so far unknown" – and knew it under the same name (sc. *spiritus sylvestris*); or that early chemists "gave the subtle elastic air produced by effervescence, fermentation and combustion the name of *Spiritus sylvestris*", that "it was considered by Paracelsus and his contemporaries to be exactly similar to respirable air" and "that Helmontius probably was the first who thought this substance worthy of more minute attention, and called it *Gas* or *Gas sylvestre*".[101]

Yet, the term *sylvestris* does occur in Paracelsus; his *sylvestres* designate one category of his elemental spirits. Like the *silvani*, the *sylvestres* are beholden to air; they are "airy men" or "airy spirits". The chaos of the *sylvestres* is the air – they are *luftleute*, denizens of the air. It is in air that they can "live", that is move freely and unimpeded, just as the gnomes of the earth move freely through mountains, earth, and rocks. The *sylvestres* share their chaos (air) with us; like ourselves they are sustained by air, burn in fire, are

---

100 Van Helmont, *Supplementum de Spadanis fontibus*, IV, 6, *Opp.* p. 652. Bernardus Sylvestris, *De mundi universitate libri duo seu Megacosmus et Microcosmus*, I, 1, verse 18, ed. C. S. Barach and J. Wrobel (Innsbruck, 1876), p. 7. For Bernard's cognomen Sylvestris see E. R. Curtius, *Europaeische Literatur und Lateinisches Mittelalter* (Bern, 1958), pp. 116 et seq.

101 E. O. von Lippmann, "Zur Geschichte des Namens 'Gas', II", in idem, *Abhandlungen und Vorträge zur Geschichte der Naturwissenschaften*, 2 vols. (Leipzig, 1906–13), ii, 381. T. Bergman, *Physical and Chemical Essays*, Vol. III (Edinburgh, 1791), pp. 155–6. J. F. Gmelin, *Geschichte der Chemie seit dem Wiederaufleben der Wissenschaften bis an das Ende des achtzehnten Jahrhunderts*, 3 vols. (Göttingen, 1797–9), i, 217.

drowned in water, and suffocate in earth. For "each remains whole in his *chaos* and perishes in another *chaos*".[102] However, unlike man, they have no soul and in this resemble animals. They may be desert dwellers, or of considerable size, and able to beget giants. They are, in short, monsters (*bruta*), but definitely not men.[103]

Any possible correspondence between the Paracelsian *sylvestres* and the Helmontian *gas* must depend on the following points. The former are spirits; they are uncouth or wild in appearance and behaviour; they are not wholly spiritual, but possessed of a material body of "subtle flesh"; they are offspring and dwellers of air, and are bound to air as their specific chaos. For its part, the Helmontian *gas* is a volatile spirit; it is wild, *sylvestris*, "uncouth" when restrained in a vessel, and escaping in its entirety when freed; it has a material basis, that is, water, the material basis of all natural things; in precise terms, it is water sealed with the almost indelible stamp of specific information. It is airy, in that it is volatile, although it is certainly not air; it is bound up with chaos (hence the term *gas*), expressing individual specificity (of ambit and source of subsistence, in the original Paracelsian meaning of chaos).

These points may, or may not, be regarded as indicating a real correspondence. If the former, there would nonetheless be no more than a general Paracelsian context in Van Helmont's mind when he came to invent a formula for the new type of "spiritual bodies" which he had observed and wished to contrast with such non-specific general *volatilia* as air and water-vapour. It seems reasonable to conclude that the points of comparison are too far-fetched to be significant.

Though a likely terminological root of *gas*, chaos is, as Darmstaedter has shown, not the only contender.[104] *Gaesen* is a close

---

[102] Paracelsus, *Philosophiae tractatus quinque*, tract. IV, "von dem underscheit der corporum und spirituum", ed. Sudhoff, xiii, 350–1. *Philosophiae magna*, VII: *De nymphis, pygmaeis*, etc., tract. II, "von irer Wohnung", ed. Sudhoff, xiv, 124. *Astronomia Magna*, I, 10, ed. Sudhoff, xii, 246 (von dem dono inanimatorum).

[103] *De nymphis*, tract. I, 2, ed. Sudhoff, xiv, 120 et seq., 129; ibid., tract. III, ed. Sudhoff, xiv, 135; ibid., tract. V, p. 144. *Astronomia Magna*, I, 10, ed. Sudhoff, xii, 244.

[104] E. Darmstaedter, *Chemiker-Zeitung* (1929), p. 565, favoured *geesen* as against *chaos*. E. O. von Lippmann, *Beiträge zur Geschichte der Naturwissenschaften und der Technik*, Vol. II (Weinheim, 1953), pp. 73–6 (reprinted from *Chemiker-Zeitung*, 1929, p. 869) rejects *geesen* in favour of *chaos*. It would seem, however, that the two terms are etymologically related rather than mutually exclusive. Consider-

runner-up and, we would suggest, so is *gest*. Paracelsus speaks of a fermentation called *vergesen*. This can take place in mucoid material and is bound up with digestion, separation, and decoction. It can lead to deposition of tartar.[105] In the same work it is recommended that a certain plant-mixture be allowed to ferment – *vergesen* – in wine must. The cognate *gest* means ebullient foam out of which rocks are formed as the "fruit" of the element water. The foam develops in lapidary matter.[106]

Van Helmont was undoubtedly acquainted with and impressed by the Paracelsian descriptions of the elemental spirits. He mentions and believes in beings intermediate between man and animal such as nymphs, dryads, nereids, naiads, and satyrs. He saw these as monsters resulting from the "co-mixture of Man before the Floud, with Nymphs...and likewise the copulation of Faunes with Maids".[107] This is essentially Paracelsus's view, which includes reference to the several specific habitations of the monsters, their rational thinking, and ability to learn diverse arts. Paracelsus had already stressed the abhorrent nature of these monsters that lack the image of God and are excluded from heavenly bliss.[108] Obviously the Paracelsian account of elemental spirits, though adopted by Van Helmont, bears no connection with the latter's *inventio* of *gas*.

It may be concluded, therefore, that Van Helmont was original in his conception, observation, and cosmosophic as well as chemi-

ing Van Helmont's interest in digestive fermentation, *geesen* could as well have been in his mind as *chaos*, even if "water gas...das grosse water chaos" does occur in one sentence, which is the point proffered by Lippmann.

[105] Paracelsus, *Das Buch von den Tartarischen Krankheiten*, cap. 3, ed. Sudhoff, xi, 33.

[106] That is, *vergesen* with reference to medicinal herbs, derived from middle-high German *verjesen*, i.e., *vergären*: see Paracelsus, *Die Kärntner Schriften*, ed. K. Goldammer (Klagenfurt, 1955), p. 274, with ref. to *Das Buch von den Tartarischen Krankheiten*, cap. 17, p. 228. Ibid., cap. 17, ed. Sudhoff, xi, 106. *Phil. de gen. et fruct. quat. elem.*, tract. IV, cap. 2, ed. Sudhoff, xiii, 108.

[107] Van Helmont, *Demonstratur thesis*, 98, *Opp.* p. 642; *Oriatrike*, p. 685. For the biblical forerunners of the *sylvestres* – field-demons, "*Feldteufel*", *ss'ijrim* – see J. Fürst, *Hebräisches und Chaldäisches Handwörterbuch*, 3rd edn., 2 vols. (Leipzig, 1876), ii, 482.

[108] Paracelsus, *De natura rerum neun Bücher*, lib. I, "de generationibus rerum naturalium", ed. Sudhoff, xi, 317: the children of *sylvestres* and of nymphs are *homunculi*; they are gifted with great power against their enemies and know secrets and occulta removed from human knowledge. Ibid., lib. IX, "de signatura rerum", ed. Sudhoff, xi, 375. *Fragmente zu Anatomie und Physiologie*, I, 1, ed. Sudhoff, iii, 464.

cal interpretation of *gas* and the gases. No more than faint fore-shadowings can be found in the Paracelsian "essential spirit", the "impetuous" spirits that develop on the resolution of salts and the specific arcana. A correlation of the Paracelsian *sylvestres* with Van Helmont's *spiritus sylvestris* is vague and not convincing.

What Paracelsus had to say on chaos and spirits in essential beings were vague pronouncements which cannot be regarded as anticipating Van Helmont's concept of *gas*. The position is different with regard to Daniel Sennert. A more extended comparison of his principles in natural philosophy with those of Van Helmont will not be attempted in the present work beyond the points given in note 109. In looking for possible sources of inspiration in the discovery of *gas*, it cannot be denied that Sennert had clear insight into the object-specificity of volatile effluvia and their difference from air and water-vapour. Smoke from oak-wood, he said, is substantially different from fumes given off by wood from other trees or from manure. Effluvia emanating from the cadaver of a dog differ in quality from those of any other animal, as is indicated by their smell. Moreover, all these are different in kind from vapour which is but water volatilized and hence neither identical with air nor object-specific. Metal-fume is atomised metal and as such inhaled and deposited in the miner's lung. Sennert was a near-contemporary of Van Helmont. His relevant works appeared before those of the latter, but at a time well after Van Helmont may be estimated to have finished the bulk of his chemical experiments and to have reaped their intellectual fruit, notably his concept of *gas*. A direct influence of Sennert in this issue is therefore unlikely. Nevertheless, there are some additional points of contact, although their natural philosophies as a whole differ widely.[109]

---

[109] Daniel Sennert, *De Chymicorum cum Aristotelicis et Galenicis Consensu ac Dissensu* (1619), cap. XI, in *Opera*, 5 vols. (Lyons, 1666), i, 218a; ibid., cap. XIV, i, p. 275a. Points of contact between Sennert and Van Helmont include the essential role of form in composing mixed bodies, *Hypomnemata physica*, III, 2 in *Opera*, p. 121a–b; the rejection of *contraria* (union of components by sympathy rather than "pugna elementorum"), ibid.; the persistence of "subsidiary forms" in mixed bodies under the jurisdiction of "dominant forms", *De Consensu*, XII, in *Opera*, pp. 227b and 230a; the independence of generation of the stars, ibid., IX, p. 203a and *Hypomnemata physica*, IV, 2, p. 124a–b. Differences between them chiefly lie in Sennert's broad admission of the elements and humours of the ancients together with the "Three Principles" of Paracelsus, the latter being regarded as products of the former.

ODOURS

In the same category as and associated with *gas* by Van Helmont are odours, ferments, and putrefaction. Bodies in the ordinary or solid state fail to reflect reality and truth. Only when volatile and spiritual do they reveal their true selves. Hence the significance of *gas*, the spiritual body, matter that is sealed specifically and stands for an individual object. Odours, ferments, and putrefaction bring about transmutations through the elevation of matter as *gas*. They play an essential part in all generation, notably in spontaneous generation. This occurs in putrefaction and is revealed by the odour connected with decay. It is odour that in its turn forms the active principle in ferments, the most powerful agents of transmutation through bringing solids into their gaseous states.[110]

It is ferments that dispose empty matter or water to receive the "idea or first shape of a possible thing".[111] This disposition is "drawn" by matter from the odour of the ferment. It is a disposition for transmutation in the widest sense and goes through a sequence of stages. First, matter undergoes a vague and general loosening. Next, there is the image of the object into which matter has to be transformed. This image together with odour constitutes the ferment. It is, finally, the ferment to which the conversion of non-specific matter into the specific *gas*, that is the essence of an individual object, is due. It elevates matter and makes it effervesce. Having accomplished all this the ferment assumes the position of archeus, the vital principle of the object. As such it is called upon to control and coordinate the functions of the unit to which it gave and gives life. Nevertheless, odour has not ceased to exert its high influence. "The Odour of the Herbe Basil being enclosed in the Seed, produces that Herbe." Toxic symptoms in disease are from a fermental odour that settles upon a part of the body, and do not derive from heat or humour. The presence of this agent demands that it be driven out by another, beneficial odour. A medicine deprived of its odour

---

[110] Van Helmont, *Imago ferm. impraeg. mass. sem.*, 8–10, *Opp.* pp. 108–9.

[111] Ibid., 12, *Opp.* p. 109. In more general terms: *Causae et initia naturalium*, 23–30, *Opp.* pp. 34–5. *Magnum oportet*, 25, *Opp.* p. 148. *Imago ferm.*, 8, *Opp.* p. 108; 18, p. 110; 23, p. 110.

has lost its virtue, especially in the case of ointment for wounds and ulcers. It is an odour that touches off an epileptic fit.[112]

Odour operates by virtue of its penetrative power. It finds its way into its object, joining another odour which already resides in that object. This latter odour is the *odorabile*, the *gas* of the object. Odour, ferment, and *gas* thus concur in representing what is essential and relevant in any individual unit, the object itself in its highest purity and essence. They share a creative function, the range of which primarily depends upon the dispersion of odours throughout matter in nature at large, their power of penetration, and consequently their mutual replacement.[113] In cosmological terms, odours and ferments in their role as essential components of the semina play "their universall part in the world"; they dominate the world-stage, conferring all variety and specificity on otherwise uniform and empty matter, the watery matrix of all. Indeed, all generation and corruption is by the interaction of ferment and water (*the* element): there is no mixture, no congregation or dissipation of several elements. Instead the way always leads from water to water through a variety of fermental "informations". It is the latter which are responsible for the emergence of the sum total of individual objects and species that exist at a given time in world history, and for their mutual relationships.[114]

To separate and specify the hierarchy of psycho-physical agents that form the individual object is a somewhat artificial undertaking which Van Helmont nevertheless attempted (See Table 2). He distinguished (1) the odours. These are capable of penetrating and of transmitting (2) the images – the directional plans, "blue-prints" of structure and function. The ferments (3) join odour to image

---

[112] *Imago ferm.*, 13, *Opp.* p. 109; ibid., 11, p. 109. Ibid., 14, p. 109; *Oriatrike*, p. 113. *Imago ferm.*, 15–16, *Opp.* pp. 109–10; *Oriatrike*, p. 114. *Imago ferm.*, 17, *Opp.* p. 110; *Oriatrike*, p. 114.

[113] *Imago ferm.*, 19, *Opp.* p. 110; *Oriatrike*, p. 114. *Imago ferm.*, 16, *Opp.* p. 110; *Oriatrike*, p. 114. *Magnum oportet*, 36, *Opp.* p. 151. *Magnum oportet*, 2, *Opp.* p. 144. *Imago ferm.*, 20, *Opp.* p. 110; *Oriatrike*, pp. 114–15. *Imago ferm.*, 16, *Opp.* p. 110. *Magnum oportet*, 26, *Opp.* p. 149; *Oriatrike*, p. 155.

[114] *Imago ferm.*, 33–4, *Opp.* p. 112; *Oriatrike*, pp. 116–17. The ferment is the "seminal principle", the agency *through* which, by contrast with water, the material "element" *from* which. The ferment "disposing" matter produces the semina therein: *Causae et initia naturalium*, 23, *Opp.* p. 34. Ibid., 25–6, pp. 34–5: ferments were "planted" by the creator in the earth as "gifts and roots, continuously propagating, self-sufficient and durable to the end of time for the awakening and making of semina from water".

Table 2. *The seminal agents productive of specific individual objects*

The instruments of semen
    SEMEN
           — contains in a scale of ascending subtlety:
      ARCHEUS (*gas spirituale*)
      FERMENTUM
           ODOUR: impregnating, "dealing", and
                    "disposing" putrifying matter by
                    means of Ferment
           IMAGO: transfers knowledge of what has
                    to be done to Odour and Ferment

Their genealogy
    Parent generating
      GENERANS
      — by means of:
        LIBIDO
        — conceiving:
        IMAGO (IDEA of SELF)
                   — thereby activating:
        SEMEN
        — containing:
        SEMINAL ARCHEUS – which is a:
        GAS of BALSAMIC nature (Salt)

---

and inform matter. The *gas* (4) is the ready-made object in a volatile state, "disposed" matter. The archeus (5) is *gas* of higher grade, informed by luminous aura and splendour. Lastly the semen (6) of sexual generation contrasts with the "naked" ferment of spontaneous generation; it is an organism in miniature endowed with ferment, image, and odour, the "dispositional knowledge of things to be done", and the archeus.

The order in which these spiritual agents are presented seems to be determined in the first place by their relative complexity, as shown in the progression from odour, the simplest, to the most composite, the semen. A further criterion is the closeness of the agent to matter. Here *gas* marks the turning point. It is closest to matter, as it is by definition matter that has retained the object-specific seal. Equally, archeus and semen are matter-bound, whereas ferment, image, and odour are only loosely and by choice connected with matter. In sharp contrast, forms and lights occupy a position high above matter. They derive directly from God and act without intermediary.

Thus, Van Helmont attributed to the odours a universal creative and generative role. He regarded them as the active principle in ferments, and the latter as the driving force in the semina of all natural objects. An object-specific odour is productive of the *gas* that is the essential spiritual nucleus of the individual object, its archeus. Interaction between bodies can be interpreted in terms of a traffic between specific odours, one besetting or replacing another. With respect to sources from which Van Helmont could have derived inspiration for his high appreciation of odours, it seems that he was influenced in this (as on so many other topics) by the alchemists, by renaissance Neo-Platonism, and by Paracelsus.

Aristotle had defined odour as a smoke-like exhalation from fire, a *kapnodes anathymiasis ek pyros*. Though diffused through air and water, odour was definitely not an exhalation of or from water; it was not an *atmis*, a watery exhalation. For the latter was cold, static, or tending to move downwards, whereas odour, a smoky exhalation, was dry, hot, dynamic, and in upward motion. It was perceived, like sound, through connate *pneuma*. The passages pre-formed for the transmission of odour and sound are full of connate *pneuma*. It is by means of these passages that the body communicates with the ambient air.[115]

Among these Aristotelian statements the Helmontian would give pre-eminence to the distinction between water-vapour and odour (the "dry smoky exhalation"). Van Helmont insisted that the essential odour, the *gas* of the object, was a "new spirit so far unknown" that had nothing to do with water-vapour or air. It could be made evident through heat, by heating, distillation, or other chemical manipulation at the hands of the *philosophus per ignem*. The odour or *gas* essential and specific to the individual object was, therefore, in Aristotelian parlance, from fire (*ek pyros*). It was not evaporation, that is watery or airy, but a smoke with individual characteristics. By contrast with the Aristotelian view, the Galenic references to the concept held nothing of interest for the Helmontian.[116]

[115] Aristotle, *De sensu*, 2, 438b20. *De partibus animalium*, II, 2, 649a22. *Meteorologica*, II, 4, 359b32; ibid., I, 3, 340b, 27, 29. *De sensu*, 5, 443a21. *Problemata*, IX, 3, 5, 908a25. *De generatione animalium*, II, 6, 744a.

[116] For Galen's references to: aromatica in epilepsy, *De remediis parabilibus*, II, 2, 6–7, ed. Kühn, xiv, 402; vaporous smells arising in cerebral ventricles, *De simplicium medicamentarum temperamentis ac facultatibus*, IV, 22, ed. Kühn, xi, 698. *De placitis Hippocratis et Platonis*, VII, 5, ed. Kühn, v, 628. *De instrumento odoratus*, 3, ed. Kühn, ii, 864–5.

The sweet smell (*euodia*) of the heavenly worlds and the banishing of demons by the smell of the consecrated ointment are among specific gnostic doctrines relevant in this context. In alchemy, an offspring of gnosticism and Aristotelian doctrine, *odores* and unguent (*unctuositas, humidum unctuosum*) are fundamental in the generation of minerals and metals. Their basic humidity by which they are fusible is not water, but a thick and unctuous moisture. It resists the heat of the furnace, thus inviting comparison with the radical humour of animated beings, which is not easily exsiccated by heat because of its fatty nature. The viscous or unctuous prime matter of all metals is thus incombustible; it is subtle and mixed with earthy matter. Unctuousness is retained in the roots of the metals. Glutinous, hot, and subtle oiliness (*oleaginositas*) was said to be the semen of silver and gold. Metal loses its essential virtue when it loses its unctuous moisture on being dissolved and made volatile.[117] It is by means of a "radical unguent" that metals are engendered in the viscera of the earth. The "soul" of the Philosophers' Stone is an "oil" (*oleum lapidis*), the "unguent of the Philosophers"; it "glows without fuel" and is not subject to combustion. God anoints the alchemist with the "oil of joy" (*oleum laetitiae*) to ward off destructive forces. The oily root of mineral or metal is related to its fatty sulphur component, at the same time fulfilling the role of its soul, that is the psycho-somatic link which joins the spirit ("mercury") with body (*faex, terra*), the "earthy dregs". This is the "sulphuric soul" (*arche theiode*) which is of caustic or fiery nature, a fire that purifies the body and thus enables the spirit to penetrate and to maintain it alive – as the ancient Hellenistic alchemists had it.[118] This Hermetic concept of oily-combustible sulphur as the soul of mineral and metal is closely related to the astral body of Aristotelian ancestry. Its persistent appeal is manifested in

---

[117] Ewaldus Vogelius, *Liber de lapidis physici conditionibus*, in *Theatrum chemicum* (1613), iii, 544, 548.

[118] Sendivogius, *Orthelii Commentarius in novum Lumen Chymicum*, tract. XII, in *Theatrum chemicum*, 6 vols. (Strasbourg, 1659–61), vi, 448. *Clangor Buccinae* in *Artis auriferae*, 3 vols. (Basel, 1610), i, 315. *De alchimia opuscula*, ed. Cyriacus Jacobus (Frankfurt, 1550), fols. 41v, 52r, 33v. *Rosarium philosophorum* in *Artis auriferae*, ii, 147. *Scala philosophorum*, in *Artis auriferae*, ii, 97. *Allegoriae super librum Turbae*, in *Artis auriferae*, i, 91. Thomas Aquinas, *Aurora*, in *Harmoniae inperscrutabilis chymico-philosophicae*, II, coll. Johannes Rhenanus (Frankfurt, 1625), p. 183; and ibid., *Comment. in Turbam*, p. 267. *Collection des anciens alchimistes Grecs*, ed. M.P.E. Berthelot, 3 vols. (Paris, 1887–8), ii, 152 and iii, 152; ii, 192 and iii, 196 (Zosimus).

the ideas of many thinkers of the renaissance and most notably in Paracelsus.[119] The unctuous-combustible and sulphurous metal-soul is by its smoky nature connected with smell; it is an *odorabile* and as such relevant to Van Helmont's conception of *gas*. Both sulphuric soul and *gas* are *vincula*, links that bridge the gulf between matter (water) and spirit. It is through this link that "empty" matter is "sealed" with the stamp of specificity and transmuted into the individual or specific object.

Closer to Van Helmont than the alchemical sources so far mentioned, however, was the commentary to the "Hermetic golden tract on the Secret of the Stone" (1610), probably by the elusive Paracelsist Israel Harvetus. The tract itself was much older, dating from the Latin Middle Ages and the reception of Arabic alchemy. Its first edition was in 1566.[120] One of the principal topics discussed in this tract is the "unctuous" kernel of metal (mercury) – to wit, "sulphur". The "radical sulphurous fatness of minerals" of the older alchemical sources acquires in this tract a wider cosmological significance. It is the "intermediary ointment" that unites celestial light with earthly darkness, achieving the marriage of heaven and earth which Pico saw as the task of natural magic. Two contraries are thus brought together by an intermediate agent (a "mean" or "mediocre"); consequently each natural object has three components, namely fluid (*utilis aqua*), ointment (*unguentum*), and body (*faex, terra*, dregs).[121] The intermediary (*unguentum mediocre*) is identified with fire and hence bracketed with the *sulphura*, that is the ignitable and igniting.[122] Through its relationship with combusti-

---

[119] Pagel, *Harvey*, pp. 263–78. Idem, *Das medizinische Weltbild des Paracelsus. Seine Zusammenhänge mit Neuplatonismus und Gnosis* (Wiesbaden, 1962), pp. 54–62; 105–8. On the emergence of the "Hermetic" middle-soul, that is sulphur in Paracelsus, see W. Pagel, "Paracelsus: Traditionalism and Mediaeval Sources" in *Medicine, Science and Culture, Historical Essays in Honor of Owsei Temkin*, ed. L. G. Stevenson and R. P. Multhauf (Baltimore, 1968), p. 61.

[120] *Hermetis trismegisti tractatus aureus de lapidis physici secreto...à quodam Anonymo scholiis illustratus*, in *Theatrum chemicum* (1613), iv, 731 et seq.; also in J. J. Manget, *Bibliotheca chemica curiosa*, 2 vols. (Geneva, 1702), i, 400–45. First printed in *Ars chemica* (Strasbourg, 1566), pp. 7–31. On the presumed author of the *Scholia*, Israel Harvetus, see C. Gilly, "Zwischen Erfahrung und Spekulation. Theodor Zwinger", p. 74. Features reminiscent of Gerard Dorn (in a preamble called *Gnosicus Belga*) were suggested by Pagel, "Paracelsus: Traditionalism and Mediaeval Sources", pp. 58–61.

[121] Pico, *De hominis dignitate*, in *Opera* (Basel, 1601), p. 217; *Hermetis trismegisti tractatus aureus*, p. 731.

[122] *Hermetis trismegisti tractatus aureus*, in *Ars chemica*, p. 18.

ble sulphur it is odour and *odorabile*. In establishing the marital conjunction of heaven and earth it qualifies as that subtle body of which Ficinian Neo-Platonists said that it is almost soul just as it is soul that is almost body.

The commentary (*scholia*) to the Hermetic text just considered demonstrates its indebtedness to Neo-Platonism of the Ficinian stamp when dealing with *odorabilia*, such as the philosopher's ointment and sulphurous middle spirit. Indeed, odours play a prominent part in nourishing spirit and hence in prolonging life, according to Ficinus. People of small stature and indifferent digestion live, favoured by a hot climate, on the "odours of the sun". Odour sustains spirit and hence life, because both are specific vapours and like sustains like.[123]

The forty-third chapter of the first book of Agrippa's *Occult Philosophy* is devoted to the power of incense (*suffitus, suffumigationes*). This enables air and spirit to capture celestial gifts that are carried by stellar rays. Thus, divine inspiration is acquired in forecasting events through fumigation.[124] For our spirit is a subtle vapour of blood that is pure, lucid, airy, and unctuous. Agrippa had thus insisted on the association of odour with air and the significance of this association. The latter is given even greater emphasis in the work of Paracelsus. Odour is an "air" (*geruch ein lufft geheissen wird*). As such it is "impressed" into something which makes it part of its body. Air may thus receive an impression from sulphuric ore whereby it becomes a specific air that is recognisable by its odour and may be ignited. A fiery air imbued with a sulphuric impression gives plants such as lilies their specific odour. A specific air contained in fire enables the salamander to live in fire. A sulphurous odour that poisons the cells of the brain causes epilepsy by virtue of its stupefactive properties. The odour of excrement differs with species and even with individuals. Putrefaction arising in earth gives off an odour that is different from that arising in the stomach.[125]

---

[123] Marsilio Ficino, *De triplici vita, II: de vita longa*, cap. XVIII in *Opera* (Venice, 1516), fols. 148v–149r; ibid., *III: de vita coelitus comparanda*, cap. XXII, fol. 165v. *Asclepius*, cap. XIII, ed. Ficino, in *Opera*, fol. 132v. Trans. as *Hermes Trismegistus his second book called Asclepius* (London, 1657), p. 116. *Lucii Apuleii Opera omnia*, ed. G. F. Hildebrand (Leipzig, 1843), cap. XXXVIII, p. 262. *Corpus Hermeticum*, ed. and trans. A. D. Nock and A-J. Festugière, 2nd edn. (Paris, 1960), pp. 348–9.

[124] Agrippa, *De occulta philosophia*, I, 43 (Lyons, 1550), p. 87; I, 44, p. 90; I, 45, p. 91.

[125] Paracelsus, *Von der Bergsucht*, II, 2, ed. Sudhoff, ix, 493; *Elf Traktat*, ed. Sudhoff, i, 143. *Bruchstücke...des Modus Pharmacandi* (aliquae aegritud. ex Physica. De

Life and all activity are bound up with odour and sulphur. The latter may itself be called alive, in as much as it stinks and burns; the life of sulphur is a combustible stinking fatness. Similarly, the life of effervescent excrement lies in its evil and morbific smell. Having lost its smell, excrement is dead. Whatever has a strong, good smell – bisem, musk, ambra, or civet – is alive, until it loses its fragrance. Hence the connection of life with balsam, which is marked out by its fragrance. Man's life is but an "astral balsam, a balsamic impression, a celestial and invisible fire, an enclosed air and a tinging spirit of salt". It is a spirit of salt that prevents putrefaction and evil-smelling decay in flesh and blood. The ease with which metal is made fluid depends upon its fatness – the harder the metal the less its fatness. Odour is one of the factors that determine the specificity of things and their lives. Of the Paracelsist forerunners of Van Helmont, Severinus also connected life with odour. Who would, he said, pronounce as dead whatever is endowed with the valour and power of flavour and odour?[126] This line of thought was not, of course, confined to Paracelsists. Before Severinus and independently of Paracelsus, Cardano had accorded odour a privileged position in biology (*odoris privilegium*). Of all sense-impressions odour alone has direct access to the brain. Hence it can ruin, or recreate, man. It is the divine part in us that is delighted by fragrance, just as incense was burnt to propitiate the gods. Smells form a link connecting soul and body; they are of the finest corporality, are vapours that are bound up with the bodies on which they are impressed. In this they resemble touch and taste, but they also exist independently of body, unlike sound and vision. Creatures distinguished by their sharp sense of smell, such as dogs and vultures, are rightly regarded as more sagacious. On this as on many other relevant points Cardano was borrowing from Aristotle. Naturally Scaliger, Cardano's implacable critic, found much to object to in this context.[127]

stercore), ed. Sudhoff, iv, 488. *Neun Bücher Archidoxis*, VIII, ed. Sudhoff, iii, 172–3: musk (*sibeta*) banishes faecal smell, aromatic medicine banishes disease. Stronger smells (eg. musk) overpower weaker ones (eg. the fragrance of roses). Hence musk is preferred in medicines. Unconscious persons who cannot take medicine benefit from *odorifera* which move the blood and refresh beyond description.

[126] Paracelsus, *De natura rerum neun Bücher*, IV, ed. Sudhoff, xi, 330–2; Severinus, *Idea medicinae philosophicae*, cap. II, p. 25.

[127] Cardano, *De subtilitate* (1559), lib. XIII, pp. 499–500. Aristotle, *De sensu*, cap. V, 444a; *Ethica Nicomachea*, III, 10, 1118a18 and *Ethica Eudemia*, III, 2, 1231a5. Julius

FERMENTATION

In according ferments a central position in his natural philosophy, Van Helmont would seem to have been indebted to alchemy in the first place and to Paracelsus in the second. In the ancient sources fermentation is closely associated with effervescence and the role of acid and salt therein. The basic term is "leaven" (*zyme*) and its derivatives. Thus, black bile was said to ferment like leaven and the stomach to be "seething" (*zeousan*) and "in ferment" (*ezymomenen*) before coming to rest.[128] "Seething and fermentation" were believed to enable black bile to erode earth and similarly to support gastric digestion by virtue of its acid nature.[129] Fermentation was also thought to be instrumental in acid putrefaction.[130] It becomes a generative agent in Plato and more definitely in Aristotle. In Plato's *Timaeus* an acid and saline ferment is said to suffuse the elemental mass of soft flesh and to play a part in the development of blood-borne particles to hollow transparent water bubbles forming around "air".[131] Aristotle compared the growth of a grub-like primordium (*scolex*) in certain animals, with the growth of yeast. Equally, eggs were said to grow by virtue of the yeasty matter (*perittoma zymodes*) which they contain.[132]

In mediaeval pharmacology, fermentation became significant with Avicenna's speculation on compounds that act *tota substantia.* A fermentative interaction between their several components was thought to lead to a new product which had properties unique to the individual substance and which transcended in quality the quality of its constituents. *Fermentum* was the stock-in-trade of the *Antidotaria*. Henry of Mondeville (*c.* 1260–1320), for example, re-

---

Caesar Scaliger (1484–1558), *Exotericarum exercitationum liber XV* (1559; Frankfurt, 1650), Exerc. CCCIII, p. 906; see also, CIV, 4, p. 384 and CXLI, 1, pp. 477–8; CXLII, 2, p. 485 (non ab odore venena). Scaliger's main criticism concerns the linking of odour with soul and spirit and Cardano's support of Neo-Platonism.

[128] Hippocrates, *Peri diaites oxeon* (On regimen in acute diseases), ed. Kühn, ii, 60; ed. Jones, ii, 116. *Peri archaies iatrikes* (Ancient medicine), XI, ed. Jones, i, 32–3.

[129] Galen, *De methodo medendi*, XIV, 9, ed. Kühn, x, 973–4; Pliny, *Naturalis historiae*, XVIII, 11, ed. L. Jahn, 3 vols. (Leipzig, 1878), iii, 111.

[130] Galen, *De simplicium medicamentorum temperamentis ac facultatibus*, V, 17, ed. Kühn, xi, 760; vi, 6, p. 882; *De alimentorum facultatibus*, I, 2, ed. Kühn, vi, 482.

[131] *Timaeus*, 74c. See F. M. Cornford, *Plato's Cosmology. The Timaeus* (London, 1937), p. 297. Ibid. 66b; Cornford, pp. 271–2.

[132] Aristotle, *De generatione animalium*, III, 4, 755a18–23.

fers under *fermentum* to the Arabic *chamir* which is "cold" because of its acidity.[133]

These concepts of fermentation are of no direct significance for Van Helmont. The same cannot be said with respect to alchemical ideas on ferments. The connection is implied even in the title of one of his fundamental naturalistic treatises. In the *Image of the Ferment Makes the Mass Pregnant with Semen*, several attributes assigned by alchemists to ferments are epitomised. There is first the conversion of the "mass" (dough) by the ferment into something akin to the ferment – in Helmontian terms its "image". Then, it is a material mass that is thus transmuted; an example of real conversion of one substance into another, a transmutation. This is compared with pregnancy, recalling the saying of the alchemists that metallic ferment, the philosophers' stone, converts all metals into itself by making itself pregnant and giving birth to itself. Indeed, further ferment is engendered by the fermented mass ad infinitum. At the same time it is up-graded in quantity, virtue, and perfection. Thus exalted, it gains the position of soul which must be incorporated to render bodies reactive. The soul-like ferment vanquishes matter – *fermentum pastae vincit pastam*. Its "luminous" quality enables ferment to enter bodies which are thereby exalted and sublimated, reaching a level intermediate between the elemental and the spiritual, a mercurial existence.[134] A close relative of ferment is tincture.[135]

Paracelsus had bracketed ferment with such powerful arcana as elixir and semen. These are seen as predominantly spiritual and it is through fermentation that corporality is lost and bodies "ascend to their exaltations". The "highest ferment which is reserved in nature" brings about the maturing of fruit by means of digestion

[133] M. R. McVaugh, "The Conceptual Background of Medieval Pharmacy", in *Arnaldus de Villanova, Opera medica omnia, II, Aphorismi de gradibus* (Granada and Barcelona, 1975), pp. 17–18. *Die Chirurgie des Heinrich von Mondeville*, ed. J. L. Pagel (Berlin, 1892), *Antidotarium*, pt. 139, p. 568.

[134] From the broad stream of pertinent alchemica only a few can be cited, e.g., Arnald of Villanova, *Liber perfecti magisterii, qui lumen luminum nuncupatur* in *Theatrum chemicum* (1613), iii, 118. Idem, *Rosarius philosophorum*, 19, in *Opera omnia*, ed. N. Taurellus (Basel, 1585), cols. 2016–17. *Pretiosa margarita novella de…philosophorum lapide*, ed. Janus Lacinius (Venice, 1546), cap. IV, "de fermento", fol. 109r. *Theatrum chemicum* (1622), v, 676–7, 678. Gerhard Dorn, *Philosophia chemica* in *Theatrum chemicum* (1613), i, 459.

[135] For tincture, a highly valued secret efficient or *arcanum specificum*, see Martin Ruland, *Lexicon Alchemiae* (Frankfurt, 1612), pp. 474–5.

and growth. Elixir is "medicine fermented from the seven metals". Christ, the "food of the soul", the divine word, is called *fermentum* in pseudo-Paracelsian tracts; it is said to be contained essentially and substantially in each thing and to dwell therein.[136]

From such statements it is clear that such powerful agents as tincture and ferment are not limited to the organic world. Indeed, all that happens in the universe is subjected to their rule. At all events, cosmic processes invite interpretation in terms of animal physiology and pathology in the world of alchemy and of Paracelsus and his followers, just as the reverse is true. The semina of metals and minerals grew and were delivered from pregnant and fertilised earth, in the same way as animals and plants came into being. Consequently, fermentation occupied a position of high dignity in vitalist chemistry and geology. Of Van Helmont's contemporaries the most significant in this respect is Edward Jorden (1569–1632). In the Bible, Jorden argued, seeds were created before plants. By analogy this should apply to minerals and metals, thus implying the existence of mineral seeds. Terrestrial fermentation, as visualised by Paracelsus and the alchemists, should be invoked as the driving force in mineral generation, rather than the interplay of the elements or celestial emanation in which the ancients believed. The alchemist Jean d'Espagnet, another Helmontian contemporary, believed in "nature's ferment". This he visualised as a spirit intermediary between the stars and the elements on earth; it transmitted astral forces to the "womb of the earth", in which it generated its fruit by fermentation.[137]

Anton Günther Billich (1598–1640), the son-in-law and defender of the distinguished chemist Angelo Sala and himself a keen chemist, took an active interest in contemporary controversies on the structure and transformation of matter. The preface of Billich's work on fermentation is dated 1632, at Oldenburg where he worked

---

[136] Paracelsus, *Elf Traktat*, II, ed. Sudhoff, i, 30 (vom schwinen). *Kolleghefte zu den Büchern der Paragraphen*, ed. Sudhoff, v, 308; *Das Buch Paragranum*, III, "von der alchimia", ed. Sudhoff, viii, 187–8. *Aus Kollegienheften De gradibus*, III, ed. Sudhoff, iv, 109. *Liber Azoth*, 2, ed. Sudhoff, xiv, 557, 560.

[137] A. G. Debus, "Edward Jorden and the Fermentation of the Metals: an Iatrochemical Study of Terrestrial Phenomena", in C. E. Schneer, ed., *Toward a History of Geology* (Cambridge, Mass., 1969), pp. 100–21. Idem, *The English Paracelsians* (London, 1965), pp. 162–4. Jean d'Espagnet, *Enchiridion physicae restitutae* (Paris, 1623), cap. 147, p. 115; ibid., caps. 45–6, pp. 33–4 (substituting the "copulating" – fermentative – *amor naturae* as generating agent, for the Aristotelian corruption as preceding all generation).

as physician by permanent appointment to the local ruler and died in 1640. The editions of his works usually quoted are those of 1639 and 1643, respectively.[138] Billich's ideas were thus published at a time when Van Helmont was still active, and should have come to his notice during the last decade of his life. He may well have greeted them as support for his own concepts.

There are in Billich's discussion two points which invite comparison with Van Helmont, both of them supporting the position of high dignity accorded to fermentation by the latter.[139] First, common to the anti-Paracelsian Billich and Van Helmont is the extension of its significance to every realm of nature as the magisterial and seminal process that is responsible for all events. Similarly, both authors firmly separate fermentation from putrefaction and corruption, thus deliberately distinguishing themselves from the ancients. Billich, however, allows the classical elements a prominent role in bringing about fermentation, although he regards fire as the leader. Van Helmont could not have agreed with any explanation in elemental terms. It should be remembered nonetheless that he extolled fire as the universal muse of chemical philosophy and, as the *philosophus per ignem*, ascribed luminous and hence "numinous" power to the ferment.

Not long after, Billich's conclusions were supported and extended to apply to any change in natural objects by Jacob Ziegler. Ziegler made fermentation the universal agent to account for "how

---

[138] See Anton Günther Billich, *Anatomia Fermentationis Platonicae* (Leyden, 1646), printed as Appendix to Hermann Conring, *De sanguinis generatione et motu naturali*, 2nd edn. (Leyden and Amsterdam, 1646), pp. 463–547, followed by Conring, *De fermentatione exercitationes ad A. G. Billichii anatomen fermentationis Platonicae*, pp. 547–626. First printed as part of Billich, *Thessalus in chymicis redivivus*, ed. J. Baier (Mainz, 1639): see J. J. Manget, *Bibliotheca scriptorum medicorum*, 4 vols. (1731), i, 310. On Billich, see H. Kangro, *Joachim Jungius. Experimente und Gedanken zur Begründung der Chemie als Wissenschaft* (Wiesbaden, 1968), pp. 196–217, 290; M. Salomon in Hirsch, *Biog. Lex. hervorr. Ärzte*, i, 459. Partington, *History of Chemistry*, ii, 280–1.

[139] This was criticised by Sennert in a letter appended to Conring's edition of Billich (Frankfurt, 1643), pp. 623–6. Fermentation is again bracketed with putrefaction as the dissolution of a mixed body in moist heat in Sennert, *Institutionum medicinae*, V, 3, 2, cap. 7, in *Opera*, pp. 637–8. Conring in his turn (1642) extended the competence of fermentation beyond Sennert's restrictions, especially in disease, associating it with contagion and its semina. In general terms he regarded fermentation as an "agitation by some sort of putridity and degeneration": Conring, *De fermentatione . . . ad Billichii*, app. to idem, *De sanguinis generatione* (1646), pp. 557–64; also pp. 565, 568, with reference to inflammatory swellings caused by poisons, or tumours.

one thing can naturally vanish and another be generated from it". Fermentation therefore embraced not only generation, but also corruption. More important and more original was Willis's treatise, which followed in 1659. He, too, accorded fermentation a leading role "in the spacious field of nature where all is full of fermentation".[140] Not only minerals and plants and animals but the whole sublunary world – a single united mass – is seeded and made pregnant by fermenting particles. These are in constant motion and agitation in all directions, angles, and regions, moving like ants, meeting, associating, and separating from each other, marrying and divorcing and thus mastering generation, corruption, and transmutation.

Here Willis echoes Billich as well as Van Helmont, with the difference that the issue is no longer to do with spiritual agencies like Van Helmont's, but rather with particles of matter, or at best spirits in which the term meant no more than constant movement and agitation of matter. Associating the elements of the ancients with the three Paracelsian principles, Willis indulges in materialistic speculations which would have been distinctly unacceptable to Van Helmont. On the other hand, Willis subscribes to the idea of Helmontian semina and their intrinsic Spirits as being significant in the maintenance and perfection of the individual.[141] He also adopts the Helmontian parasitic existence of "foreign guests" from outside that reside in the host organism; but again it is not foreign archei with their middle-lives, not foreign vital units which must be kept or subjugated in a reduced state, but fiery particles joined with saline particles. These must be separated from each other by earthy matter lest they develop destructive heat. If they do, dissolution of the individual object follows. This *qua compositum* bears the germ of decomposition in itself because of the multiplicity and variety of components which must be kept together in harmony. The greater the object's heterogeneity the shorter the way to its decomposition. Having reached maturity and perfection, natural bodies do not persist much longer. Their active principles, spirit,

[140] Jacob Ziegler, *Fermentatio generationis et corruptionis causa. Ein kurtzer Bericht wie ein Ding natürlich vergehen und ein anders daraus werden könne* (Basel, 1647). Thomas Willis (1622–75), *De fermentatione*, in *Opera Omnia* (Lyons, 1676), pp. 1–62: cap. 5, p. 20, with the subtitle: "sive de motu corporum naturalium inorganico".
[141] Willis, *De fermentatione*, cap. 3, p. 11; ibid., cap. 8, p. 32. For a detailed and perceptive account see A. B. Davis, *Circulation Physiology and Medical Chemistry 1650–1680* (Lawrence, Kansas, 1973), pp. 50–8, 81–92.

sulphur, and salt are in perpetual motion, the spirit inclined to fly away, the sulphur to be liquefied, and the salt to evaporate slowly, leaving a foul smell.[142] With this the kinship of fermentation with putrefaction seems to be endorsed.

Although accepting the "great necessity" (*magnum oportet*) of Van Helmont as the general principle underlying corruption, Willis left blurred the clear line drawn between putrefaction and fermentation by Billich and Van Helmont. He believed in "fiery" particles and their role in fermentation, thus recognising the importance of "fire" as postulated by Billich, without, however, according it the exclusive rights which the latter had claimed for it. The fiery particles are vaguely identifiable with spirit, which in the object is responsible for its maturing and perfection through sublimation ("exaltation"), unfolding, and transformation of its thicker particles. There is also room in Willis's speculations for spirit as an ethereal substance of highest subtlety, a divine "breath" that the father of nature established in this sublunary world. Recollecting, no doubt, the Helmontian *blas*, Willis makes this universal spirit rise and subside inside the canals and cavities of the body, thus governing the rhythmic repetition of vital motions and thereby animation, vegetation, and growth as much as the locking and unlocking of the bolts which hold the object together.[143]

Willis thus recognised with Van Helmont (and Billich) the universal significance of fermentation, but replaced the archei by particles of matter and corporeal spirits. He devised elemental patterns, associating the elements of the ancients with the three Paracelsian principles – concepts alien to Van Helmont. On the other hand, like Van Helmont, Willis extolled the semina with their intrinsic spirits that motivate matter and lead individuals to maturation and perfection. Indeed, the tendency to perfection figures prominently in Willis's definition of fermentation: "The intrinsic motion of particles or principles of individual bodies with a tendency towards perfection of the individual body or for its transmutation into something else."[144] The perfection of a body through domi-

---

[142] Willis, *De fermentatione*, cap. 6, in *Opera*, p. 21. Ibid, cap. 8, pp. 31, 34. Ibid., cap. 8, p. 32.

[143] Ibid., cap. 2, p. 3.

[144] Ibid., caps. 3 and 8. Brief mention may be made of a work of minor significance, but indebted to Van Helmont: Martin Kerger, *De fermentatione* (Wittenberg, 1663).

nating spirits like the semina which make matter pregnant are, of course, alchemical echoes common to Willis and Van Helmont.

A somewhat surprising application of fermentation to cosmology may be found in the *Hypothesis physica nova* which the twenty-five-year-old Leibniz submitted to the Royal Society of London.[145] Here divine ether is made to penetrate the major part of matter which becomes the earth, and to be enclosed in *bullae*. These are formed through the interaction of contrary rectilinear and circular motions engendered by the penetrating ether. It is the universal motion in our "Terr-aqu-aereo" globe which serves as the basic pattern for all natural processes, rather than the figures of atoms or the varieties of particles and whirls (*vortices*). In the beginning, then, innumerable *bullae* arose varying in size and thickness, through the interaction of the circular motion of the earth and the straight motion of light. These *bullae* are the semina of things, the warps of species, the receptacles of ether, the foundations of bodies, the causes of their consistency, of their variety, and of the momentum in their motions. All things solid are held together by virtue of the *bullae*; they are secured by their gyration around proper centres. Thus, earth no doubt consists of *bullae*. In forming *bullae*, fermentation is liable to change a substance by turning it inside out, whereby what looked alkaline may prove to be acid and vice versa.[146] Like Willis, Leibniz preferred interpretation in chemical rather than atomistic and figurative terms. It is the chemical explanation which incorporates the significance of the *bullae*. Again, Leibniz expected notions of the exhaustion and distension of *bul-*

[145] Gottfried Wilhelm Leibniz, *Hypothesis physica nova qua phenomenorum plerorumque causae ab unico quodam universali motu, in globo nostro supposito, neque Tychonicis, neque Copernicanis aspernando repetuntur. Nec non Theoria motus abstracti.* Londini, impensis J. Martyn, Reg. Soc. typographi ad insigne Campanae in Coemeterio Divi Pauli, 1671. 74 pp. Sm.–12°. The *Hypothesis physica* was reprinted in Vol. IV of *Leibnitii Epistolae*, ed. C. Kortholt (Leipzig, 1742), pp. 279–345. The *Theoria motus* was dedicated to the Académie Royale des Sciences. The imprint in Kortholt is: Moguntiae, typis Christophori Küchleri anno 1671 in 12°.

[146] *Hypothesis physica* (1671), paras. 36–9, pp. 38–41. Kortholt edn. (1742), pp. 313–14. Ibid. (1671) para. 45, pp. 43–4; Kortholt edn., pp. 316–17. Here the recognition by Pierre le Givre of the alkaline nature of mineral waters previously reputed to be acid may have been relevant: *Le sécret des eaux minérales acides . . . qui montre que l'opinion commune touchant l'acidité des eaux minérales ne peut subsister* (Paris, 1667). Partington (*History of Chemistry*, ii, 694) only cites *Arcanum acidularum principiorum chimicorum* (Paris, 1670), and points out that le Givre was endorsed by Friedrich Hoffmann. The acid taste of a water which gave an alkaline reaction to indicators was attributed by le Givre to "spirits".

lae to increase our understanding of muscular motion, which had
been attributed by Willis to the discharge of innumerable tensile
shooting devices. For Leibniz, Van Helmont's archeus is really
the ether that operates through the *bullae* and, using acid and alkali
as its instruments, brings about natural processes, in particular
fermentation – the *digestio rerum fermentantium*. Equally, the archeus
is the "mercurial principle" which accounts for the perpetual internal motion that takes place in all things, but particularly in
fluids, owing to the circulation of ether. It embraces the plastic
force in semina, in salt, and in mercury. It shows itself when an
elegant "tree" is formed on mercury amalgamating with metal.[147]

Leibniz thus plainly connected fermentation with the bullous
ground-structure of all things, thereby making it a basic cosmic
process. He developed this line of thought in his *New Physical
Hypothesis* in which he promises to explain most natural phenomena in terms of a singular universal movement in our globe which
should "displease neither the followers of Tycho nor those of
Copernicus".[148] Leibniz singles out fermentation among the natural phenomena that find their cause in the internal ethereal motion
of the *bullae* which constitute the universe. He does not say in so
many words that everything is due to fermentation, but the obligatory ebullition, and *bulla*-formation connected with it, would
have rendered fermentation worthy of his particular attention and
thus affirmed its pre-eminence as asserted by Van Helmont. The
latter's name and authority frequently recur in Leibniz's treatise
and there are not a few points of contact between Leibniz's *Monadology*
and Helmontian ideas.[149]

In conclusion, the following points about the nature of ferment
can be regarded as being held in common in the sixteenth and

[147] Leibniz, *Hypothesis physica*, para. 57, pp. 57–8; Kortholt edn., pp. 328–9. Ibid.,
para. 60, pp. 70–2; Kortholt edn., pp. 341–3 (paras. 71–2). I.e., the *arbor Dianae*
well known in alchemical and Paracelsian tradition, the "philosophical tree", a
product of the "cohobation" (repeated distillation) of metal-salt solutions such as
silver-nitrate with mercury. See Paracelsus, *De natura rerum neun Bücher*, lib. 2,
"de crescentiis rerum", ed. Sudhoff, xi, 322; E. Darmstaedter, *Arznei und Alchemie.
Paracelsus-Studien* (Leipzig, 1931), p. 26.
[148] As expressed in the title quoted in note 145, above.
[149] W. Pagel, *Religious and Philosophical Aspects of Helmont's Science and Medicine*
(Baltimore, 1944), pp. 27 et seq. Idem, "The Speculative Basis of Modern
Pathology. Jahn, Virchow and the Philosophy of Pathology", *Bull. Hist. Med.*,
18 (1945), 1–43 (at pp. 18–21). See an earlier suggestion in Heinrich Ritter, *Geschichte
der christlichen Philosophie*, Vol. VI (Hamburg, 1851), p. 165.

seventeenth centuries. It is (1) a spiritual force joined to a body (*massa*); capable (2) of multiplying itself ad infinitum; of (3) subjugating or seminally impregnating any object; of (4) making the object similar ("assimilating" it) to itself, thereby perfecting it by (5) effervescence, (6) acidity, and (7) some relationship – obligatory or accidental – with putrefaction. All these points can be located in and defined against the ideas of Van Helmont, which are readily seen as providing a climax in their naturalist-chemical as well as cosmological and metaphysical aspects.

BLAS

In all fields Van Helmont's concern was the individual object and what lent it those characteristics by which it differed specifically from other objects. This is clearly evident in his concept of *gas*, the object-specific smoke, in contrast to such general "exhalations" as water-vapour and air, of which all individual objects had their share. And yet Van Helmont recognised one general and "astral-cosmic" force which he made responsible for all motion and change in the universe. He called it *blas*. This in the first place directed and determined motion; it was *blas motivum*. Motion brings about change, as is seen in the motion and change of wind. Hence there is also a *blas* of change, a *blas alterativum*. The idea is reminiscent of Platonic "fare" (*phora*); this embraced motion (*kinesis*) and change (*alloiosis*).[150] Van Helmont himself likened *blas* not to this, but to the Hippocratic *enhormon*, the intrinsic impetus that is operative in the organism just as much as in the universe where it is manifested in wind. In this he found the deeper meaning of the Hippocratic treatise *On winds* which he regarded as the most authentic and important part of the Hippocratic corpus. Unlike the "fictitious booklet" *On the Nature of Man*, its key-note was provided not by matter, to wit the elements and their complexions, but by a spiritual driving force, corresponding in all essentials to his *blas*.[151]

The cosmic *blas* is a gravitational force that governs the motion of the stars and meteorological change. This *blas meteoron* is an active ("male") agent of motion in the stars no less than on earth,

[150] Plato, *Theaetet*, 181c. Idem, *Parmenides*, 138b. See Zeller, *Philosophie der Griechen* (1875), ii, 1, p. 581.
[151] Van Helmont, *De flatibus*, 1, *Opp.* p. 399. *Humidum radicale*, *Opp.* pp. 678B–679A. *Blas humanum*, 52, *Opp.* p. 182. *Vacuum naturae*, 2, *Opp.* p. 80.

in air, and in water. By contrast, heat and cold and hence condensation and rarefaction fall under the *blas* of change (*alterativum*).
Weather in general is conditioned by the higher atmospheric stra-
tum in which the astral *blas* produces heat; one effect of the heat of
the sun is manifested in rain, snow, and hail.[152] Cold at high altitudes keeps the atoms of *gas aquae* together; when loosened by
solar heat they descend as rain.[153] Indeed, everything in the universe is in constant motion. There is no room for the Aristotelian
"unmoved mover", and even such quiescent-looking objects as
the semina ceaselessly agitate the matter in which they operate.[154]

The *blas* of man is in the first place the agent responsible for the
generative power of human semen – the "product of the lust and
desire of a manly will", in conformity, that is, with the will of the
creator. The human *blas* also finds its manifestation in the pulse.
To Galen the purpose of pulse was to expel smoke, a by-product
in the formation of vital spirit, and to cool the cardio-vascular
system. Cooling had to be by dispersion of air through the pulse.
Moreover, heat had been regarded as intrinsic to the heart, even
though the cold-blooded frog displays a heart that beats like ours,
pales on contraction, and reddens on expansion. Van Helmont
further points out that traditionally since Galen it had been left out
of account that heat cannot provide vital forces like the pulse; it is
not a provider, but a companion of life, an instrument of the basic
life-force; it can only modify and moderate functions. Nor, finally, is there an innate heat or "fiery focus" in the heart which had
been supposed to consume a "radical moisture" – if there were,
Galenic "smoke" would indeed arise and "besmirch" heart and
vascular system.[155]

Yet it cannot be questioned that heat constantly flows from the
warm-blooded heart. How, then, is it generated and sustained,
what is the tinder which once ignited continues to burn? It is not
some mysterious "non-burning fire", as traditionally believed. It
is the pulse which, far from cooling, serves to propagate heat. For
it is the pulse that restores warmth and consciousness after fainting.

---

[152] *Blas meteoron*, 5, *Opp.* p. 78. Ibid., 9–11, p. 78; ibid., 11, p. 78.
[153] Here Van Helmont employs the three Paracelsian "principles" (*tria prima*) which
he elsewhere depreciates as mere metaphors of little real value. The icy salt and
mercury of the *gas aquae* particles are softened up, the mercury at the same time
"enveloping" and liquefying their salt and sulphur.
[154] *Blas humanum*, 1, *Opp.* p. 172.
[155] Ibid., 8, *Opp.* p. 173; ibid., 16, *Opp.* p. 174.

Equally, it is the pulse that sustains the vital spirit, a "fermental light", though it does not generate it. The pulse in its turn is "made" by the heart, more precisely by the latter's intrinsic motion, its "luminous" *blas*. This cardiac *blas* is responsible not only for pulse and heat but thereby also for the "tinder" that nourishes and sustains the vital spirit. Reciprocally, it is the vital spirit that induces and keeps up motion of the heart and the arteries which are "rhythmically lifted up" and thus spread "spirit and light" throughout the body. Heat, "fermental illumination", and constant movement – *blas* – lend excellence to arterial blood. This acquires a "salty", "ethereal" "thinning out", whereby it becomes an "immediate inn" (*hospitium*) for the vital light. The pulse beat is the means that ensures homogeneity of the spirituous blood, which is comparable to the equal distribution of scent by shaking the flask.[156]

No serious attention, Van Helmont went on to claim, had been given to the chemistry of blood, arterial or venous. Mildly heated arterial blood – the bearer of vital spirit – is volatilized, whilst venous blood – the carrier of nourishment for the organs – leaves a deposit that finally becomes coal. Having served the organs, however, venous blood is also made volatile and converted into *gas*. It is thus disposed of by respiration and perspiration without leaving a deposit. In order that the "whole Venal bloud . . . may depart into a Gas, it hath need of two wings to fly, the air and a ferment".[157] "Ferment" contained in vital spirit and air breathed in "dispose the venal blood into a totall transpiration of itself". In other words, venous blood, having served its purpose in nourishing the organs, can now be "breathed away" by the lung and through the pores of the skin into the outside world.

The conversion of venous cruor into "breath" (*gas*) is further illustrated in chemical terms. These are concerned with the production of salt, fixed and volatile. Fixed salt is alkali; its particles are stable and form a deposit when a substance containing it is liquefied by heat. In settling down it "snatches" particles of less stable nature – so-called sulphurous particles – which are thus

---

[156] *Blas humanum*, 19, *Opp.* p. 174; ibid., 21, *Opp.* p. 174; ibid., 23, *Opp.* p. 175. Here Van Helmont still endorses the interventricular pores of Galen whereby venous "cruor" from the right is converted into arterial spirituous blood by virtue of a "ferment" intrinsic to the left chamber of the heart. *Blas humanum*, 23–4, *Opp.* p. 175.

[157] *Blas humanum*, 31, *Opp.* p. 177; ibid., 35, *Opp.* p. 178.

incorporated in the deposit. The fixed salt being unable to fix all the sulphur particles, the rest, which have escaped being snatched, follow their natural tendency to become volatile and in their turn force some of the salt to evaporate with them. Thus, volatile salt is generated. When heated in an open vessel all salt contained in the substance evaporates. This is what happens to the cruor of the blood in the "open vessel" of the lung, that is where it is in contact with the air. All its salt has become volatile whereby it is made disposable without residue by the breath. Conversely, there are substances such as pine-wood which on heating are completely "calcined" into fixed salt or alkali (*Weedaschen* and *Potaschen*). Additionally, some of the volatile salt of any object can be turned into fixed alkali. Thus, on distillation sixteen ounces of vinous tartar yield two and a half ounces of alkali-salt, whilst the remaining thirteen and a half ounces persist in volatile condition. In decaying matter fixed alkali is depressed through intensified and accelerated formation of volatile salt. Both – the fixed and the volatile – are identical in substance, though different in form and condition. In all this Van Helmont found the Paracelsian three principles helpful, however much he may have militated against them elsewhere.[158] He also here clearly identified alkali, for which he may claim additional laurels from the historians of chemistry.[159]

To return to pulse, blood, and respiration, this discussion may be concluded by noting the range of functions of the pulse stipulated by Van Helmont: (1) transmission of the blood from the right chamber of the heart to the left through interseptal pores; (2) promotion of the formation of vital spirit in the left chamber of the heart and the arteries depending upon it; (3) cooperation in the conversion of venous cruor into thinned-out sub-yellow (*subflavus*) arterial blood by providing the necessary agitation or "beating" of the thick material cruor; (4) help with the gradation of arterial blood in the brain, its information by the mind; (5) maintenance of the continuity of the vital light and spirit throughout the organism; (6) provision of heat, as against the traditional belief in the cooling action of the pulse; (7) volatilization of the used-up ve-

---

[158] Ibid., 38, *Opp.* p. 179; ibid., 39–41, *Opp.* pp. 179–80.

[159] D. Goltz, *Studien zur Geschichte der Mineralnamen in Pharmazie, Chemie und Medizin von den Anfängen bis auf Paracelsus* (Wiesbaden, 1972), p. 237. Van Helmont, *De lithiasi*, III, 25, *Opp.* II, p. 16 and ibid., V, 17, p. 34. See also: Partington, *History of Chemistry*, ii, 200, 225.

nous blood, making it disposable – "blowing it away" – by the breath without residue; and finally (8) cooperation with breathing in the disposal of cruor by coordination of function.[160]

Blas humanum, then, assumes its position of highest dignity in the relationship between the "blowing" pulse and the origin, movement, and maintenance of the vital spirit. Pulse plays an essential part in the reciprocal action by which the heart generates the vital spirit, and this in its turn keeps the heart moving in order to distribute pulse and its fermental light of life and its heat at equal rates. In this explanation, air is allowed no claim to the essential role attributed to it in Galenic and traditional physiology. As there is no fiery focus in the heart there is no need for smoke to be blown out, or for keeping the fire alive or damping it down by air-cooling. Cooling, indeed, would be counterproductive where all effort is obviously centred on heat, its production, distribution, and maintenance. Rather, air is essential in the lung, in the exchange of venous and arterial blood, or, more precisely, in the ultimate disposal of residual venous blood, its coarse material cruor. The discharge of the venous cruor is accomplished by its conversion into a volatile salt, which is blown away with the breath. It is a ferment in the air that makes the conversion possible. In other words an exchange takes place in the lung: an aerial ferment (*magnale*) is received into the venous blood, which is thereby rid of useless residue. A further point of interest in this remarkably advanced concept is its connection with Van Helmont's original identification of alkali. In the present context alkali stands for the fixed salt that forms the residue of venous blood. It is converted into volatile salt by the access of air and its ferment – both in vitro, and in vivo, in the lung.

It is Van Helmont, then, who stipulates the separation of breathing from heart and pulse, along lines different from those followed by Harvey and Cesalpino, but coming to the same result. This he achieved without in any way endorsing the circulation of blood, although its discovery as such is unlikely to have escaped his notice. Breathing seen as the vital instrument in balancing blood chemistry by the exchange of "residue" for "ferment", that is of a constituent of the blood for a catalyst from the air, anticipates in some respects the fundamental recognition of the chemical and

[160] Van Helmont, *Blas humanum*, 57, *Opp.* p. 183.

functional difference between arterial and venous blood. This advance belongs to the second half of the seventeenth century, to Richard Lower (1631–94), John Mayow (1645–79), Walter Needham (*c.* 1631–91), and Robert Hooke (1635–1703); it was alien to Harvey.[161] The last-named adhered to the Aristotelian singleness (*henotes*) of the blood, a feature that may well have inspired his discovery.[162] Moreover, it was Van Helmont who rejected the traditional concept of a "fiery focus" in the heart. This was not finally disposed of until well into the second half of the century, although Conring had inveighed against the notion of a luminous heat-source only a few years after Van Helmont's death.[163]

Closely connected as it is with *meteora* such as weather and wind, the *blas* obviously operates in air. For Van Helmont the latter shares with water the dignified position of a true element. As such it is inconvertible. Even the highest pressure cannot change it in such a way as (for example) to convert it into water. Air can be compressed, however. When air under high pressure is suddenly released it acquires the hitting power of a fire-arm. Van Helmont reckoned that air could be reduced to one half of its original volume under pressure. Consequently the other half must have consisted of empty space and therefore be non-corporeal. When the flame of a candle burning on top of a water surface and enclosed in a cylinder has consumed the air, the water rises in the cylinder and extinguishes the candle.[164] On the other hand, heat from an enclosed burning candle causes air to dilate and the flame to become larger than its normal size.

Hence there must be empty interstices in the air; if there were not, the process would amount to the annihilation of elementary matter. Therefore what is really consumed by the flame is not the air, but its empty interstices. The direct effect of the heat – the extension of the air – is masked, however, by the filling of the

---

[161] Partington, *History of Chemistry*, ii, 564 (Hooke), 568 (Lower), 567 (Mayow), 573 (Needham). See, more recently, R. G. Frank Jr., *Harvey and the Oxford Physiologists* (Berkeley, 1980), p. 109 with reference to Van Helmont's influence on Ralph Bathurst. Cf. W. Pagel, review in *Med. Hist.*, 23 (1981), 426–31.

[162] Pagel, *New Light on Harvey*, pp. 23, 47.

[163] Ibid., p. 165. Hermann Conring, *De calido innato sive igni animali liber unus* (Helmstädt, 1647), p. 154, cap. XV.

[164] Van Helmont, *Vacuum naturae*, 7, *Opp.* p. 80. The experiment confirms that (a) flamma est fumus accensus, (b) fumus est *gas*, (c) fuligo (soot) ascendit ex apice combusti (d) aliquid loci in aere vacuum, (e) consumpta aliqua pars *in* aere: ibid., 9, p. 81.

interstices with smoke, whereby the air is stifled and compressed. At the same time the flame is unable to compete with the adverse effect of the smoke and is extinguished. It is not extinguished for lack of nourishment after having consumed the air, since fire is no "substance" and hence not in need of aliment. Neither air nor water suffer compression calmly: when air is blown under heavy pressure into an air pocket on top of water in a closed vessel, not only abundant air but also much of the water gushes out when the vessel is opened.[165]

Vacua, then, evidently do occur normally and of necessity, however much this is denied in Aristotle and his scholastic followers. Nevertheless, though empty of body, the interstices of the air are not completely empty. What they contain is something that was created and hence exists in reality and not merely hypothetically. This is the *magnale* or spirit of the air (*Lufft-Geist*), a "middle third" (*tertium quid*) between soul and body. It is not a constituent of air, but co-exists with it as if by marital connection. *Magnale* is the vector of astral *blas* by which the latter can communicate over large cosmic areas.[166]

It follows that what impresses us as dilatation and contraction of air is really augmentation or diminution of *magnale*.[167] Such is the effervescence of beer, which floods the table when the flask is opened.[168] However, no such prosaic function does justice to the main, cosmic significance of *magnale*. This rests with its dignity as the donor and sustainer of life. Indeed, it is what is called the soul of the world, or "universal mercury". As such it is responsible for the omnipresent sympathy and antipathy and magnetic effects that manifest themselves at great cosmic distances. *Magnale* is an ether which is much more subtle than air; as a constituent of water it, rather than air, maintains the life of fishes. Above all it is *magnale*

---

[165] *Vacuum naturae*, 11, *Opp.* p. 81. Ibid., 18–19, *Opp.* p. 83.

[166] Ibid., 19, *Opp.* p. 83. Ibid., 20, p. 83. Ibid., 21, p. 83 and 22, p. 83.

[167] Ibid., 27, *Opp.* p. 84: air and water finally dispersed through scattering of atoms and appearing as a *halitus* remain substantially air and water. Rarefaction is not *of* the air, but *in* the air – an enlargement of the *magnale*.

[168] Van Helmont, Letter to Mersenne, in *Correspondence du Mersenne*, ed. Tannery and de Waard, iii, p. 34, which gives the line-drawing of a flask with cock to illustrate compression of air and water. Of all editions and translations of the *Ortus* and the *Works* (including the *Dageraad*) none includes this sketch except the German translation of 1683, the *Aufgang* (p. 124). Could its editor Knorr von Rosenroth, friend and collaborator of Franciscus Mercurius Van Helmont, have had access to manuscript – and letter – material otherwise unknown?

and not air which keeps us alive when we breathe. *Magnale* is continuously consumed by us. It "dies in fire", for *magnale* is the opposite of fire. The latter is destructive; magnale is the "life" of everything. All life is in the *magnale*, all life dwells in ether and through this *magnale* is revealed to be the soul of the universe.[169]

The immediate sources from which Van Helmont derived his notion of *magnale* are not difficult to trace. There are two, the first being the Neo-Platonic idea of the intermediary between spirit and body. This is the astral body, the *tertium quid*, which has a long history dating back to Hellenistic speculations. It was propounded by Ficino and Agrippa von Nettesheim.[170] The second source is Paracelsus. He quite commonly speaks in admiration of the *magnalia* of God and nature, these meaning to him the indefinable virtues of arcana that derive from the creator. They are supernatural, deriving from a sphere where there is no annihilation or decay. Each of us can experience them through his own astral body, the unconscious that teaches us in dream and vision. More concretely and specifically, Paracelsus's *magnale* represented the intermediary through which man is linked to heaven. Paracelsus presents it as an "ether" finer than air, and as a receptacle for astral influences and impressions. Magnalian odour, tastes, acidity, or bitterness may pollute water and thereby fishes or human bodies, afflicting them with disease or death of astral origin. Paracelsus's *MM* – his *mysterium magnum*, a version of the *magnale* – is closely linked with air, on which it confers its exalted position in life. Less concretely again, *mysterium magnum* and *magnale* stand for prime matter, the sum total of actions that are possible and realised in nature.[171] Even in

[169] Van Helmont, *Supplementum de Spadanis fontibus*, II, 12, *Opp.* p. 648. See also *Mons domini*, *Opp.* p. 743. Letter to Mersenne, 21 Feb. 1634, in *Correspondence du Mersenne*, ed. Tannery and de Waard, iii, 111.
[170] Marsilio Ficino, *De vita coelitus comparanda*, III, 3 (Venice, 1516), fol. 153r. Agrippa von Nettesheim, *De occulta philosophia*, I, 14, p. 33. E. R. Dodds, ed., *Proclus. The Elements of Theology* (Oxford, 1933), App. II, p. 313. G. Verbeke, *L'Evolution de la Doctrine du Pneuma* (Louvain, 1945), pp. 287 et seq. Pagel, *Medizinische Weltbild des Paracelsus*, pp. 38–40. See Chapter 3, "Odours".
[171] Paracelsus, *De vera influentia rerum liber* (*Philosophiae magna*, 10), tract. 2, ed. Sudhoff, xiv, 230; ibid., tract. 1, ed. Sudhoff, xiv, 215; *Astronomia Magna*, I, 8, ed. Sudhoff, xii, 196; *Philosophia ad Athenienses*, I, 1, ed. Sudhoff, xiii, 390. *Volumen medicinae Paramirum*, I, 6, ed. Sudhoff, i, 182; *Bruchstücke zum Volumen medicinae Paramirum*, ed. Sudhoff, i, 237. *Volumen medicinae Paramirum*, I, 6, ed. Sudhoff, i, 182; Pagel, *Paracelsus*, p. 299, and pp. 141, 342 with ref. to *ens astrale* and Agrippa. *Paracelsus*, pp. 91, 140, and p. 319 (Erastus's criticism of Paracelsus); Pagel, *Medizinische Weltbild des Paracelsus*, pp. 81, 95, 113.

this context they represent celestial forces sustaining life on earth. Paracelsus's *magnalia* remain a concept too vague to compare with Van Helmont's *magnale*, which is a concrete natural force that to him was even measurable – in terms, that is, of the volume of water raised by its energy.

4

Biological ideas

ARCHEUS: THE HARMONIOUS BLACKSMITH

Individual units – monads – constituted Van Helmont's world. Truth and reality found expression in things as they were created by the source of all truth. Hence "thingliness" was the subject of Van Helmont's research. Things themselves rather than relations between things, their differences and specific properties rather than what they had in common, engaged his sustained interest. It followed from his first principles in natural philosophy that these monads could not be determined by matter, which to him was nothing but inert, empty water. On the other hand the monad was not pure spirit; matter had to play its part in the emergence of the individual unit. It could be regarded as matter specifically "disposed", as something in which matter and spirit had been united to become inseparable and indistinguishable in a new being. This was neither matter nor spirit, but had something of both, namely a physical and a psychoid aspect, either of which could be turned to the surface. "Disposal" and "information" of matter lay in the hands of a trustee and executive of the divine creator. This agent had not only to hammer out and confer empirical existence upon the individual object but also to ensure its harmonious performance toward maturity and perfection in life. Indeed, this was the vital principle which abides with the individual object from its first seminal beginning to its destined end: the archeus. To Van Helmont this was not a mere concept, not an *ens rationis*, the product of human reasoning; it could be demonstrated in vitro, as an object-specific smoke, its *gas*. Whatever happens to the individual from within itself and, indeed, any reaction to outside influences, was controlled by the will, connivance, or opposition of the archeus.

The archeus is at his purest and most concentrated in the sem-ina. To these he lends a "subtle material breath of life". He forms the link between the material husk of the semen and the seminal idea or image.[1] This latter is the shadowy blue-print which prefig-ures the object to be formed. Again this is not a concept, but something real, an idea that is operative or plastic and indeed is the agent that makes the semen fertile.[2] There is, then, a tripartite stratification in the semina: the material husk, the seminal breath of life (aura) or archeus, and the operative idea or image. Again in accordance with Helmontian first principles it is the spiritual di-mension, the idea or image, that has a claim on hegemony in the stratified unit of the semen. The idea is the force that drives the semen towards germination and generation. However, to be trans-lated into empirical reality the idea needs a connection with mat-ter. This cannot be direct. The intermediary is the vital principle or archeus. To be effective an image requires imagination. Through the archeus, matter is disposed on the lines prescribed by the prologizing idea or image. Archeal imagination enlivening and directing the semen belongs to the sphere of the will of the archeus and his "knowledge of what has to be done".[3] Through the same imagination the vital image of a living being is transferred to the spirit of the semen through lustful imagination of the parent – an image that unfolds itself more and more in the course of genera-tion. Intent on corporeal effects, the seminal spirit is soon clad in a bodily garment. It perambulates through its germ – locating here the heart, designing there the brain and – as governor of the whole economy – appointing a local administrator to each of the organs, parts, and members.[4]

In this Van Helmont reveals himself as an epigenesist. Devel-opment is by free formation of organs and parts from a homoge-neous semen, de novo and not from any pre-formed material, visible or invisible. The process is not one of apposition, but a "disposal" and true transmutation of matter, brought about by the directing operative idea. The latter is in no need of matter already diversified, nor does it induce diversification. Instead there is a uniform "flow towards perfection, the maturing of properties, the

---

[1] Van Helmont, *Archeus faber*, 4, *Opp.* p. 38.

[2] Ibid., 5, *Opp.* p. 38. See also Pagel, *Harvey*, pp. 285–323.

[3] *Archeus faber*, 3, *Opp.* p. 38.

[4] Ibid., 5, *Opp.* pp. 38–9; ibid, 7, *Opp.* p. 39.

manifestation of hidden features and consummation of regular periods to the destined end."[5]

There is, then, first the archeus, the organizer that is concerned with the designing of individual organs and members. He particularises his "monarchy" in accordance with the local requirements of each of them. He establishes for each part a "stomach" or "kitchen", entrusted with the reception and preparation of the nourishment carried to the member by the blood. He appoints the "particular pilots of the members" – the subarchei, specialised in their tasks and limited by the requirements and boundaries of individual members. By contrast the "master" who appointed them is a central authority; he remains as "internal president, curator and rector", an organismic archeus "floating about", "full of light" and never at rest.[6] Obviously this *archeus influens* surpasses in potency and spirituality the subordinate *archei insiti*. These are "fixed" to their places, comparably to fixed matter and in contrast to its volatile counterpart which is "male", active, "alive" and freely moving. Conversion of the former into the latter had been one of the goals of the alchemist. A further point that should be noticed is the microcosmic analogy. Both types of archei display a parallelism with astral movements. Hence, in the "bowels the planetary Spirits do most shine forth".[7] Equally the changes and forces of the firmament are mirrored by the influent archeus. These astral analogies explained the ability of some chronic sick to forecast the weather and its changes. Here Van Helmont had recourse to a version of the Paracelsian idea in which an influence of the stars on the living being is denied, in favour of a parallelism between the courses of the stars and the periodic functions of organisms.[8] On the whole, however, Van Helmont depreciated such microcosmic analogies and admitted them only as symbols without significance for the quest of knowledge. In earlier works, his reference to them conformed to tradition. The influent archeus and spermatic spirit plants the solar spirit into the heart, the lunar into the brain, that of Jupiter into the liver, and so on. That of Mercury served as a mediator between the planets and animal sense in the region of the

---

[5] *Scholar. humorist. pass. deceptio*, I, 65, *Opp.* II, p. 166; *Fluxus ad generationem*, *Opp.* p. 686; *Ignotus hospes morbus*, 38, *Opp.* p. 468.

[6] *Archeus faber*, 7, *Opp.* p. 39.

[7] Ibid., 8, *Opp.* p. 39; *Oriatrike*, p. 25.

[8] See Pagel, *Paracelsus*, pp. 67–72.

stomach.[9] The influent archeus possesses properties of the eighth sphere, because he is the true buttress and firmament in us, and is also called the firmamental archeus.[10] However, at the same time the "natural astrology" of the human semen – the instructions for arranging the order of the developing parts – are definitely stated not to be "begged" from outside.[11] The terminological precedent for Van Helmont's distinction between "influent" and "insitus" was provided by Jean Fernel (1485–1558). "Insitus" is a term commonly used by Fernel but it was not taken up by most of his contemporaries.[12] Fernel's lead was followed by, for example, Johann Heinrich Alsted (1588–1638), the encyclopaedist and millenarian, who distinguished a radical or insitus spirit from a threefold influent spirit.[13]

The decisive conceptual inspiration for the archei – as well as for the term itself – remains Paracelsus. He called the archeus "the workman who gives origins by drawing and forging all from nature", who is responsible for the "peculiar nature and form" that appertains to each individual unit. The archeus is also seen as the chemical separator, an occult natural artist and physician, the supreme "physician of nature" who distributes to each object its vital principle in occult ways. As the "blacksmith" he separates the useful from the waste, the assimilable from the indigestible, the solution from the residue. The essential features of the Helmontian concept are here foreshadowed. There is the individualising and specifying function of the archeus: his connection with genera, species, individual objects and, importantly, their several organs and members. As an inchoative force and distributor of divine gifts he enjoys a position of high dignity in proximity to the creator.[14] There was a Paracelsian basis to the Helmontian perspec-

---

[9] See *Ortus: Archeus faber*, 8, *Opp.* p. 39. The more detailed account in the *Dageraad*, as given in *Aufgang*, p. 41, in *Von dem Archeus oder dem inwendigen Werck-Meister der Samen*, 8, may have been thought suitable for a more popular version in the vernacular.

[10] Passage from *Dageraad*, as in *Aufgang*, pp. 41–2, relating to *Archeus faber*, 9 and *Archeus faber*, 7, *Opp.* p. 39.

[11] *Archeus faber*, 9, *Opp.* p. 39.

[12] Jean Fernel, *Physiologia*, IV, 10 in *Universa medicina*, ed. J. and O. Heurnius (Utrecht, 1656), p. 92. *Physiologia*, IV, 8, in *Univ. Med.*, pp. 89–90; IV, 5, in *Univ. Med.*, p. 85. *De abditis rerum causis*, I, 5, in *Univ. Med.*, pt. II, p. 424.

[13] J. H. Alsted, *Theologia naturalis* (n. pl., apud Ant. Hummium, 1615), lib. II, cap. 29, p. 596.

[14] For a summary of references to archeus and *ares* in Paracelsus, see Ruland, *Lexicon alchemiae*, pp. 52–4.

tive of a general and central archeus as separated from those archei that were bound to individual organs.[15] Van Helmont gave all this a much more concrete and proto-scientific complexion. He linked archeus with a chemically demonstrable substance – his "new" *gas*. It was the archeus who disposed empty matter (water) and thereby "dedicated" to each object its beginning, its emergence from this matter as an individual with all its specific characteristics. Hence, Van Helmont saw the archeus as operating in semina, as a generative force. Embracing the seminal image of the object to be formed, the archeus possessed all the genetic information necessary to fulfil the plan of the creator under the guidance of the *idea operatrix*. Van Helmont's redefinition of the archei was to provide the context in which Glisson, Charleton, and Willis evolved their own versions of these agents and their functions.

In Van Helmont, each of the individual organs enjoys the tutelage of a resident custodian, its indigenous *archeus insitus*. The latter is in charge of selecting and assimilating the nutriment proper to the organ; he presides over its own kitchen, its own stomach.[16] However, he in his turn is answerable to a higher court. This consists of the central stomach of the organism as a whole, the organ of "digestion of all digestions", where first and decisive action is taken. Informed by the closely connected spleen, its cardiac part embodies the immediate executive of the vital principle. Being near the spleen it is near the site where the immortal mind joins that part of the soul which is vegetative, sensitive, and mortal.[17] In this view the spleen is elevated to a position of high dignity and responsibility. This drastically differs from its ancient and traditional appraisal as a cesspool in which impure food is disposed of and the loathsome "black bile" is produced. Moreover, it was made to serve as the "receptacle of insanity", that is, the state of hypochondria, an irrational and brutish passion.[18]

The duumvirate of stomach and spleen, then, issues orders that

---

[15] On the Paracelsian archeus see Pagel, *Paracelsus*, pp. 104–12, esp. p. 108.

[16] The idea of nutritional centres, "stomachs" or "kitchens" attached to the individual organs is Paracelsian: see for example Paracelsus, *De modo pharmacandi*, I, 1, ed. Sudhoff, iv, 441.

[17] Van Helmont, *A sede animae ad morbos*, 12, *Opp.* p. 281; *Jus duumviratus*, 60, *Opp.* p. 296.

[18] *Duumviratus*, 16, *Opp.* p. 329. See A. Wear, "The Spleen in Renaissance Anatomy", *Med. Hist.*, 21 (1977), 43–60.

overrule the local government of the *archei insiti* of the organs.[19] No material carriers such as blood, lymph, or vapour – ascending or descending – nor pre-formed anatomical channels are called upon to execute the higher commands. They are carried out by *actio regiminis*, an "imperious nod" (*nutus potestativus*), a light radiating.[20]

The subordination of individual organs to central regulation is particularly conspicuous in metabolism and in nervous function. In obesity, for example, most of the fat may be converted into water and thus excreted by the kidneys.[21] The latter have nothing to do with the obesity, but are merely executives of a higher authority. It was this, the central archeus, the duumvirate of stomach and spleen, that made the person obese in the first place. It did so by converting body fluid into fat. Now, like a trumpet in the battlefield, it calls upon the fat or oil to return to its pristine fluid state, to be drawn back into the veins and to be discharged by the kidneys. All this happens without the slightest involvement of the kidneys. These may be largely destroyed by stone, yet obesity can still develop. Nor is this condition related to overeating. There are compulsive eaters who remain thin and obese Capuchins who are wont to fast. Instead it is the stomach which stands for the root of the tree which directs the whole stage-play (*comoediam*) that is performed in foliage, fruit, and bark as well as in wood, pulp, and branches.[22] Glandular phenomena are on the same level: nobody would suggest, for example, that it is vapours ascending from the testicle rather than its "imperious nod" or "action of regimen" that are responsible for growing a beard.[23] Similarly, in the field of nervous function, involuntary action allows no time for consulting the brain – a mere gesture of tickling will make a person jump away.[24] The brain is largely an executive subordinated to the stomach. Hellebore, regarded as a specific for brain lesion and insanity, is a powerful emetic.[25] A brain's being asleep in coma, and thus

---

[19] *Duumviratus*, the combined regulating activity of stomach and spleen is the subject of the two treatises *Jus duumviratus* and *Duumviratus*. The latter is a short corollary to the former dealing with the duumvirate as the seat of fantasy, love, sleep, and soul.

[20] *Duumviratus*, 15, *Opp.* p. 329.

[21] *Jus duumviratus*, 58, *Opp.* p. 296.

[22] Ibid., 58–9, *Opp.* p. 296.

[23] *Duumviratus*, 14, *Opp.* p. 328. *Ignota actio regiminis*, 40, 42, 46, *Opp.* pp. 321–3.

[24] *Jus duumviratus*, 61, *Opp.* p. 297.

[25] Ibid., 26, *Opp.* p. 291.

insensitive, cannot prevent dreams, which reveal the deeper sensitive soul residing "below the ribs" to be still awake.[26] Rich food causes vertigo and nightmares; carbon-monoxide poisoning clearly affects the stomach in various ways, as Van Helmont experienced himself. Opium suppresses cough as long as it remains in and "under the jurisdiction" of the stomach. Its action is gastrogenic and digestive through conversion of sticky sputum into a fluid that can easily be discharged. Its efficacy thus derives largely from the stomach. The stomach works in conjunction with the spleen, which is marked out by its rich vascular plexus as the original "seat" of imagination and fantasy.[27]

MAGNUM OPORTET AND MIDDLE-LIFE: DIGESTION, CORRUPTION, AND DISEASE

Bodies are subject to invasion by other bodies. The invaders may disappear without leaving any trace, for example, through digestion. Others may be retained unassimilated and in a state of reduced vitality, a "middle-life". Such "sticky" invaders who "adhere" and "persist", endowed with some (albeit reduced) activity, are potential causes of disease. They require continuous vigilance on the part of the vital principle, the archeus, of the body invaded. This state of affairs was called by Van Helmont the "great necessity", the *magnum oportet*. This very term as well as essential parts of the concept are derived from Paracelsus. "Middle-life" and "middle corpus" are also Paracelsian terms.[28]

The *magnum oportet*, now part of our normal lives, was acquired as one of the penalties for the Fall of man. Up to then man's life and body were under the direct control and direction of the divine soul. There was no question of unassimilated and potentially dangerous invaders. Digestion meant complete dissolution comparable to the indescribable virtue of the universal chemical solvent, the liquor alkahest. After the Fall the lower, sensitive soul came

---

[26] *Ibid.*, and 53–5, *Opp.* pp. 295–6. *Duumviratus*, 15, *Opp.* p. 329.

[27] *Jus duumviratus*, 19, *Opp.* p. 289; ibid., 65, *Opp.* p. 298; ibid., 32, *Opp.* p. 292; ibid., 1, *Opp.* p. 285.

[28] Paracelsus, *Grosse Wundarznei*, lib. II, tract. 2, cap. 2, ed. Sudhoff, x, 290. For Paracelsus on middle life see *Opus Paramirum*, I, 3, ed. Sudhoff, ix, 53; ibid., I, 5–6, pp. 65–7; ibid., II, 3, p. 97. *Astronomia Magna*, I, 11, ed. Sudhoff, xii, 257. *De secretis creationis*, in *Chirurgische Bücher und Schrifften*, ed. J. Huser (Strassburg, 1605), Appendix, p. 114.

between the divine soul (*mens*) and man's body. Ever since, food has acted as a kind of contagium or contamination through preservation of its middle-life, which survived the weakened power of digestion. There may occur a hostile interaction between the archeus of the host, and the archeus of the undigested residue or of the invader as a whole. This interaction is visualised not as a straightforward combat between contraries – nature does not know of contraries (*natura contrariorum nescia*), Van Helmont had stipulated. It was rather an act of sympathy, namely a seduction of the host-archeus away from its own schedule (regimen) in favour of the archeal schedule of the guest; a morbid desire and imagination on the part of the host attracts the guest-invader and lets the host forget and neglect his own duty and loyalty to the organs and the organism that should be under his constant direction and control.

To illustrate the co-existence of two archei in the same organism, Van Helmont gives the example of pigs that feed in certain places on shrimps and mussels, whereby their meat assumes a fishy taste. Nevertheless, the meat is still pork, with all its specific qualities, and remains prohibited for the Jews.[29] Similarly, urine may retain the smell of turpentine, nutmeg (*macis*), or asparagus when one of these has been ingested. These are not food-residues accidentally carried in excrement, but active participants in that true and deep transmutation by which, through digestion, food is converted into flesh and blood. This process is carried out under the direction and jurisdiction of the archeus, which has the power of changing matter and pre-disposing it to the assumption of forms, smells, colours, and other accidental properties.[30]

Van Helmont departs from Paracelsus in his view of solid deposits or calcification of the tissues, notably gravel and stone – the tartar of Paracelsus. In the latter's view this was material which had resisted digestion. It was present as such from the outset, before being deposited as such at some place remote from its portal of entry. Here it stuck like tartar deposit in a wine vat. It was dead matter that by its mere presence caused morbid responses such as those attending obstruction. Van Helmont looked down upon this as a materialistic concept, as of a collision between matter and matter. He translates the phenomenon into the vitalist and spiritual sphere. In his view there is not the simple fact of a passive

[29] Van Helmont, *Magnum oportet*, 4, *Opp.* p. 145.
[30] Ibid., 5, *Opp.* p. 145.

collection of inert material. This material is rather the final result of a dynamic process. It is maintained by the interaction of two vital principles (archei), namely that of an invaded host and that of his foreign guest. The latter resists the efforts of the host at subjugating or assimilating him by sticking to the invaded host in a state of reduced vitality, or middle-life. This state has its bodily equivalent in the tartar deposit, which may appear lifeless on the surface, but is in fact active and "alive", as witnessed by the bouquet, taste, or medicinal efficacy which it displays in the body or the excreta of the host. Equally, a drug does not act by adding a certain material to the body, nor does the mere impact of some material on body-matter cause disease. Both substances are actively involved in the vital transmutations that are brought about by digestion and metabolism. They are thus involved through the preservation and activity of their middle-lives. If not interfered with by other archei beyond a tolerable level, an individual archeus lives out his own life to a certain destined end. However, he cannot avoid trafficking with others whom he must subjugate and make subservient to his own schedule of duties for the common weal of the organism. He has to curb the "foreign uneasiness" arising from a "consort-archeus" by fitting him into his own economy.[31]

If there is middle-life, there must be also a first and an ultimate life. A first life sprouts in the semina. The embryo already lives a middle-life, proceeding to ultimate life when perfect and mature. At this stage, in his ultimate life, he becomes parent to the first life of the offspring. Nevertheless, in ultimate life the parent also retains his middle-life; his archeus constantly maintains it and thus ensures the possibility of survival at the low level of *vita minima*, for example, in a parasitic existence. Reversion from ultimate to middle- and even to first life can occur; this notably applies to food and drugs, and depends upon the extent to which the consuming host can repress the outside influence. Ultimate lives may be annihilated through putrefaction.[32]

Levels of life can be distinguished in minerals and metals more clearly than in plants and animals; there is less confusion caused by a multitude of features and shapes, and there are no malformations. The types and forms of minerals and metals are housed in the "cellars or store-houses of divine bounty" and hence endowed

[31] Ibid., 3, pp. 144–5.
[32] Ibid., 28, *Opp.* p. 149.

with miraculous medicinal power. This, however, cannot come to fruition unless the mineral is first reduced to its "middle-life".[33] Mineral at this stage meets the eye of the miner who has scratched the surface of a gallery, in the form of a greenish soap-like fluid, the *bur*.[34] This is the mineral in the form of a seed that has already passed its first life; the latter remains unknown to us in its nature and appearances. In its promotion to middle-life, a *gas* hovering on water containing sulphur, and transmutation of the latter by condensation, are instrumental.[35] Ultimate life of the mineral or metal is established when it is stored, stable and fixed in a metallic vein.[36] Analogous to *bur* in the mineral world is the "juice of the earth" – *leffas* – the germinal medium of plants.[37]

Paracelsus located all change and commotion in the middle-life through which an object passes between its existences in its prime and in its ultimate matter, just as all activity in the sublunary world has its source in the middle region in which the stars dwell.[38] Middle-life thus makes survival possible in a state of reduced vitality. It is not itself subject to destruction when the individual unit as a whole is dissolved. A rose decayed or food assimilated after digestion is not destroyed, but has kept a "shadow of middle-life". In its first life the rose with all its splendour and fragrance has no medicinal virtue; it acquires this when it decays or is manipulated by the chemist. This virtue indicates its survival at a low level. Any substance can thus acquire medicinal qualities, by being made into an arcanum by the adept who "reduces its life". By contrast, the sick person starts a new life when, on being cured, he leaves the reduced, the middle, life of sickness.[39]

[33] Ibid., 41, *Opp.* p. 151. The "angustae potestates" of all editions should read "augustae", as adopted by *Oriatrike*, p. 156, "famous power of healing" and *Aufgang*, p. 205: "vortreffliche Kraft".

[34] *Imago ferm. impraeg. mass. sem.*, 31, *Opp.* p. 112.

[35] A local semen (*fermentum saxosum*) in the earth "begets the sulphur of the water with childe, condenseth the water": *Oriatrike*, p. 155, correct as against *Aufgang*, p. 204, incorrect.

[36] *Magnum oportet*, 40, *Opp.* p. 151.

[37] *Imago ferm. impraeg. mass. sem.*, 32, *Opp.* p. 112. "Leffas" is borrowed from Paracelsus ("predestination of herbs"): *Philosophiae ad Athenienses*, III, 3, ed. Sudhoff, xiii, 420.

[38] Paracelsus, *Elf Traktat*, cap. 3, ed. Sudhoff, i, 47; *Astronomia Magna*, I, 11, ed. Sudhoff, xii, 257; *De natura rerum neun Bücher*, I, ed. Sudhoff, xi, 318; *Opus Paramirum*, II, 3, ed. Sudhoff, ix, 97.

[39] *Opus Paramirum*, I, 3, ed. Sudhoff, ix, 53, and I, 5, pp. 65–7.

The concept of middle-lives and their preservation inside the host-object has implications for the true nature of corruption. This cannot mean annihilation. When an object corrupts, it is its shape – the surface by which it is recognisable – that disappears. Its components remain in middle life and wander in new combinations into new objects. The paradigm is the clear fluid that contains a variety of substances which can be recovered in solid form on addition of other substances to the fluid. The presence of middle lives is predominantly detected by taste and smell; when, for example, anise and nutmeg transfer to the baby with the nurse's milk and emerge in the baby's urine. Equally, generation does not start from nothing, nor does it require annihilation or corruption of a preceding object. There is no "stripping of every accidental" or "overcoming of previous dispositions so that every generation should be preceded by corruption or privation", as postulated in Aristotelian tradition. In other words, generation is not from a tabula rasa, such that anything "might be indifferently generated from anything". It is true that there is no pre-formation of parts; generation is de novo, by epigenesis, but non-material "dispositions and ferments" persist. These account for aromatic traces in the urine of ingesta which are relics and not new formations.[40]

Associated with its middle-life are the specific qualities of a given substance. Such seminal qualities do not vary with proportional mixtures of material components, even when the quality concerned is of a "simple" and "corporeal" nature, still less when the substance is charged with "speciall aromaticall savour [as] in Cinnamon, Saffron, Cloves etc.", and least of all in the third class of qualities, which embraces the poisonous, medicinal and "magnetic" properties. These last act by virtue of pure form, not unlike light, and hence penetrate easily and deeply. Their "seals", or middle-lives, which are impressed on the vital principles of objects are difficult to master and to assimilate. They inevitably cause grave disease, "piercing the archeus throughout the whole light thereof".[41]

ON TIME, DURATION, AND LASTINGNESS

Van Helmont's treatise *On Time* is worthy of close attention. It is of major significance in his natural philosophy as a whole and it

[40] Van Helmont, *Magnum oportet*, 44, *Opp.* p. 152; ibid., 48, p. 152.
[41] Ibid., 52, p. 153; ibid., 53, p. 154; *Oriatrike*, p. 158.

has something to offer those who are interested in "biological time" and its history today. That Van Helmont himself valued it highly is indicated by the exalted position which it occupies in the *Dageraad*. Here it forms the proemial leader under the title: *Van tijdt, duringe, oft weringe* (Of time, duration, and lastingness). It thus immediately conveys the deeper metaphysical meaning that transcends in Van Helmont's concept the common notion of time. The position allocated to it in all editions and translations of the *Ortus* or *Opera* is quite different. Bearing the simple title *On Time*, it occurs unobtrusively at the very end. Here it is still a leader, but merely introduces a theosophical collection that is largely concerned with original sin, eucharistic redemption, longevity, and immortality.[42] These, and their naturalistic and alchemical aspects, will be considered separately.

There is some justification for this placing, however. The treatise has a distinct theological message. Its main proposition is that time is identical with eternity, or eternal duration.[43] In this Van Helmont found himself in collision with the accepted doctrine of the church as well as, and perhaps more importantly, the Aristotelian syllabus of the schools. If time coincides with eternal duration, what about our human time? Does it participate in the former? The answer is emphatically in the affirmative. Our time is the rhythm of life that is specific to and typical of a given individual or species. In this sense time is understood as the specific duration of individual objects, and as such embraces the duration of life. It emanates from divine creation and is intrinsically bound up with each individual seed, with the semina which embody "all necessity of nature".[44] It is to that extent that our time (*duratio*) participates in true time, which is divine and eternal. Individual objects and

---

[42] *Dageraad* (1660), pp. 1–15. *Ortus medicinae*, pp. 629–42; *Opp.*, pp. 604–752. The treatise has been little noticed; see, however, T. A. Rixner and T. Siber, *Leben und Lehrmeinungen berühmter Physiker am Ende des XVI. und Anfang des XVII. Jahrhunderts*, Vol. VII (Sulzbach, 1826), pp. 45–9, and a short note in R. Eisler's *Wörterbuch der philosophischen Begriffe*, 3rd edn. (Berlin, 1928), iii, 648. For a translation and analysis of the philosophical section, see W. Pagel, "J. B. Van Helmont *De tempore* and Biological Time", *Osiris*, 8 (1949), 346–417, and H. Weiss, "Notes on the Greek Ideas Referred to in Van Helmont *De tempore*", *Osiris*, 8 (1949), 418–49; and idem et eadem, *Isis*, 33 (1942), 621–3 and 624.

[43] Van Helmont, *De tempore*, 2, *Opp.* p. 594.

[44] "Semina and Time", ibid., 18, *Opp.* p. 595; *Aufgang*, p. 1145. *Imago ferm. impraeg. mass. sem.*, 7, *Opp.* p. 108, following Paracelsus, *Astronomia Magna*, I, 7, ed. Sudhoff, xii, 177.

their specific life-spans can claim this privilege as the products of divine creation. The individual seed is thus responsible not only for the formation of the body but also for the timing, the speed and duration, of its functions. These notably depend upon the extensiveness and intensity of individual responses, in short, the rhythm that is specific to an individual and determines his life-span in the framework of divine predestination.

Time thus defined as emanating from divine eternity would appear to be static rather than dynamic – once given, it abides by its appropriate semen on its progress in a certain direction and to a certain destination. As such it is essentially different from all motion and its attributes. Time is not a measuring unit and definitely not the "number that measures motion", as Aristotle had defined it. Nor is it measured by, for instance, the days and years of the calendar or the movements and constellations of the stars. Conventional time as a measuring yardstick is not made as such by nature. It is brought into the realm of nature by human reason as it were from outside; it is an *ens rationis* rather than an *ens naturae*, it is an *extera consideratio* rather than an *intimum rebus ipsis*.[45] It is "thingliness", individual specificity, with which Van Helmont is concerned in all aspects of nature, from gas and earthquake down to the passions of the soul, rather than with the strait-jacket of mathematical or numerical patterns that human reason has fabricated around them.

Time, then, exists in sublunary objects as well as in the celestial bodies, but notably above heaven in that infinite place that is of the spirit, and devoid of body. Motion rather measures time, than time measures motion. Year, day, night, month are "accidental" to time, they measure what happens *in* time, but not time itself. What is night to one is day to another. Nor do seasons inform us of time – they merely announce changes in the air.[46]

Time as the number that measures motion had been underpinned by the concept of a continuum of infinite moments or "now-points". Each of these had been supposed to be indivisible. In this Van Helmont finds an inconsistency: infinity is incompatible with indivisibility, as this by itself brings in a limitation and thus finiteness. If time were, as the scholastic followers of Aristotle said, a

---

[45] Aristotle, *Physica*, IV, 11, 219b2; Van Helmont, *De tempore*, 19, *Opp.* p. 596.
[46] *De tempore*, 46, *Opp.* p. 601; ibid., 4, *Opp.* p. 594. *Dageraad*, p. 2; *De tempore*, 5, *Opp.* p. 594.

conjunction of infinite indivisible points of duration, these could not be indivisible as they are productive of something divisible by dint of their conjunction – a divisible continuum, namely "time". Moreover, a mathematical point that is indivisible is infinitely small and thus unable to produce something real, positive, large, or small – it is just nothing.[47]

Van Helmont's next target of attack is succession. Just as there are no "points" in true time, there is no succession of such "points" in it to form a continuum. This is a fabrication of human reason and hence alien to nature. The same applies to the association of time with number, and in particular to the degradation of "the one" as implied in ancient numeral philosophy. In this it had been stipulated that the smallest number is two. Against this Van Helmont argues that it is through a summation of ones that numbers are generated. This in itself militates against the confusion of the one with zero which has been committed. Above all, were time essentially a series of successive numbers it would consist in a permanent becoming, rather than being.[48]

Time, then, is neither long nor short, neither before nor after, neither measure nor measurable, nor, in particular, can it measure or judge which of two motions of the same duration is the quicker. By contrast, time must be found where determined durations are located, namely in the semina of created objects. For, "innate in all semina there is not only a principle of each motion, but also the determined period of durations appropriate to each motion". The duration of motions is therefore "essentially, intimately and originally inherent in the semina as their forming and directing principle". In other words what makes the semina active, and determines the way in which they are activated, is object-specific time, their *duratio* as predetermined by the creator. It is thus that time is real, is a matter of "thingliness" rather than of human reasoning, internal and intrinsic in things rather than of things. The continuum is a notable example in question: it is not a thing, but a consideration of things; it is based on measuring and hence an *ens rationis*, regardless and devoid of the *species essentiales*, the specificity of things and

[47] *De tempore*, 6–7, *Opp.* p. 594. Cusanus, *De ludo globi* in *Opera*, fol. 153r. Cf. Scharpff, *Des Nicolaus von Cusa wichtigste Schriften*, pp. 220, 255; Francis Glisson, *Tractatus de natura substantiae energetica* (London, 1672), pp. 463, 466.
[48] *De tempore*, 12, *Opp.* p. 595; ibid., 11, *Opp.* p. 595; ibid., 14, *Opp.* p. 595.

their individuality. It replaces species by mathematics and the individual by number.[49]

What is true of the semina and of individual objects is true of nature as a whole. Nature "stands rooted in time – *duratio* – as it flows without intermediary from eternity itself". In fact, *duratio* was before creation, which happened at a certain "then" (*dum*) in *duratio*, when it pleased God to create. It is thus that *duratio* is outside and above and at the same time most intimate to individual objects. Indeed, it is more intimate to things than these are to themselves.[50]

Two sets of conclusions can be drawn. It can be said of duration, first, that it is divine, and secondly that it is indistinguishable from eternity, and allotted to each individual object according to a measure predetermined for each recipient. It follows for time that, having no parts, it is incompatible with the idea of continuum, and that, devoid of succession, it cannot measure anything large or small, plain, round, deep, broad, or duration, long and short. Equally it cannot predicate priority and celerity. Nothing finite can appraise time, which being inseparable from eternity connotes an actual infinite. Finally, the light of divine providence reveals itself in the intra-seminal determination of individual duration, in time which is the rule that directs the creature rather than being the creature itself.[51]

With these considerations the theoretical part of the treatise concludes. They outline the position of time in its theological, metaphysical, and biological aspects. It is Van Helmont's first concern to dissociate time from motion, and in particular from successive and numerically measured and measuring time.[52] Obviously these negations were directed against the Aristotelian and scholastic syllabus. They occupy a considerable part of the whole treatise.[53] Of the original Aristotelian positions some were misunderstood and others even inadvertently agreed to by Van Helmont, as the detailed analysis by the late Helene Weiss has shown.[54] There remain, however, such basic Aristotelian points as the association of time

[49] Ibid., 16, *Opp.* p. 595; ibid., 18, *Opp.* p. 595. *Aufgang*, p. 1145. *De tempore*, 18, *Opp.* p. 595; ibid., 20, p. 596.

[50] *De tempore*, 26, *Opp.* p. 597; ibid., 29, *Opp.* p. 597.

[51] Ibid., 30, *Opp.* p. 597; ibid., 32, *Opp.* p. 598; ibid., 46, *Opp.* p. 601.

[52] *De tempore*, 30, *Opp.* p. 597.

[53] Ibid., 6, seq. to 44, *Opp.* pp. 594–601.

[54] As cited above, this chapter, note 42.

with motion, the succession of "pointed" moments, and the measuring and numbering function of time. These were tenaciously sustained by the scholastic authorities of Van Helmont's period. Succession by means of indivisible instants which marked the divisible parts of time was made responsible for its flow by Suarez. The *continua* of time fall into parts through its indivisible "points, lines and surfaces", according to Hurtado de Mendoza. Certain qualifications were admitted, as for example by Keckermann. Similarly, Fromondus argued against a distinction between divisible parts of time and indivisible instants. Time has infinitely divisible parts, but these are not the instants, which act as *copula* in a *continuum* without existing as such "really and positively". Motion and time are magnitudes, each with a certain beginning and end, but the flow of time cannot be associated with instants – neither it, nor the instants exist in reality, according to Revius.[55]

That there was "created *duratio*" and that it was free of succession had been a scholastic commonplace. Moreover, *duratio* had been linked with the individual object; it was intrinsic to each individual being and only as such was it subject to variation. Hence it could not serve as a measuring yardstick for all. It was by this very feature, however, according to Suarez, that it was distinguished from that *duratio* which was time, for time was bound up with extension, succession, and motion.[56] This is the point at which Van Helmont disagreed, following the Plotinian lead in identifying time with *duratio* and beyond this with eternity. Philosophers and naturalists of the renaissance (Bruno, Cardano) came quite close to Van Helmont's concept.[57] To the metaphysical and cos-

---

[55] Franciscus Suarez (1548–1617), *Metaphysicarum disputationum libri duo* (Geneva, 1636), lib. II, pp. 453 et seq.; Pedro Hurtado de Mendoza (d. 1651), *Commentarius in universam philosophiam* (Lyons, 1624), p. 332, "de continuo", sect. II, "sintne in continuo indivisibilia realia?"; Bartholomäus Keckermann (1573–1609), *Systema physicum*, 3rd edn. (Hanover, 1612), I, 7, "de tempore", p. 43; Libertus Fromondus (1587–1653), *Labyrinthus sive de compositione continui, lib. I* (Antwerp, 1631), pp. 29 et seq. and cap. XXXII, p. 99 and cap. XXXVIII, p. 137; Jacobus Revius, *Suarez repurgatus sive syllabus dissertationum metaphysicarum Franc. Suarez cum notis* (Leyden, 1644), sect. IX, pp. 19–26.

[56] F. Suarez, *Disputat. L. de rerum duratione*, sect. V, p. 14 (Geneva, 1614), II, 464.

[57] Giordano Bruno, *De immenso et innumerabili*, I, 12 and VII, 7, ed. F. Fiorentino (Naples, 1884), i, 244 et seq. Idem, *De triplici minimo et mensura* (Frankfurt, 1591), p. 22 in cap. VI. Idem, *Acrotismus adversus Peripateticos* (1588), art. XXIX (Naples, 1879), pp. 53 et seq., 146. W. Pagel, "The Reaction to Aristotle in Seventeenth Century Biological Thought", in *Science, Medicine and History, Essays in Honour of Charles Singer*, ed. E. A. Underwood, 2 vols. (London, 1953), i,

mological considerations of Plotinian critics of Aristotle, Van Helmont added a religious dimension. From this he arrived at a biological application of his new insight, into the true, divine nature of time. He finds this to lie in a *duratio* that was specifically predestined by the creator for each individual object and as such lent to the semina. It is through these divine *primordia* that life is distributed and unfolded. The dominating position accorded to the semina in Van Helmont's natural philosophy is perceptibly and avowedly Augustinian. However, Van Helmont had regretfully to disagree with the venerable Father's ideas on time. For in spite of his doubts and his recognition of time as "some extension" connected with the soul, St. Augustine in principle subscribed to the Aristotelian "measure of motion".[58] Above all he strictly separated time and eternity according to the dualistic Platonic and Christian tradition. It was at this point and in the wake of Plotinian monism that Van Helmont consciously departed from Christian doctrine. He was not quite isolated in this, however. The Lutheran theologian J. J. Hainlin (1588–1660), rejecting Aristotle, declared in 1646 that all time is from eternity or from God who is the principle of all things existing. Indeed, time is the influx of God's virtue into his creatures. It preserves them until they reach their destined end after having passed through a certain span of duration defined by God and measurable by the celestial motion.[59] So far the closeness to Van Helmont is striking. However, Hainlin was prepared to grant objects a root in number, a *radix numerica* that is accessible to arithmetical consideration. This "root" allotted to time was the mystical *septennium* by which it progresses *in infinitum*. Van Helmont had deliberately removed time from all numerical connotation and could hardly have consented to Hainlin's transfer of the septennial "root of time" to empirical chronology and the solution of its problems by drawing up chronological tables.

489–509: pp. 493–4. S. Hutton, "Some Renaissance Critiques of Aristotle's Theory of Time", *Annals of Science*, 34 (1977), 355–8. Cardano, *De subtilitate* (Lyons, 1559), XXI, 671.

[58] Augustine, *Confessionum libri*, XI, 29, ed. K. von Raumer (Stuttgart, 1856), p. 298; ibid., 31, p. 299; 33, p. 300; 14–17, pp. 291–3; 36, p. 302.

[59] Johann Jacob Hainlin, *Sol temporum sive Chronologia mystica...item elenchus chronologicus novus* (Tübingen, 1646), pp. 16 et seq. Cf. Thomas Jackson's *Treatise of the Divine Essence and Attributes* (London, 1628), I, 6, sect. 1–2, pp. 62–3, 65. I owe the latter reference to Sarah Hutton.

Van Helmont's *De tempore* was to introduce his treatises on longevity. He saw the main factor in longevity as the rhythm of life which varies by animal, species, and individual in accordance with divine and seminal predestination. This is that "biological time" which is best circumscribed by the difference between "mouse-time and elephant-time" (Joseph Needham).[60] As such Van Helmont's notion of time can claim to be a forerunner of quite modern concepts in which time is considered to be separate from "clock-time" and quantification, and linked with biological and even sociological specificity. This is indeed the *duratio* of Van Helmont, the divine gift of the semina that is responsible for the specific differences between individuals. Such differences lie in variations that are specific and typical of the movements of the individual and the velocity of alterations depending upon them.[61] This could be taken as the Helmontian notion of life-rhythm and biological time, in which specific individual time is measured by specifically attuned motion and motion is not measured by time. With this Van Helmont transferred the old Plotinian postulate to the realm of individual life and its specific rhythm (*duratio*); he thus gave it a biological relevance.[62]

The bulk of Van Helmont's *De tempore* is epistemological, religious, and metaphysical, but not all of it. It has a short technical and scientific postscript. In this the fallacies of time-measuring by the clock as due to temperature changes are substantiated.[63] Van Helmont himself recommended the pendulum. He had found it reliable in working out the swiftness and efficacy of projectiles and the factors influencing them. He realised that the duration of the swings of a pendulum is constant and depends upon the pendulum's length, but believed that it is gradually diminished, the

---

[60] J. Needham, "Chemical Heterogony and the Ground Plan of Animal Growth", *Biol. Review*, 9 (1934), 79.

[61] Van Helmont, *De tempore*, 18, *Opp.* p. 595.

[62] For modern biological time see H. Bergson, *Time and Free Will*, tr. E. L. Pogson (London, 1910), p. 107. On time outside the sphere of the rational intellect: Van Helmont, *Confirmatur morborum sedes in anima sensitiva*, 7, *Opp.* p. 533. See also J. Uexkuell, *Theoretische Biologie* (Berlin, 1928), p. 56; idem and G. Kriszat, *Streifzüge durch die Umwelt von Tieren und Menschen* (1934; 2nd edn., 1956), p. 30; K. E. von Baer, *Welche Anschauung der Natur ist die richtige?* (Berlin, 1862), p. 24; see J. Ritter, ed., *Historisches Wörterbuch der Philosophie* (Basel and Stuttgart, 1972), ii, 345–6, under "Eigenzeit" by T. von Uexkuell; Le Comte de Nouy, *Biological Time* (London, 1937).

[63] Van Helmont, *De tempore*, 48–9, *Opp.* p. 602.

angular velocity of the earlier swings being greater than that of the later swings. By means of a sun-dial the pendulum may be gauged and thus time more accurately measured.[64] This discussion is followed by yet another polemical piece – this time against the humoralist number-mysticism of the critical days, and its astrological embellishments.

A whole system of time-conditioned rules had been built up in traditional humoralist medicine. The system was based on crises: the rhythm of "critical days" that recurred at regular intervals in all cases and decided – "decreed" – the outcome of the disease. Crises indicated an internal combat between contraries; they were eagerly studied, expected, and promoted. Van Helmont, for whom nature was "ignorant of contraries", was bound to totally reject all this. The task of the physician, as he saw it, was to avoid crises, and to arrest diseases before such cataclysms set in – instead of waiting passively with the humoralists for the "critical" elimination of humours which were believed to become the agents and bearers of disease through their decay. By contrast, active therapy was indicated, as Paracelsus had postulated.[65] What was true of the critical days applied in principle to the "climacteric year". The forty-ninth and the sixty-third years of life in particular had been held to be critical years implying danger to life and health through the connection with the seven and the nine.[66] All this was heathen deception in Van Helmont's eyes, and against scripture. Years – as such – remained years and could not have any significance; they were, in Bergsonian terms, "homogeneous continua", whereas life had its specific "history" in which no moment was equal, in terms of "historical" content, to any other moment.

The biological insight of *De tempore* may seem to be overshadowed at least in bulk by its religious concerns and criticism of scholasticism. The work cannot be understood, however, without taking Van Helmont's whole religious philosophy and biological

---

[64] *De tempore*, 50, *Opp.* p. 602.

[65] Van Helmont shared Paracelsus's views on the biological and medical aspects of time, but opposed their extensive astrological connotations. See Paracelsus, *Andere Ausarbeitung über Terpentin*, 3, ed. Sudhoff, ii, 187; *Deutsche Kommentare zu den Aphorismen des Hippokrates*, I, 2 (et tempus), ed. Sudhoff, iv, 501; *Sieben Defensiones*, ed. Sudhoff, xi, 127; *Astronomia Magna*, I, 1, ed. Sudhoff, xii, 23. For astrological aspects see Pagel, "Helmont *De tempore*", p. 401.

[66] See, for example, Claudius Salmasius, *De annis climactericis et antiqua astrologia* (Leyden, 1648) and Bartolomeo Castelli, *Lexicon medicum* (Leipzig, 1713), p. 184.

and medical work into consideration. Its key-note is life as a leading divine principle guiding the reader through a labyrinthine world.
This is a world of singular specific individuals that are alive by
virtue of an inbuilt divine duration which also determines the
rhythm and length of their several lives. Being the product of
divine creation, the essence of duration or true time cannot be
penetrated by the human intellect or by any numerical or mathematical manipulation. It must be taken as the divine endowment
of the semina that compose the world and make nature their subject and vassal. In Van Helmont's concept of time, religious and
naturalistic motives are as inseparable as in all the other fields of
natural philosophy to which he dedicated his endeavour.

De tempore introduces a collection of treatises which were products of Van Helmont's old age – of, he says, an old man in the face
of approaching death. The pessimistic trend which pervades his
work as a whole consequently here receives a still more pointed
expression and so does its grand theme: original sin. Humanity
has since the Fall been in the grip of fraud, which has dominated
the medical scene in particular through stubborn adherence to
traditional theory and ineffectual therapy. Van Helmont glimpses,
however, a "coming age"[67] which will rid itself of this and listen to
him, the "adept of secrets" who had been spurned as an "apostate
from Galen, a Paracelsist and occultist".[68] Though in decline himself he now raises the question of the "medicinal extension of the
natural boundaries of things", that is, whether life may be prolonged through a "universal medicine".[69]

Van Helmont's answer is in the affirmative: there must be a way
to longevity through natural means, since long life is a natural
event, especially in certain regions and climates. What was natural
in Nestor of old must be feasible in later times by discovering the
appropriate arcanum of long life. In this prescription "art is sure
and short and life is long", by contrast with the "kitchen cooking"
and massage, prescribed by those for whom "art was long and life
was short", as the first of the Hippocratic Aphorisms had it.[70] This
arcanum Van Helmont believed to have been shown in a dream of

---

[67] Van Helmont, *Arbor vitae*, *Opp.* p. 750a; *Aufgang*, p. 1267, par. 17. *Praefatio*,
Opp. p. 592.
[68] *Praefatio*, *Opp.* pp. 592–3.
[69] *Vita longa ars brevis*, 4, *Opp.* p. 605b.
[70] *Vita longa ars brevis*, 6–8, *Opp.* p. 606a–b.

the "tree of long life" on the Mountain of the Lord.[71] The cedar was that tree which lent the material for ark and temple, and the twig which the leper was bidden to carry. Cedar contained the life-prolonging substance through an "extraordinary mysterium" (*insigni mysterio*). By means of the liquor alkahest, the universal solvent, the wood was converted into a milky juice within a week and, after another two weeks, into an oil. Kept at moderate heat for three months it would eventually be reduced to the prime essence, the arcanum, of the cedar tree, in the form of a soluble salt.[72] This sounds simple enough. However, nobody has ever revealed the nature of the alkahest, neither Paracelsus, its source, nor Van Helmont, its advocate, nor any of their followers. Van Helmont himself spread a cloak of mystery on the matter. The choice of cedar was both traditional, and a feature of contemporary writing.[73]

How did death become part of human experience? Van Helmont answered the question in simple and naturalistic terms. Man brought death upon himself through the lust which made him partake of the apple in Paradise. This contained an aphrodisiac. It was thus that Eve's blessed state of virginity was lost,[74] that semen and with it the sensitive soul was intercalated between man and his immortal mind (*mens*) and he was made mortal. Man "ate his own death".[75]

Though a celestial mystery, invisible and inscrutable, the union with God in the eucharist had an earthly association and significance. It recalls Jesus's saying to Nicodemus: "If I have told you earthly things – to wit the rebirth of those born of water and the

---

[71] *Arbor vitae, Opp.* p. 749; *Aufgang,* p. 1266, par. 14. *Mons domini, Opp.* p. 744; in *Aufgang,* p. 1261, par. 6.

[72] *Arbor vitae, Opp.* p. 750; p. 1267, par. 17 in *Aufgang.* Additionally a daily intake of a distillate of sulphur reduced to an oil was recommended for the prolongation of life and a pertinent case reported: *Arbor vitae, Opp.* p. 752; *Aufgang,* 23, p. 1270. This is consistent with Van Helmont's high appreciation of sulphur as a preservative against putrefaction and consumption.

[73] See, for example, William Mennens (1525–1608), *Aureum vellus* (1604) in *Theatrum Chemicum* (1622), v, 467.

[74] In this context Van Helmont ascribed a preferential status to woman which, although assailed, was still recognisable in, for example, the different mortality rate of the sexes: *Demonstratur thesis,* 100, *Opp.* p. 643. Elsewhere, however, it is not loss of virginity, but sexual differentiation in general which Van Helmont views as the "Fall of Nature", the descent from divine unity and homogeneity to duality and impurity. See Paracelsus, *Liber azoth,* cap. II, ed. Sudhoff, xiv, 563, and ibid., pp. 574–5.

[75] Van Helmont, *Mortis introitus,* 9, *Opp.* p. 608; *Aufgang,* p. 1160.

spirit – and ye believe not, how shall ye believe if I tell you of heavenly things?" The "gift of purity" may therefore justifiably apply to a perfectly natural ("earthly") event such as long life and its achievement on earth.[76] If regeneration of those to be saved and their participation in life everlasting are the key-note of the eucharist, its earthly simile must lie in the projection of the gold-making stone. Van Helmont assures us that in his hands it converted commercial mercury into an equal quantity of pure ("virgin") gold – a metal, base and corruptible, into a metal, immortal and incorruptible. Comparable to the disproportion between the immense number of the elect and the modicum of celestial bread that "saves" them, mercury a thousand times heavier was redeemed by a minimal quantity of the stone. Van Helmont had received but a quarter of one grain[77] of the heavy yellow "powder" that glittered like ground glass; this was "projected" over one pound of boiling mercury. Immediately there was a noise, and all of the seething metal stopped moving and settled into a cake. Developing intense heat, it yielded eight ounces of purest gold: one grain of the "powder" had converted 19,200 grains of the impure metal into gold and that in one instant.

In confirming the alchemist's dream of transmuting baser metals into gold Van Helmont seems to go against the better chemical insight of his earlier days. Then, he had judiciously interpreted the deposit of copper from acid solution on addition of iron as metal exchange rather than transmutation. Perhaps it was a kind of messianic yearning which brought him to the belief in the philosophers' stone when he felt death approaching after a life of frustration and bitterness. In this light his symbolical eucharistic view of transmutation appears less surprising. To view it as the terrene complement of the eucharist was nothing new. The *Lapis-Christus* parallel was an old alchemical principle in which the stone stood for that renovation, redemption from corruption, and prolongation of life which the alchemist strove to achieve in vitro as well as in his soul.[78] Nonetheless, Van Helmont speaks everywhere as a chemist rather than in the secret jargon of the alchemists. With

[76] John, 3: 12. *Demonstratur thesis*, 57–8, *Opp.* p. 631.
[77] I.e., one grain equalling 1/600th of an ounce.
[78] The parallel was endorsed by Luther. See H. Kopp, *Die Alchemie in älterer und neuerer Zeit*, 2 vols. (Heidelberg, 1886), i, 210–15; and, more comprehensively, C. G. Jung, *Paracelsica* (Zürich and Leipzig, 1942), p. 174, and idem, *Psychologie und Alchemie* (Zürich, 1944).

him transmutation acquired the rank of chemical reaction at large. In his natural philosophy it is a principle of general validity far beyond its narrow sense of conversion of metals. It is the powerful instrument wielded by the archeus, the vital principle – as, for example, in generation and digestive assimilation. Moreover, he may have found in the eucharistic parallel with transmutation yet another instance of a heavenly prologue to a natural process that takes place on earth, a further evidence of the prerogative of the spirit over matter. Indeed, the close interweaving of the natural and the supernatural, the search for possible natural equivalents and explanation of the "occult" are the characteristic features of all his speculations. In his work the philosophers' stone is appropriately found among the theosophical treatises on *Long Life* and the *Tree of Life*.

THE IMMANENCE OF FORM IN "DISPOSED" MATTER AND NATURAL PERCEPTION

Van Helmont's theoretical biology can be designated as vitalist monism. By virtue of its specific function each object is alive and its living substance represents at the same time body and soul, matter and form. It is a unified and unique whole. In other words, soul and form are not added to matter and body, but are in it or with it. Matter as such is empty and of no significance. It is nothing but water; for all objects can in the last resort be reduced to it. By contrast it is "working matter" that claims the attention of the naturalist; matter, that is, which is charged with a specific disposition and endowed with a unique schedule or plan of form and function. This life can be recognised at all levels of nature – in mineral, plant, animal, and man. Nor are the several ways of living of these different beings different from each other in principle. They are rather *modi* of a single identical force, which at the lowest level, is innate sensation (*naturalis perceptio*) and common to all. It accounts for the sympathy and antipathy that prevails between objects throughout nature. Thus, Van Helmont speaks of a "deaf perception" which appertains to any object – perceiving as well as perceived – and also of a rudimentry *sensus* in any inanimate body.[79] The next higher stage is vegetation and nutrition, to

---

[79] *Imago mentis*, 36, *Opp.* p. 260; as also the earlier *De magnetica vulnerum curatione*, 32, *Opp.* p. 708.

be followed by *sensus* and irritability, intrinsic properties of animal tissue, and finally by *intellectus* – the divine *mens* which is the prerogative of man.

"Life", then, embraces sensory power that starts at the lowest level of *naturalis perceptio* and ascends to a kind of "tissue-intellect". The latter enables a tissue or organ to judge or to "know" what is good or harmful for itself and the economy of the organism as a whole. This discriminating virtue is intrinsic in the tissue and there is nothing structural or functional acting between tissues, notably no higher authority, such as a soul, or the nervous system serving as a regulator or transmitter of stimuli. The knowledge required is inherent in the local working-matter. Thus, the pylorus knows when to open and when to close. It is the *rector digestionis* in its own right by virtue of its rhythmic tonic contraction and relaxation. These movements are peculiarly different from those, say, of the anus or the womb. When initiating vomiting the pylorus closes and sends a wave of motion along the body of the stomach toward the oesophagus. *Gnarus est pylorus rerum agendarum in stomacho* – "the pylorus knows the agenda of the stomach." Likewise when the pylorus fails to open it is because it knows or judges (*censet*) that it is harmful to let bad or badly digested food through. It reacts as if it were an animal in itself, being subject to emotions such as fury, reactive, for example, to an injury received to the leg. Such an accident may be followed by vomiting that stops when the leg is mended. Similarly, poison may cause pyloric indignation and subsequent paralysis.[80]

A further example of the same tissue-bound psychoid mechanism is peristalsis. Observing an infant with a large umbilical hernia Van Helmont saw how, through contraction of the transverse fibres of the gut wall, the iliac lumen was closed and the contents moved downwards. This rhythmically repeated movement reminded him of the lute-player who "opens finger after finger and relaxes the one that has just pressed". A gas bubble propelled with the contents, returned upwards to its original place as soon as the lumen had re-opened. It is thus shown that it is not by outside stimulation but by internal urge (*sensu*) and continuity, that our organs work, and never become idle (*non feriari*), even when we are asleep.[81]

[80] *Pylorus rector*, 10–11, *Opp.* pp. 216–17 and 29, p. 221.
[81] *De flatibus*, 38, *Opp.* p. 404; *Aufgang*, p. 728.

Primitive perception, sense, and reactive response are common to all objects in nature. They are conspicuous in "flesh", that is in muscle. However, each kind of reactive or living substance has its own type of activity. Life, though universal in all things, is specifically diversified, and there is a pattern of life, that is of reactivity, that is peculiar to muscle.[82] This pattern appertains to the muscular constituent of an organ such as the stomach or uterus, but the particularised tissue-life of muscle is overruled in such organs by the life of the part as a whole, its "monarchy". Thus, the womb as a whole engineers the epileptical convulsions that may occur in parturition.[83] Similarly, the life of the vein as a whole accounts for the fluidity of blood.[84] Yet blood itself is eminently alive in its own peculiar way. Though not sensitive to touch, it has a "sense" through which it co-operates harmoniously with the vital principle. It is alive qua sympathetic and "con-sensing" with it – *sympathetice sentit.*[85] When considered as lifeless matter, one blood is no different from any other blood, but alive, and endowed with sensitive spirit, it exhibits diversity of properties and movement. This is true not only of the blood of different individuals but also of the blood in different regions of the same body. Coursing in the vessels, blood does not care about weight, mass, and gravity or about "what is above and below".[86] Equally, blood alive in the vessels is protected against putrefaction in which forces are operative which extinguish sensation and life. As the scriptures tell us, blood is the treasure and seat of life.[87]

Irritability thus comprises motion as a reaction to *sensus* and emanates from a unit of live substance. This usage reflects the monist view of the immanence of psychoid impulse in tissue as against the dualist idea of a superadded "soul" which enters and enlivens dead bodily matter, endowing it with sensation and stirring it up to move. Haller (1708–77) restricted irritability to muscle, regarding it as the energy specific and intrinsic to that tissue. Van Helmont had already emphasised muscle as the locus in which irritability is prominently displayed, but also attributed it to all tissues and indeed to "life" as present in all objects of nature. In his

[82] *Vita multiplex in homine, Opp.* p. 685b.
[83] Ibid., *Opp.* p. 685a; *Ignota actio regiminis*, 43, *Opp.* p. 322.
[84] *Vita multiplex in homine, Opp.* p. 685b. *Pleura furens*, 15, *Opp.* p. 379.
[85] *De lithiasi*, IX, 93, *Opp.* II, p. 83.
[86] *Supplementem de Spadanis fontibus*, I, 8, *Opp.* p. 645; I, 11–12 and 21, p. 646.
[87] *De febribus*, II, 22, *Opp.* II, p. 100.

own time this was the view of Glisson, who is usually regarded as the original observer of irritability and its significance.

However, older sources apart,[88] Glisson was, on his own showing, influenced in this matter by another contemporary, namely William Harvey (1578–1657), and by Van Helmont. Glisson's works appeared between 1650 and 1677, the last containing his most extensive and pertinent account of irritability. He was undoubtedly familiar with Van Helmont's *Ortus*, probably since its first appearance in 1648. Perhaps so also was Harvey, but twenty years earlier, Harvey had already developed the idea of sensitive and reactively moving matter with regard to the blood, in *De motu cordis et sanguinis* (1628). He regarded blood as the prototype of such "working-matter" for two reasons: first, its primogeniture in the developing embryo and secondly, its supreme dignity and significance in the perfected individual. He speaks of its "obscure palpitations, movements and waves" that are independent of the driving force of the heart. They are evidence of a primordial *sensus* and desire to be moved hither and thither, intrinsic to the blood.[89] In more general terms, Harvey had described motion as reactive to irritation (and the sensation thereby caused) in his lecture notes on the local motion of animals, a year before *De motu*, in 1627. However, he had already in 1616 pronounced blood to be identical with spirit, and in 1627, "muscle and motive spirit to be the same thing".[90]

Harvey's ideas on irritability were seminal and original, as is already evident from the fields in which he developed them: cardiovascular physiology and embryology. It can be said in general terms that they have in common with those of Van Helmont the recognition of live working-matter on vitalist and monist lines, while there is no trace of Harvey and Van Helmont having influenced each other. Glisson's observations and speculations, on the other hand, were avowedly stimulated by those of Van Helmont

---

[88] See O. Temkin, "The Classical Roots of Glisson's Doctrine of Irritation", *Bull. Hist. Med.*, 38 (1964), 297–328, and idem, "Vesalius on an Immanent Biological Motor Force", ibid., 39 (1965), 277–80.

[89] Harvey, *De motu cordis* (1628), cap. XVI, p. 63; ibid., cap. IV, p. 28. On the movements intrinsic to blood see Johannes Müller, *Handbuch der Physiologie*, Vol. I (Coblenz, 1833–4), p. 137.

[90] Harvey, *De motu locali animalium*, ed. G. Whitteridge (Cambridge, 1959), p. 110; Harvey, *Praelectiones anatomiae universalis* (London, 1886), fol. 85v. Idem, *De motu locali animalium*, p. 102. Pagel, *Harvey*, p. 343 and note 17.

and to a larger extent by Harvey.[91] Glisson elaborated and firmly established a notion of irritability before Haller and probably influenced Leibniz's monadological concepts. The pivot of Glisson's doctrine was the autonomy of tissue reactivity, its independence of the nervous system. This very point had been clearly stipulated by Van Helmont and more scientifically by Harvey. In 1650, in his first book *On Rickets*, Glisson enlarged on the *tonus* of tissues as a moving force for fluids under the direction of nerves.[92] Four years later, in his work *On the Liver* he traced the copious flow of bile caused by irritant cathartics and emetics, to the irritable bile-ducts: these sense the stimulus and respond with motion. The function of the latter was to counteract possible damage and thus was comparable to diarrhoea and vomiting as healthy reactions for the evacuation of injurious matter.[93] All these movements, Glisson argued, are due to *sensus* and hence are "nervous". The *consensus* of stomach and gut is similarly explained in terms of nervous activity – that is, by the common nervous network which operates through the "sixth pair", the *nervus vagus*. If it was the tone of the tissues in general which was made to account for the movement of fluids in the book on rickets, this role was now attributed to the tone of the nerves.

It was nearly twenty years before the nervous outlook was revised and irritability liberated and made independent of the nervous overlord. This Glisson achieved in his philosophical work on the "energetic nature of substance or the life of nature",[94] and it was here that the concept was presented as a continuation of Harvey's ideas. A long passage from Harvey's *On generation* was reproduced in connection with the immanence of the soul in the body, as opposed to its accession and super-addition to the body. Glisson was in no doubt that the plastic force intrinsic in semen "uses natural perception in forming the foetus, and is directed by

---

[91] Attention was first drawn to Harvey's anticipation of Glissonian irritability by J. Needham, *A History of Embryology* (Cambridge, 1934), pp. 129–30.

[92] Francis Glisson, George Bate, and Assuerus Regemorter, *A Treatise of the Rickets*, tr. Philip Armin (London, 1651), VII, p. 58 and XIV, pp. 114 et seq. Temkin, "Glisson's Doctrine of Irritation", p. 302.

[93] Glisson, *Anatomia hepatis* (Amsterdam, 1665), cap. XLIV, p. 366 and cap. XLV, pp. 420–1; Temkin, "Glisson's Doctrine of Irritation", pp. 299–303.

[94] Glisson, *Tractatus de natura substantiae energetica*. Briefly analysed in Pagel, "The Reaction to Aristotle", pp. 503 et seq.

it".[95] Indeed, it is natural perception which produces and maintains life in all the kingdoms of nature, albeit at its basic and most primitive level. No more than its modification is needed to arrive at higher levels and finally at the form or soul that informs the genitures and subsequently the building-up of the foetal body. It is the same single soul that stands for the individual unit embracing its bodily and psychoid aspects, the two sides of the identical coin.

It is at this point that Glisson introduces the archeus of Van Helmont. The chemists, he says, were the first to give the appropriate name to matter specifically "disposed": archeus. It presides like a major-domo over the natural constitution of an object. Consequently, Glisson identifies archeus with natural perception and its wide range of activity, from its role in constructing the whole fabric of an organism and in "knowing" what has to be done by the organs, to the Hippocratic *physis*, the natural healer of disease. As the plastic force it works in the semen; as embodied life it repairs faulty organs, consolidates where continuity has been severed, brings waste to the point of discharge, and preserves all object-specific characteristics in their natural states. Without it no medicine can be effective.[96]

It may be noted that in his last work Glisson showed less sympathy with the concept of *gas*, especially as representative of the archeus in the blood. He supported, however, Van Helmont's view of the "irritated and perturbed archeus" as the first mover in disease. The wide range of archeal activity is recognised in the same late work (as before in 1672), by its identification with natural perception. Indeed, the archeus is made responsible for the whole fabric of the body and the use of the organs. Glisson also accepted the Helmontian principle of middle-life, the impression that is made by unassimilable substances that remain in a state of reduced vitality. He paid little attention to acid gastric digestion, preferring an account in terms of a chain of "coctions", and he was unwilling to allow bile the position of dignity to which it had been reinstated by Van Helmont. However, he rejected the role attributed by Van Helmont to the spleen in digestion. Catarrh, a con-

---

95 Glisson, *Tract. de nat. substant. energet.*, sig. C2r (Ad lectorem), and sig. A2r, with reference to Harvey's criticism of Scaliger, Fernel, and Sennert: see Pagel, *New Light on Harvey*, pp. 24, 84–92.

96 Glisson, *Tract. de nat. substant. energet.*, Ad lectorem, sig. C4r.

cept denounced by Van Helmont as madness, still retained an important place in Glisson's pathology.[97]

Van Helmont presented a fully developed case for the subordination of the nervous system to the vital principle. Nothing should be allowed to come between the organism and what organises it, which is the vital principle, the sensitive soul. This receives and responds to outside stimuli directly, by virtue of its intimate interconnection with bodily matter. In fact it is but one aspect – the psychoid – of the live unit, and, as such, is convertible into physical effects when its physical counterpart is turned to the surface. Thus, for example, inflammation not only signals, but is in itself the "fury, indignation or disturbance" of the vital principle resident in the part or tissue affected. It directly senses what "rushes upon it" from outside.[98]

By contrast, the brain works through mediators. It maintains its traffic with the body by means of spirits and humours which travel along pre-formed anatomical channels; hence there is a time-lag before these reach their destination. This is clearly seen in voluntary motion, by contrast with autonomous muscular motion, which is independent of cerebral impulse. Thus, catalepsy, spasm, vertigo, and similar conditions are not primarily from the brain, but have repercussions on it – they are felt to arise in the *pre-cordia*, the residence of the vital principle. Catalepsy from poisoning and madness may leave motion and sensation intact and hence is not caused by the nervous system. The same is true of carbon-monoxide poisoning, as Van Helmont had experienced himself.[99] That motion can be independent of the brain is shown by the decapitated fly that continues flying, or the violent muscular contractions in a man who has been beheaded.[100]

As compared with the deep-seated vital principle, then, the nervous system is something much narrower in scope; it is specialised, and attuned to a particular group of sensations and responses. Hence, it is subordinate to the vital principle which is "open to and tolerates" all sensations, is omnipresent, and immediately ready for its task without "consulting or having recourse" to the brain.

[97] Glisson, *Tractatus de ventriculo et intestinis* (London and Amsterdam, 1677), XXV, pp. 443, 457; VIII, p. 161; XIX, p. 274; XXV, p. 479.

[98] Van Helmont, *De lithiasi*, IX, 31, *Opp.* II, p. 67.

[99] Ibid., IX, 57, *Opp.* II, p. 76; IX, 129, p. 89; IX, 54, pp. 74–5 and IX, 81, p. 82; IX, 54, pp. 74–5 and IX, 83, p. 82; IX, 54, p. 74.

[100] Ibid., IX, 56, *Opp.* II, p. 76.

Timing, if nothing else, excludes the brain from consultation, as only instantaneous action can avoid harm.[101]

The primacy of the vital principle and the secondary role of the nervous system are reflected in the phenomenon of pain. This expresses the "boiling, seething or raging" (*aestus*) at some irritation or indignation experienced by the sensitive soul. Translated into its physical effect it spells contraction of a member or group of muscles. Nature in itself is prone to elicit cramp – "crispation and corrugation", as is shown in the scrotum at the onset of defaecation. A chemical equivalent is the conversion of nutritious matter into a corrosive salty acid in painful wounds, as part of a vicious circle in which pain is both consequence and cause of the humoral change.[102] Pain may be acute – in the nature of cramp; it may be chronic as in ulcers through the development of corrosive acid; or it may be deep-seated numbing or gnawing, as in faulty digestion and assimilation indicating a "morose" rather than a "furious" *anima*. At all events it is not the irritant that is active, it is not the nettle that stings; rather the stinging lies in the "*anima* stung". Nothing not alive, such as a piece of skin out of its vital context, can be stung.[103]

If it is not the nettle that makes the blister, but the *anima* or vital principle, what is the latter's purpose? Briefly this is the mitigation, blunting, or extinguishing of the chemical irritant that has formed after an injury, which is normally an acid. The blister thus expresses irritation sustained as well as counteracted. Such efforts may be overdone, however, when there is too much rage and fury, with resulting degeneration of tissue-fluid into acid or a still more corrosive ichor. Hence the chronicity and recalcitrance of some ulcers. On the other hand, irritation may become less on repeated exposure to a certain irritant.[104]

Pain manifests itself in contraction – often, but not necessarily, of muscle. Contraction or cramp produces pain, but conversely pain invites contraction and thus increases pain in a vicious circle. A wound is painless as long as its lips remain soft. A thorn thrust into the skin hardens and contracts it. Small, hitherto invisible arteries emerge, and the pulse hardens. All this is due to traumatic

---

[101] Ibid., IX, 90, *Opp.* II, p. 83.
[102] Ibid., IX, 116, *Opp.* II, p. 87.
[103] Ibid., IX, 116, *Opp.* II, p. 87; IX, 103, *Opp.* II, p. 85.
[104] Ibid., IX, 103, *Opp.* II, p. 85; IX, 108, *Opp.* II, p. 86.

pain, attended by tension and contraction of the arteries, for it is the property of pain to "pull up and to contract". Under the impact of pain and contraction, parts such as the penis may become almost invisible, whilst others are widely opened such as the pelvis in child-birth. Intestinal colic is nothing but spastic contraction; it has nothing to do with the quality of the contents of the gut. Contraction is the motion proper to muscle. It expresses the sensation of injury sustained, a kind of "sorrow" felt.[105]

Diseases in general had traditionally been appraised as privative in character, some loss opening the door to imbalance and anarchy. Van Helmont argued against this, pointing out the positive existence of diseases as classifiable entities each with a specific irritant cause. Thus, apoplexy had been defined symptomatically as loss of consciousness and of motor and sensory activity. In this definition no provision was made for its cause, the specific irritant responsible. This should be a specific poison of a "stupefying and cadaverous" nature, which is reacted upon by the vital principle residing in the precordial region. Here a "virulent narcotic prelude" leads to an affection of the brain – a decidedly secondary event.[106] Apoplexy, then, is as little a disease primarily of the brain as the blister is a condition caused by the nettle.

Of the stupefying drugs relevant to these questions only opium, hyoscyamus, and mandragora had been considered, and that indiscriminately as variants of the same substance, differing from each other only by degree. Van Helmont saw essential differences between those drugs which blot out sensation and the mind whilst leaving motion intact – a condition typical of epilepsy – and those through which motion is impaired or motion as well as sensation. Still others cause a drunken stupor and nothing else. All these have in common the two stages of action, which provide the pattern for apoplexy: the primary "prelude" of interaction of the poison with the vital principle, and the secondary overpowering of the brain. The form in which the brain lesion is manifested, however, whether as vertigo, falling sickness, fainting, somnolence, palpitations, or stroke, depends upon the specific characteristics of the individual poison, be it introduced from outside or developed from within.

---

[105] Ibid., IX, 132, *Opp.* II, p. 90; ibid., IX, 135, *Opp.* II, p. 91; ibid., IX, 132 and 134, *Opp.* II, p. 90; ibid., IX, 129, *Opp.* II, p. 89; ibid., IX, 136, *Opp.* II, p. 91 and 120–2, pp. 87–8.
[106] Ibid., IX, 81, *Opp.* II, p. 82.

The "apoplectic poison" creates "fear in the sensitive parts" with subsequent contraction and paralysis.[107]

In Van Helmont's view, far too much attention had traditionally been given to opium. Opiates are capable of inducing madness: it is therefore utterly wrong to believe in their curative power in madness (*mania*). For "opiate" itself implies deprivation of senses. In the demented subject, more than ten times the normal dose would be needed to induce sleep. Even so, sleep would but increase his derangement and, in dreams, add a further set of vanities to those which tormented him when awake. Sleep can indeed be healthy and initiate recovery in the mentally sick; if induced by opiates it is certainly not, for these are "lethal through sleep".[108] A similar case is made out against laxatives. They but suck out healthy blood from the mesenteric veins in order to convert it into putrescent material. They operate through an occult intrinsic poison. Whatever they touch they ferment, dissolve, and make putrid.[109]

Understanding of drugs and poisons had been further obscured by grading them according to the qualities of the ancients. Thus, opium was said to act by virtue of its cold quality. However, its hypnotic effect is bound up with its bitter component, and bitter things are "hot", according to the scholastics. A much more beneficial hypnotic is sweet, namely the *sulphur vitrioli* of Paracelsus. Its sweetness is demonstrated in the preference shown for it by animals. It causes "sweet sleep", with restoration of the principal faculties.[110] By contrast, opium-induced sleep is "laboured sleep", an evil harbinger of "disturbance and tempest". This effect of opium places it in the same category as the poisons that cause stroke, vertigo, epilepsy, coma, and palpitations.[111] It should, however, be noted that the dangers wrought by opium had not been ignored by traditional physicians before Van Helmont's time

---

[107] Ibid., IX, 82–3, *Opp.* II, p. 82.
[108] Ibid., IX, 85, *Opp.* II, p. 82; IX, 84, p. 82; *Promissa authoris*, I, 9, *Opp.* p. 8.
[109] *Potestas medicaminum*, 33, *Opp.* p. 455.
[110] *De lithiasi*, IX, 86, *Opp.* II, p. 82. *Jus duumviratus*, 40, *Opp.* p. 293 with reference to the *spiritus vitrioli antepilepticus* or *dulcis* of Paracelsus, probably a mixture of alcohol and ether. See W. Pagel, "Paracelsus' aetherähnliche Substanzen und ihre pharmakologische Auswertung an Hühnern. Sprachgebrauch (*henbane*) und Konrad von Megenberg's *Buch de Natur* als mögliche Quellen", *Gesnerus*, 21 (1964), 113–25; J. S. Gravenstein, "Paracelsus and his Contributions to Anaesthesia", *Anaesthesiology*, 26 (1965), 805–11.
[111] Van Helmont, *De lithiasi*, IX, 86, *Opp.* II, p. 82.

who "graded" and "qualified", for example, Leonhard Fuchs (1501–66).[112]

In conclusion, then, Van Helmont's vitalist first principles are here clearly embodied in several respects. There is first the prerogative which he accorded to the immediate action of the sensitive soul by contrast with the mediated forces of the nervous system. Secondly, there is his opposition of matter specifically disposed to empty matter. Enmattered psychoid impulses stand against soul super-added to matter from outside, and *sensus* omnipresent in nature and primary to all activity therein is opposed to interaction of matter with matter. Thirdly, he defines *sensus* as "active judgment of the soul", as against *sensus* as passively receptive; and *impetus* as reactive to *sensus*, as against *impetus* as primary and solely active.[113] Finally, Van Helmont gives pain a positive character as a "judgment" or assessment made by the vital principle, as distinct from the view of it as privative or something passively suffered. The translation of the spiritual sensation into its bodily equivalent is instantaneous and immediate, without transmitters such as humours and vapours and without the use of pre-formed anatomical channels. In all this the characteristics of irritability are clearly recognisable.

The vitalistic trend finds further expression in the relegation of heat, non-specific and indistinct, to the rank of an auxiliary, not really efficient, in favour of a distinct and specifically effective chemical, namely acid. Acidification is the physical side of the "acid" sentiment, the "indignation and furor" of the vital principle being the other face of the same coin: a single, identical, and indivisible action of living substance. In this action sensation and motion bear the brunt of stress and strain, but contraction and paralysis, pain and insensibility, are close companions. They not only follow each other in rhythmic succession but may also change into each other. Thus, becoming accustomed to an irritant may reduce sensitivity, whilst as part of a vicious circle pain itself may touch-off further contraction and intensified sensibility. A parallel to this is found in the ambivalence and paradoxical effects of drugs which may merely add another disease to the one they were meant to cure. This Van Helmont found particularly true of opiates and

---

[112] Leonhard Fuchs, *De componendorum miscendorumque medicamentorum ratione* (Lyons, 1563), III, 3, pp. 775–81 (at p. 778).
[113] *De lithiasi*, IX, 97, *Opp.* II, p. 84.

laxatives, the all-too-ready expedients of traditional medicine. Here, then, are applications of the general vitalist principle of irritability that became cornerstones of medical reform.

THE DISCOVERY OF GASTRIC ACID DIGESTION

The elucidation of gastric digestion, its working by virtue of an acid "ferment", and the nature of the acid concerned, owes much to Van Helmont. However, he observed, experimented, and argued in this field, as in so many others, on Paracelsian lines. Nor can he be called the "discoverer" of gastric acid, for its existence and significance were recognised by contemporaries who were also opposed to the traditional Galenic explanation of the process in terms of heat and "cooking". Moreover, an account by Johannes Walaeus (1604–49) that surpasses Van Helmont's in its experimental thoroughness, quantification, and synchronisation of the stages of gastric digestion, was arrived at during the last period of Van Helmont's life, although published a year after his death (Walaeus, 1645). Nevertheless it was through Van Helmont that definite chemical principles were established in place of Galenic concepts of heat and cooking. *Heat Does Not Digest Efficiently, but Excitingly* did not appear until it was included in his collected works, the *Ortus medicinae*, when he had been dead for four years (1648).[114] Nor does the title of the treatise do justice to its positive contents, which include the proof of the acid nature of the digestive agent and much substantial observational, experimental, and chemical material contributing to its closer identification. This may have conduced to the long delay in the acceptance of his findings and those of other contemporary opponents of Galen's doctrine of digestion.

An understanding of the true nature of gastric digestion constituted a major challenge to Van Helmont. In his opinion it was through this – the separation of the good from the harmful in our food – that first and final decisions for health and disease were arrived at. It was in the stomach that Van Helmont located the centre and seat of the vital principle, the *anima sensitiva*. To it and its region had to be traced the true origin even of those vital

---

[114] *Ortus medicinae*, pp. 201–6; *Opp.* pp. 192–7. *Oriatrike*, pp. 198–203. *Aufgang*, pp. 253–9; *Imago ferm. impraeg. mass. sem.*, 23–7, in *Ortus medicinae*, pp. 115–16; *Opp.* pp. 110–11 for a brief summary of *Calor non effic. dig.*

processes, healthy and morbid, which were normally referred to the brain and nervous system alone.

In his usual way Van Helmont started with a criticism of Galenic and scholastic doctrine. This had fallen a victim to the appearances of meat softened by boiling. It had escaped the Galenists that cooking fails to interfere with the ground-structure of the tissue, by contrast with digestion which does: for the latter is transmutation, a profound change which heat even of the highest degree could never bring about. There is no heat in fishes, and yet their digestion is of the first order. Nor can recourse be had to a potential heat therein, for in a process as real as digestion there is either an actual power at work or none at all.[115] This power must be specifically attuned to a specific task. It cannot be a general factor such as heat, the action of which remains the same wherever applied. The search for specific factors is here, as elsewhere, the essence of Van Helmont's work. This approach had already led him to the discovery of *gas*, which stands for a specific individual unit, as against air and watery vapour, which appertain to all things and cannot explain the differences between them. Resort to such general factors as heat, air, and vapour tends to deprive things of the reality of their existence, their "thingliness". The products and results of digestion, however, are distinctly diversified. Venous blood formed from the digested food in one animal differs from the blood in another. Heat cannot account for such basic differences; only "formal properties" can do so and these are singularly specific to any animal and perhaps even to any individual. Were heat responsible for digestion this should be particularly efficient in fever. The opposite is the case. Moreover, food kept for some time attached to a warm surface such as the skin simply putrefies instead of being digested.[116]

The true agent of digestion can be recognised from the following pertinent observations: first, glass swallowed by hens has lost its sharp edges when recovered from the stomach shortly afterwards and is found completely dissolved at a later date. As glass is known to resist even acids that dissolve metal, the agent that disposed of it in the stomach of the hens must have been particularly strong. Nevertheless this agent can be neutralised by material from tiles or bricks, by chalk or clay; indeed, this will give relief to

---

[115] *Calor non effic. dig.*, 8–10, *Opp.* p. 193; ibid., 11–12, *Opp.* pp. 193–4.
[116] *Calor non effic. dig.*, 14–15, *Opp.* p. 194; ibid., 18, *Opp.* p. 194.

those birds that are "ill at ease through the multitude of sharp-ness". It follows that the digestive agent must be a strong acid. Secondly, as a child Van Helmont played about with sparrows. Once it so happened that one of them got hold of his tongue, and he noticed the intense acidity that prevailed in its throat: hence, he had immediately concluded, the greediness and efficiency of diges-tion in these birds. Thirdly, he had on occasion noticed that a "sharp distilled liquor of sulphur" reduced the fabric of a glove to a juice in those places where it had come into contact with it. Fourthly, stimulation of appetite and digestion is brought about by "*all* things sharp", such as unripe olives, vinegar, lemon, or-ange juice, and mustard, but above all salt, and saltpetre which "hath a spirit in it that causeth hunger [*spiritus esurinus*] and most pleasingly sharp".[117]

In this way, then, knowledge of the gastric acid had "grown old" with Van Helmont himself, and he had soon realised its significance in gastric digestion. Yet (fifthly) the agent is not acid-ity as such. Neither vinegar nor lemon juice nor leavened flour will digest. Moreover, the presence of acid in the stomach cannot override specific incompatibilities of certain foodstuffs in individ-uals as well as species. Mice and pigs refuse beans, the falcon bread; cheese, wine, and milk are indigestible to certain people.[118] Hence, it must be a specific and vital, an "essential" acidity that is liable to individual and species variation. Its formal nature justifies its designation as ferment, an agent truly capable of trans-*forming* one thing into another.[119] Though originating in the spleen (like the Galenic black bile), it has nothing to do with the suppositious "melancholious sour and black excrement", the "black bile" of the ancients. This is morbid in character, the reputed main constituent of black vomit, and thus far removed from the vital digestive agent in dignity and function.[120]

In conclusion, then, acid must be the agent operative in gastric digestion. This can be supported by heat, but accidentally, not essentially. What is essential is the acid, the ferment specific to the

[117] Ibid., 22, *Opp.* p. 195; ibid., 23, *Opp.* p. 195; ibid., 24, *Opp.* p. 195.
[118] *Calor non effic. dig.*, 26, *Opp.* p. 195. *Oriatrike*, p. 201.
[119] *Calor non effic. dig.*, 28–9, *Opp.* pp. 195–6; also *Imago ferm. impraeg. mass. sem.*, 24 and 26–7, *Opp.* p. 111.
[120] *Calor non effic. dig.*, 30–1, *Opp.* p. 196: the spleen is intimately connected with the stomach topographically in animals with powerful digestion such as hens. Occa-sionally the spleen may be found to be acid when the stomach is not.

task and its performance in a given individual and species. By contrast heat is non-specific, a general factor that affects any individual or species uniformly. Though derived from the spleen, the *duumvir* harbouring the vital principle in equal partnership with the stomach, the gastric ferment is absolutely distinct from black bile, which is supposedly a splenic excrement or pathological product that has no function to fulfil, if it exists at all. Nor can the gastric ferment be compared with such a powerful agent as nitric acid (*aqua fortis*), or other acids (acid salt-spirits) that are capable of corroding and blowing up earth with effervescence. Earth is not fermentable either; it is merely dissolved by acid.[121] Heat, as well as the traditional "occult quality" favoured by Hermetic writers like Reuchlin and Agrippa of Nettesheim, were thus replaced by a well-characterised agent in Van Helmont's interpretation of gastric digestion.

In the treatise we have been considering we look in vain for any identification, let alone a "formula" of the acid "ferment". Information on this point can be culled, however, from other parts of the *Works* that at first sight seem to be concerned with different topics. There is first of all a passage in the *Dageraad*, the early Dutch collection of treatises, in which "salt-acid-spirits" are introduced. They are the *Zout-suere geesten* or, in the old German translation, *Salzsaure Geister* which, as already noted, resemble nitric acid in their properties as powerful acids, and contrast with the excrement "melancholic black bile". Hence, the strong acidity of gastric contents retained in the stomach longer than normal should have been attributed to *aqua fortis* formed inside the stomach rather than to the impotent and inert bile. In the same context in the *Dageraad* the pleasing and appetising virtue of sea-salt is attributed to its latent acidity.[122] Moreover, an acid salt, partly volatile, partly fixed, is stated in the *Opera* to be formed in the stomach.[123] It is in action similar to that of the arcana; it removes, dissolves, cleanses, and expels noxious substances. As early as the tract on the *Waters of Spa* (1624) Van Helmont had regarded the hungry salt (*sal esurinum*) as the agent enabling spa-water to dissolve mucus and to promote

---

[121] *Dageraad* (1660), p. 58 (de Uytwerckinge van Zaden). *Scholar. humorist. pass. deceptio*, I, 78, *Opp.* II, p. 169. *Oriatrike*, p. 1029.

[122] German trans. in *Aufgang*, p. 157. See also *Imago ferm. impraeg. mass. sem.*, 24–7, and *Dageraad*, VIII, pp. 53–61.

[123] *Potestas medicaminum*, 18, *Opp.* p. 541.

gastric digestion.[124] Indeed, all salts and salty condiments conducive to appetite are of an acid nature, such as notably salt of the sea, the liquors of sulphur, vitriol, salt, sal nitre.[125]

Van Helmont has thus successfully rendered the digesting agent chemically concrete: it belongs to the powerful mineral acids, including notably "acid of salt" or "spirit of salt", in other words, hydrochloric acid. Van Helmont was well acquainted with hydrochloric acid as a chemical and with its production in the laboratory. He prepared a "gas of salt" by distilling a watery solution of saltpetre, vitriol, and alum in equal parts with the addition of sal ammoniac. Even in the cold, he found, a gas is released that breaks the vessel. This was deemed to have been hydrochloric acid.[126] No doubt can prevail about its identity in another process, described at two places: the preparation of the spirit of salt by distillation of salt and dried potter's clay.[127]

What is of particular significance in the present context is the inspiration which led Van Helmont to this chemical process: the observation, that is, of the stone-dissolving property of the acid ferment in the stomach of pigeons. His idea was to employ an extract from it in the treatment and prophylaxis of calculus. This proved to be ineffective, because, as Van Helmont believed, the stone-dissolving virtue of the stomach wall had been extinguished with the life of the animal. A trial to imitate and reproduce this arcanum by the "art of the fire", that is, in the chemical laboratory, resulted in the preparation of hydrochloric acid.

Acid dissolves stone. The stomach of some animals is possessed of such an acid. It can be reproduced by preparing hydrochloric acid in vitro. It is the latter therefore that must be the digesting principle in the stomach of all animals including fishes and man. Although this chain of conclusions was not presented by Van Helmont in so many words, he must have been aware of it implicitly; hence, there is strong reason to suggest that it was he who not only established acid as the digestive agent in the stomach but also

---

[124] *Supplementum de Spadanis fontibus*, V, 1, *Opp.* pp. 653–4.
[125] *Calor non effic. dig.*, 24, *Opp.* p. 195. *Sextuplex digestio alimenti humani*, 12, *Opp.* p. 200.
[126] *Complex. atque mist. elem. fig.*, 37, *Opp.* p. 105. *De flatibus*, 62, *Opp.* pp. 407–8. Hoefer, *Histoire de la Chimie*, ii, 146. Kopp, *Geschichte der Chemie*, iii, 349. Partington, *History of Chemistry*, ii, 227ff. does not seem to refer to this process.
[127] *De lithiasi*, VII, 28 (duelech resolutum), *Opp.*II, p. 52.

recognised, or came very close to recognising, its chemical identity with hydrochloric acid.

Van Helmont's formulations may be seen as part of a long
process of refinement of the role of acid in digestion. The Galenic
view allowed an auxiliary role to acid which contracted the stomach, thus intensifying the cooking process brought about primarily by the heat radiating from the organs surrounding the stomach.
Black bile therefore was acid, but its effects in the stomach were as
likely to be harmful as supportive of normal digestion. Writers
before Van Helmont had contested this view on the grounds that
neither heat nor black bile matched in specificity the digestive
process, since as agents they were operative everywhere in the
body. In the case of the Hermeticist Johannes Reuchlin (1455–1522),
the emphasis on specificity led to the notion of an occult quality
inhering in the gastric wall as a whole. This approach seems to
have influenced Fernel, although he remained committed to a
Galenic view of the importance of black bile in nutrition and in the
generation of disease.[128] Consequently he attracted sharp criticism
from Van Helmont.

Paracelsus first elaborated the specific character of gastric digestion, separating it from digestive processes elsewhere in the body,
for example, the mouth. He was intrigued by the peculiar digestive powers of some animals, and by the therapeutic acid properties of spa-waters.[129] However, he restricted acid gastric digestion
to a particular group of animals, and allowed a function to digestive heat.[130] No conspicuous attention seems to have been paid to
acid gastric digestion by early Paracelsists, although Severinus,
author of a brilliant system of Paracelsian doctrine (1571), laid
stress on the activity of chemicals or "mechanical spirits". Severinus
gave these spirits no precise definition, however, and his references to acid relate chiefly to its morbid effects. Joseph du Chesne
(1544–1609), a Paracelsian with Aristotelian leanings and antagonist of the Parisian medical faculty, emphasised the "sharp" humour

---

[128] Johannes Reuchlin, *De verbo mirifico*, II, 6 (Basel, 1494), sig. c5r; see also Pistorius
Nidanus, *Artis cabbalisticae tom.I.* (Basel, 1587), p. 912. Fernel, *Physiologia*, VI, 1,
in *Univ. Med.*, p. 128; ibid., I, 7, in *Univ. Med.*, p. 21; ibid, VI, 9, p. 147.

[129] Paracelsus, *Opus Paramirum*, III, 2, ed. Sudhoff, ix, 134; idem, *Buch von den
Tartarischen Krankheiten*, cap. 16, ed. Sudhoff, xi, 99.

[130] *Buch von den Tartarischen Krankheiten*, cap.10, ed. Sudhoff, xi, 66. "Ignis digestionis"
in *Opus Paramirum*, II, 1, ed. Sudhoff, ix, 86. See also Pagel, "Van Helmont's
Ideas on Gastric Digestion"; idem, *Paracelsus*, pp. 159–61.

as the active principle in acid digestion, and elaborated the Paracelsian idea through which artificial "hungry acid" (*acetum esurinum*) was presented as a *vitriolatum*, comparable to the acid derivative of any metal.[131]

Van Helmont may have been influenced by his contemporary Fabius Violet, Sieur de Coqueray, who rejected heat as a digestive agent in favour of a specific dissolving spirit or hungry acid. This was transferred from the liver to the stomach.[132] The outstanding account of Walaeus, mentioned at the start of this section, must be regarded as pre-Helmontian, although not published until a year after Van Helmont's death. Walaeus not only subscribed to acid rather than heat as the agent in gastric digestion, but graded its effects by the time taken to digest a variety of foodstuffs. He found that each food took a specific time to digest in the stomach and that this was not affected by the presence of other, different foods. He denied that bile was either present or active in the stomach in digestion, and conjectured that the gastric acid must derive from the spleen, the only acid part in the body.

Walaeus's results were derived from a considerable number of observations on live dogs.[133] His contributions to physiology are thus not limited to his early experimental confirmation of the circulation of blood. It is hard to say whether Walaeus and Van Helmont were familiar with each other's work. Van Helmont's treatise on digestion was, as already mentioned, published for the first time posthumously in 1648, three years after the appearance of Walaeus's observations. The former is likely to have been composed sometime in the 1630s. Suggestions contained in Van Helmont's earlier published works, such as his treatise on the stone (1644) or even that on the waters of Spa (1624), may have been noticed by Walaeus but, in the contemporary context, were

---

[131] Severinus, *Idea medicinae philosophicae*, pp. 184, 196–7, 244–6, 332. Joseph du Chesne, *The Practise of Chymicall and Hermeticall Physicke for the Preservation of Health*, trans. Thomas Timme (London, 1605), sigs.L2r, I.1–5; idem., *Liber de priscorum philosophorum verae medicinae matera* (S. Gervasii, 1603), pp. 110–12.

[132] See Fabius Violet's important paraphrasis to Paracelsus's *Paragranum: La parfaicte et entière cognoissance de toutes les maladies du corps humain causées par obstruction* (Paris, 1635), II, 3, p. 142; III, 4, p. 296.

[133] Johannes Walaeus, *Epistolae duae de motu chyli et sanguinis*, in Caspar Bartholinus, *Institutiones anatomicae...auctae a Thoma Bartholino*, 4th edn. (Leyden, 1645), pp.443–88. See J. Schouten, *Johannes Walaeus. Zijn beteknis van de verbreiding van de leer van de blood som loop* (Assen, 1972); Pagel, *New Light on Harvey*, pp. 113–34.

not necessary to the development of his ideas.[134] Van Helmont himself argued and observed from a Paracelsian platform. My belief is that Van Helmont stood in no need of post-Paracelsian authors such as du Chesne, Pietro Castelli, and Violet, and was largely original in his observations and experiments on acid gastric digestion.[135] It may be noted, however, that all of them, including Van Helmont, derived the digesting acid agent from the spleen in accordance with Galen's idea of the origin of acid black bile as an adjuvant of gastric digestion – with the difference that black bile was no longer invoked as such.

Van Helmont defined several aspects of acid as an agent within the body. Acid has to fulfil the vitally important task of separating the pure from the harmful in the stomach where it is formed. It also prevents and can cure the stone. It is pathogenic and locally destructive, however, outside the stomach. Paracelsus had already enlarged upon the adverse effects of acid generated in an ill-digesting stomach and causing tartar. Acid, Van Helmont says, is welcome to the stomach, but a hostile invader to other organs.[136] Under the direction of the stomach-bound vital principle or sensitive soul it can be "taken down" and become a "foreign guest" in a "foreign ground". Outside the stomach the displaced acid engenders a variety of diseases such as podagra (arthritis), abscesses, ulcers, even epilepsy, vertigo, and apoplexy. The acid is so displaced when it fails to attack food in the stomach, thereby irritating the vital principle (archeus) there resident. This reactively expels and disperses it to the periphery.[137] Indeed, inflammation and abscess can be identified with dislocated foreign acidity everywhere in the body.[138] Pleurisy automatically develops when gastric acid, the "guest of first digestion", flies towards "an alien harvest". Equally, pneumonia supervenes when acid is dispersed into the pulmonary vessels, arteries, or veins.

[134] Van Helmont, *De lithiasi*, III, 24 (1644), p. 52; *Opp.* II, p. 16. Idem, *Supplementum de Spadanis fontibus*, III, 10–11, *Opp.* p. 650; ibid., V, 21, *Opp.* p. 655.
[135] For Pietro Castelli (1580–1656), see his *Epistolae medicinales* (Rome, 1626), Ep. V. ad M. A. Severinum, pp. 139–41. I am indebted for this reference to Dr. J. J. Bylebyl.
[136] Van Helmont, *A sede animae ad morbos*, 4, *Opp.* p. 279. *Aufgang*, p. 836. *Pleura furens*, 14, *Opp.* p. 379. See also *Pleura furens*, 22, *Opp.* p. 380.
[137] *A sede animae ad morbos*, 6, *Opp.* p. 279; ibid., 10, *Opp.* p. 280.
[138] *Pleura furens*, 13, *Opp.* p. 379.

And finally, all such "transport of the ferment" can be forestalled by alkali.[139]

In all this Van Helmont has recourse to the displacement of a fluid that is taken down from its site of origin to remote places along pre-formed anatomical channels, and this not instantaneously, but in stages – first, that is, from its normal site to the vessels, and subsequently to the tissues and organs. It is a process that has to account for a number of quite disparate diseases, from simple inflammation and abscess, to pleurisy, arthritis, epilepsy, and apoplexy. In general terms this is disturbingly reminiscent of catarrh, the traditional buttress of humoral pathology – admittedly with the difference that it is not the omnipotent corroding mucus of ancient tradition, but acid and acidity, that are now incriminated. However, it was Van Helmont who with an imposing array of observations and arguments demolished the "madness of catarrh". He demonstrated that this concept had been based on a humour that did not really exist, on channels freely invented, and a production and propagation ("ascent" and "descent") just as fictitious as the channels along which it was supposed to travel.[140] Instead Van Helmont insists on the local origin of all morbid changes, the true seats and causes of consumption, podagra, abscess, growth in the local nutritional centres, the "kitchens" of the particular organs concerned.[141]

The channels for the transport of Van Helmont's acid were real and not fictitious like those invented for the climbing-up of food-vapour to the brain, its conversion into mucus and its down-flow into the organs. Gastric acid was a well-characterised active chemical while the mucus of the ancients was at best an inert excrement. A non-specific universal such as heat and its interplay with cold in the brain had to serve in catarrh, that is, a contrariety of qualities, instead of a definite and real agent. However, a bodily transportation of any material along pre-formed anatomical channels would have been far too materialistic a basis of disease aetiology to find

---

[139] *Pleura furens*, 22, *Opp.* p. 380; tr. Pagel, *Van Helmont*, p. 214. *Pleura furens*, 20, *Opp.* p. 380; tr. Pagel, *Van Helmont*, pp. 213–14. *A sede animae ad morbos*, 22, *Opp.* pp. 283–4. *Aufgang*, p. 840.

[140] On catarrh theories and Van Helmont's treatment of them, see Pagel, *Van Helmont*, pp. 48–77. For a German translation with commentary of his treatise *Catarrhi deliramenta* see Van Helmont, pp. 144–78.

[141] *Van Helmont*, pp. 84, 131. For a classical example (the local origin and growth of a tuberculous cavity), see Van Helmont, *Catarrhi deliramenta*, 61, *Opp.* p. 429.

favour with Van Helmont. In fact it plays no significant part in his biological and pathological concepts. In these quite a different answer to the problem is provided, in genuine Helmontian, that is, spiritualist and dynamist terms. These exclude the bodily transmission of a ready-made acid fluid by ordinary "public transport" such as, in particular, the veins. Instead there is something luminous and "numinous", the command that is given by the archeus, the central digestive authority in the stomach, to its subordinate digestive agencies, the "kitchens" in the organs, to form acid locally and de novo. This dynamist view covers acid as the normal product of "first" gastric digestion, as well as heterotopic acid and its morbid activity in peripheral organs. No time-lag, no intermediate channel, no flow upward or downward, no law of gravity or levity, no heat or cold, no matter either fluid or solid, is allowed to come between the archeus and the executor of his command. This command, namely to form acid, normal or pathological, is given by an "imperious nod" (*nutus potestativus*) and governmental ruling (*actio regiminis*). In this light, acid is the physical aspect or manifestation of the directive. As such it is not separable from, but immanent in, tissue and fibre. What is propagated is not acid, but the error.[142]

Disease through acid, then, was due to acid arising in, not transported to, an organ. This conformed to the localist principle which Van Helmont opposed to the generalising pathology of traditional humoralism. Van Helmont's views were instrumental in bringing about a redefinition of the nature of bile. Traditionally bile was classified as excrement. Its use was rather accidental and overshadowed by the dangers inherent in its mordancy. By its bitterness alone it was disqualified from serving the purposes of nutrition. Though able to remove impurities from blood of inferior quality, it was in itself an excremental impurity in need of removal. Hence, it was aptly said by ancient writers that the absence of bile implied long life.[143] Galen essentially subscribed to this. He did not, however, deny any usefulness to bile. By "biting" the walls of the gut, for example, it stimulated evacuation; it also "washed off" dangerous mucoid deposits. Bile had, however, to be excreted by itself, for when retained it provided a major cause of disease,

---

[142] *A sede animae ad morbos*, 4, *Opp*. p. 279. See also, ibid., 11, *Opp*. p. 281; ibid., 19, p. 283; ibid., 8, p. 279.

[143] Aristotle, *De partibus animalium*, IV, 2, 677a.

notably such acute disorders as putrid fever, erysipelas, and generalised inflammation.[144]

Anti-Galenic sentiment may have been instrumental in the appraisal of bile as non-excremental by later writers such as Vesalius and Harvey. However, there was a long tradition of stressing the positive functions of bile independently of this factor. In the defence of bile the early Christian Nemesius, Bishop of Emesa, who wrote on the nature of man in the fourth century, may well have been a source for Paracelsus and Van Helmont, the Christian naturalists. Although basing his views on Galen, he elevated bile to the rank of part of the body, endowed with a vital faculty.[145] Paracelsus denied that bile belongs to the humours of the ancients. It is rather a principal member that remains stable, neither growing nor losing weight throughout life. Like heart, liver, and brain it cannot suffer reduction in substance. Nor has it the dangerous and morbific propensities which had been attributed to it because of its yellow colour and bitter taste. It is true that contradictory statements can be found in Paracelsus's writings; in these he even blames the ancients for having accorded too much importance to bile, a "redundant member", a freak of nature.[146]

Severinus, the most genuine and reliable expositor of Paracelsus, endorsed the positive view. He argued against the reception of bile into the "family of excrements". Instead it should be granted the same status as an organ enjoyed by the gall-bladder.[147] This witness as well as Van Helmont's position confirm the impression that appreciation of bile as a vital part outside the range of the fictitious humours and excrements reflected Paracelsus's true opinion. This is in any case consistent with his overriding opposition to ancient tradition. It can be supported by evidence from another Paracelsist, Violet. In 1635 he extolled bile as the "internal physi-

---

[144] Galen, *De naturalibus facultatibus*, II, 2, ed. Kühn, ii, 78 and ibid., II, 9, ed. Kühn, ii, 135–6. Galen, *De usu partium*, V, 3, ed. Kühn, iii, 349; M. Tallmadge May, trans., *Galen on the Usefulness of Parts of the Body*, 2 vols. (Ithaca, N.Y. 1968), i, 249. Galen, *De alimentorum facultatibus*, II, 6, ed. Kühn, vi, 568. Galen, *De placitis*, VIII, 6, ed. Kühn, v, 699.

[145] *Nemesius Emesianus De natura hominis*, ed. C. F. Matthaei (Halle, 1802), p. 260 (text; trans. p. 80). English tr. by George Wither (London, 1636), chap. XXVIII, p. 441.

[146] Paracelsus, *Elf Traktat*, ed. Sudhoff, i, 48 and 71. *De viribus membrorum*, II, 11, ed. Sudhoff, iii, 21–2. *De tartaro*, II, tract. 1, cap. 2, ed. Sudhoff, v, 51. *De membris contractis*, tract. 1, cap. 4, ed. Sudhoff, ii, 468.

[147] Severinus, *Idea medicinae philosophicae*, cap. XI, pp. 182, 187.

cian" who comes to the organs (notably the stomach) to prevent and cleanse them from morbific tartar deposits. It is an "internal soap" that "tames" the tartar just as spirit of vitriol vanquishes it, and, like the latter, stops decay.[148]

Van Helmont clearly followed the Paracelsian (or perhaps Nemesian) lead. To him bile is a vital balsam and "not at all excrement". On the contrary, it is a "noble part" and absolutely necessary, just as much as the wall of the stomach, the flesh of the heart, and the substance of the brain. In short, it "contains the rudder of life". Hence, it is present in all creatures alive, even in those devoid of a gall-bladder like pigeons.[149]

Bile did not easily lose its derogatory classification as excremental. It remained excrement as late as in the system of Friedrich Hoffmann (1660–1742). However, not long after Van Helmont the microscopical observations of the liver by Malpighi (1628–94) in 1669, were taken into consideration by Franciscus Sylvius (1614–72), the iatrochemist, who discussed bile quite without reference to any excremental quality. Van Helmont's vindication of bile was finally and emphatically endorsed through the experimental demonstration of its circulation and essential conservation, as against its excretion, by Maurits Van Reverhorst (1692). The latter concluded that bile is "absolutely not excrementitious". Reverhorst showed that the amount of bile obtained through a tube inserted into the bile duct by far exceeded any quantity discharged by the gut.[150] His experiments and deductions were based on and modelled after the great Harveian exemplar, the discovery of the circulation of blood.

[148] Violet, *La parfaicte et entière cognoissance de toutes les maladies*, lib. II, cap. 4, pp. 145–50.

[149] Van Helmont, *Scholar. humorist. pass. deceptio*, I, 24, *Opp.* II, p. 160; ibid., II, 8, p. 175 and II, 24, p. 179. *Sextuplex digestio alimenti humani*, cap. II, 53–6, *Opp.* p. 209.

[150] Friedrich Hoffmann, *Commentarius de differentia inter F. H. doctrinam medico-mechanicam et G. E. Stahlii medico-organicam* (Frankfurt, 1746), p. 57; Franciscus Sylvius, *Praxeos medicae*, I, 44, *Opera medica* (Amsterdam, 1679), pp. 296 et seq; Maurits Van Reverhorst, *Dissertatio anatomico-medica de motu bilis circulari* (Leyden, 1692). See further, Pagel, *New Light on Harvey*, pp. 135–7.

5

The ontological conception of disease

A new "dawn of medicine", a radical reform and complete abolition of ancient medical tradition, was the aim of Van Helmont's work. Today his laurels may be mainly reaped in the field of chemistry, but this should not obscure his part in the foundation of the modern concept of disease. This is the "ontological" view. In it diseases are visualised as if they were real beings, objects that can be considered and classified like any other objects. Such a view is in radical opposition to ancient tradition, which in Van Helmont's time ruled absolutely in medicine. This knew of no diseases as such; it knew only of individuals who were made ill by a disruption of humoral balance. Symptoms and disease-features varied according to a surplus or deficiency of one of the humours – a strictly personal affair of the patient. His own particular humoral mixture, his "complexion", was the result of a struggle between humours for hegemony, and its function was to achieve that balance which insured the healthy life of the person concerned. This was basically a materialistic view and as such it was deprecated by Van Helmont. His view was idealistic, in that he did not distinguish a multitude of patients, but rather a variety of diseases, each representing a specific idea or image with a specific cause of its own and specific organ-changes by which it became recognisable, regardless of the individual and his personal response.

Medicine was defined in one of the Hippocratic treatises as "subtraction and addition – subtraction of what is in excess, addition of what is wanted".[1] There is, in fact, but one disease. Obviously its nature and outcome depend upon the body material, humours, qualities, and mixtures of humours. "Disease" is merely an abstraction; it exists in the singular or not at all. At all events it

---

[1] Hippocrates, *Breaths (Peri physon)*, 1–2, ed. Jones, ii, 228.

concerns the organism as a whole. It is generalised from the start, engendered internally, and emerging in haphazard places. A classical example was catarrh, the domineering monopoly of mucus formed by food-vapours ascending to and condensed in the "cool" brain, descending again and "raining down" into a multitude of organs as a displaced and thereby corrosive attacker. It caused consumption, rheumatism, gout, stone, and "tumours" (*rhume de cerveau*).

Van Helmont's attack was frontal and total: "the reason of mixtures waxeth lean".[2] Disease is not an abstraction, not an *ens rationis*, it is not privative and finally a *non-ens*; it is not from a "cause of deficiency, whereunto a species, manner and order is wanting". On the contrary, disease is like any object in the world, "positive, actual and real", with a "seed, manner, species and order". It is from an external "efficient seminal cause", a "strange guest received within and endowed with a more powerful or able archeus".[3] Instead of the "too much or too little" of the ancients, mere negative and privative predications concerning the body as a whole and without specification, Van Helmont introduces specific disease-semina. Each of these represents an active individual that "assaults" our body from outside and, qua active ("alive") individual, from a position of equality with the individual assaulted.

The disease-semen owes this activity to an archeus, a vital principle of its own that regulates it and directs it towards certain ends in accordance with an intrinsic plan of life or idea. It gains access and superiority over the archeus of the host through the power and ability of its own archeus. Disease, therefore, is not due to the impact of matter – humour or humoral mixture – on the body, but to the interaction of vital principles, with secondary effects on the body. It is thus that disease is engendered and we are informed about its causation. Disease qua object in its own right is not identical with the vital principle that made it; it has its own *ens* and intrinsic morbid constitution (*essentia morbi*), and the nature of this is the subject of our enquiry. In Van Helmont's own words disease is a monster "aborted by a seminal agent"; it is not dead, however, but capable of self-propagation.[4] Before we enter into our discus-

---

[2] Van Helmont, *Terra*, 10, *Ortus medicinae*, p. 55. *Opera* (1682), p. 53. *Oriatrike*, p. 51.

[3] *De morbis Archealibus. Introd. diagnostica*, 8–9, *Opp.* p. 503. *Ortus medicinae*, p. 530; *Ignotus hospes morbus*, 20, *Opp.* p. 466.

[4] *Ignotus hospes morbus*, 63, *Opp.* p. 473. *Aufgang*, p. 916; *Ignotus hospes morbus*, 70, *Opp.* p. 475. *Aufgang*, p. 917.

sion of this "creature",[5] the position of its begetter, the archeus, should be more closely examined. We will thus arrive at sharper definitions of the essential difference between the father and the child, and of the latter's independence of the former.

Nothing can happen in an organism other than through its vital principle, the archeus. Disease, therefore, must be an affair of the archeus just as much as is normal life.[6] As we have seen, the archeus is object-specific. It represents the individual as an inseparable union of spirit and of matter (water) specifically "disposed" by it. It is a vital unit with two aspects or sides, the spiritual, that is psychoid, and the material, rather than a twin-complex of matter with super-added spirit or vice versa. There is no question of matter directly imposing on matter in the causation of disease. No corporeal agent is able to attack the body directly. It has first to find access to the archeus, which qua living substance is essentially spiritual and comparable to celestial light.[7]

On the psychoid side the first origin of disease may be found in an irritation of the archeus by something which comes from outside or is engendered from within. This something which distracts the archeus from its domestic duties is variable in nature. An irritant like cantharides, noxious fumes, or a trauma may arouse the "indignation, perturbation, terror or fury" of the archeus.[8] In response normal functions may become exaggerated, such as heat production as in fever, or muscular contraction as in tonic or clonic spasms. These reactions may be regarded as tokens of the healing power of nature and may successfully rid the organism of the irritant.

The indignation and perturbation experienced by the archeus is an opening gambit, a vague preliminary episode of "transient passion". It is only when, instead of these "non-entia", true *entia* have arisen in the form of certain disease images and ideas, that morbid changes take place. The disease process is thus connected with the archeus's choosing an image in the face of an object desired or feared, and hence with sympathy and antipathy. Normally, actu-

---

[5] *Ignotus hospes morbus*, 45, *Opp.* p. 470. Ibid., 47, *Opp.* p. 470.
[6] This has rightly been emphasised by P. H. Niebyl, "Sennert, Van Helmont and Medical Ontology", *Bull. Hist. Med.*, 45 (1971), 115–37.
[7] Van Helmont, *Tumulus pestis*, cap. IX, "praeparata sedes". *Ortus medicinae*, II, p. 35. *Opp.* II, p. 229. *Ignotus hospes morbus*, 8, *Opp.* p. 465.
[8] *Ortus imaginis morbosas*, 2, *Opp.* p. 523. *De virtute magna verborum ac rerum*, in *Opera* (1707) pp. 753–4.

ated by self-love (*philautia*), he "senses" the difference between friend and enemy, between what is advantageous and what is not.[9]

Although no disease can arise or subsist without the archeus, it is not in him that the *ens morbi*, that is, the essential that constitutes disease, is to be found. If it were, we would have to assume that there are as many diseases as there are archeal responses conditioned by individual "complexions", which would be a regression to the ancient view, with vital principles taking the place of individual humoral mixtures. To equate archeus and *ens morbi* would indeed be to miss Van Helmont's main point: that is, the real existence of each individual disease as such, the independent monster born and bred by the archeus and adhering to him as a parasite and foreign guest. It would be to deny what is uppermost in Van Helmont's idea: the "thingliness" of disease, its specificity in cause, course, and appearances – in short, his new ontological concept of disease.

There is nothing in nature, no object, no process that is not the result of seminal generation. Hence, Van Helmont says, "all that is destined to happen in nature I have assigned to the semina".[10] No matter, no interacting qualities of matter, but semina, are operative in nature in disposing matter towards specific goals. Like any other seed, the morbid semen begotten by the archeus soon achieves independence of its parent. Once externalised from the archeus it attacks and penetrates him from outside like poison. It behaves like a parasite that is hatched in and "obsesses" a part of the archeus.[11] As such it distracts the archeus from his domestic duties and may thus destroy the organism that is administered by him. The semen so acts by virtue of the intrinsic idea or image that makes it fertile and directs its development towards certain ends.

It is, then, the archeus who first conjures up or "imagines" an idea or image. This rebounds upon him, enshrined in a morbid seed. In the latter the spiritual idea or image has assumed corporality, and brings forth an overpowering monster, that is, the disease. The image has become virulent, an impression that masters the vital spirit and emerges at certain places of the body, the

---

[9] *Progreditur ad morborum cognitionem*, 10, *Opp.* p. 509. *De lithiasi*, I, 4, *Opp.* II, p. 3; ibid, IX, 29, *Opp.* II, p. 67.

[10] *Imago ferm. impraeg. mass. sem.*, 7–8, *Opp.* p. 108.

[11] *Progreditur ad morborum cognitionem*, 10, *Opp.* p. 509. *Ignotus hospes morbus*, 34, *Opp.* p. 468; ibid., 47, *Opp.* p. 470; ibid., 8, p. 465. *De ideis morbosis*, 5, *Opp.* p. 512.

"members and places" which are the immediate seats of the disease.[12] In short, the essence of disease lies in the morbific seed as material bearer of the morbific idea or image.

External agents are occasional causes, but not seminal essences of disease. They may touch-off the chain of events leading to disease, however, and are therefore of considerable importance. Moreover, apart from their role as initial stimuli they may condition the character of the morbid changes and their outcome. Van Helmont went so far as to state that "nature distinguished the species of diseases according to the species of the occasional causes" and that in disease all depends upon the occasional cause.[13] Such causes were even graded by their power of penetration and irritation of the archeus. They ranged from retained "offensive" metabolic products with mild morbific effects, to such violent agents as the saliva of the rabid dog, the plague virus, the venom of the tarantula, and the juices of wolfbane and nightshade. Causes of the latter category communicate the "image of furor" without leaving the recipient a chance of defending himself.[14] They are spiritual, "luminous" and thereby highly penetrative agents aiming at an immediate fusion with the vital principle, the archeus, a spirit like themselves. The plague-virus, for example, thus becomes the "consort" of the archeus, to whom it communicates the image, the true essence (*ens*), that is, of the disease. The virus of the plague does exist as such, but it is not in itself the disease, for it makes animals sick without eliciting plague. Man conceives the plague-image and develops the disease through a complicated chain of psychophysical events in which imagination, "magnetic" attraction of the virus, and above all fear, play a prominent part. This is the fear of having already contracted the disease when and where this is prevalent; hence, not all who are exposed to infection fall ill. Conveying the image or idea of plague, its poison, the "occasional cause", conditions the essence of the disease, lending it the character of plague and not of any other disease. The plague character is imposed on the body from outside as a certain "thing" to be received. This formulation contrasts with the ancient concept in which the

---

[12] *Demens idea*, 3, *Opp.* p. 263. *De ideis morbosis*, 26, *Opp.* p. 516, with reference to Hippocrates (*Ancient Medicine*, XV, ed. Jones, i, 40). *De morbis Archealibus. Introductio diagnostica*, 10, *Opp.* p. 504.

[13] *De lithiasi*, 123, *Opp.* II, p. 88. *De febribus*, XIII, 5–6, *Opp.* II, p. 138.

[14] *De febribus*, XVI, 4–5, *Opp.* II, p. 146. *Ignotus hospes morbus*, 42, *Opp.* p. 469. *Progreditur ad morborum cognitionem*, 10, *Opp.* p. 509.

emphasis lay on humoral imbalance inside the organism, almost to the exclusion of agents from outside. The event was appraised in purely materialistic terms, whereas Van Helmont viewed it as primarily the result of traffic between spirits, the vital principle (archeus) of the invader, and that of the patient. The same principle held good in rabies, when the saliva of the dog transfers its own form to the vital principle of the patient, converting it into its own form or character. This is an act of genuine transmutation comparable to that which the chemist achieves in vitro. In such extreme cases, involving agents with irresistible radiating and luminous power, any sharp difference between occasional cause and seminal essence of disease becomes blurred. This point loses its relevance, however, in view of the immediate, total, and "utterly pointed" fusion of the agent with the archeus. There is, as it were, no time or space for a theoretical distinction between cause and essence in a process of overwhelming rapidity and fierceness. Poisons of mineral, vegetable, and animal origin can act with similar ferocity, but poison as such need not come from without; it may be the product of pure archeal imagination. It may simply be endogenous images that are from the start as hostile, "foreign and external" to the archeus as the most deadly poison from outside.[15]

Each disease is distinguished by its type (*characteristicum*). This may be ingrained – burnt-in (*inustum*) – for example, in the wall of the stomach, the seat of the vital principle. Thus, the hereditary character of gout is "given in trust" (*concreditus*) to the stomach wall; not, however, as a bodily deposit in its folds, as tartar, but as a spiritual, specific disposition which at any time may lead to disease when the archeus is irritated by it.[16] The *character epilepticus* and the *ens apoplecticum* are similar type-specific designations of diseases and it is this type-specificity which lends "thingliness" and reality to each disease.

In conclusion, then, what is essential in diseases is neither the personal response of the patient, nor the archeus, nor any "occasional causes". The true *ens morbi* is the type-specific and classifiable idea or image that is enshrined in a specific disease-semen that has become independent of its begetter, the archeus. The offspring in its turn invades the father, the archeus of the patient, like a

---

[15] *Progreditur ad morborum cognitionem*, 10, *Opp.* p. 509.
[16] *A sede animae ad morbos*, 11, *Opp.* p. 281. Ibid., 12, *Opp.* p. 281; 17, p. 282. *Progreditur ad morborum cognitionem*, 10, *Opp.* p. 509.

parasite, a foreign guest; it distracts him from his duties for the common weal and, if not checked, may destroy him. This is the principle of the parasitic conception of disease that is akin to the modern view of individual and classifiable diseases; it is the ontological concept, which takes the place of humoral pathology and which has a history from Paracelsus to Virchow.

Though not *entia morbi*, the "occasional causes" condition disease in certain ways, interacting with the organism. Exchanges of this kind can again not lie in action of matter on matter. At the receiving end there is the archeus, the spiritual vital principle. Qua spirit he is not accessible to a direct attack by physical matter. Only a spiritual force can influence or change him. If such a force derives from an outside object, it is not the body of the object but its own archeus that enters into a relationship with the archeus of the potential patient. In other words, the archeus of the occasional cause becomes a consort of the archeus of man. There is an archeal dialogue.[17] Its result depends upon the spiritual strength of the partners. Self-preservation demands that the host is stronger than the parasite: he must "curb the foreign uneasiness of his consort archeus and make him subservient to his own commonwealth, subjugating him".[18]

Contacts with outside objects cannot be avoided. Moreover, since the Fall of man the human archeus is no longer capable of completely dissolving anything entering him, in spite of the strength of his digesting ferment, the acid, in the stomach, the residence of his vital principle. What remains undissolved is the foreign invader in a reduced state of vitality – in its middle-life. Its archeus remains, and directs its behaviour, which varies between harmless co-existence and its activities as "caltrops and thorns" reminiscent of those which the earth had to bear through man's disobedience. Hence the "great necessity", allowing sticky residues of outside objects in their middle-lives to form in our body, and to cause diseases, in the course of the conjunction of the two archei.[19] Though insistent on the *ens morbi*'s independence of the responsiveness of

---

[17] *De virtute magna verborum et rerum*, 6, *Opp.*, p. 754. This exchange with the "consort"-archeus can result in immunity acquired by the host-archeus through mild sensitisation. There are irresistible poisons like the saliva of the rabid dog, but others may on a single contact stimulate the necessary natural power of healing.

[18] *Magnum oportet*, 3, *Opp.* pp. 144–5.

[19] *Magnum oportet*, 52–4, *Opp.* p. 154.

the individual, Van Helmont was fully alive to the significance of the latter factor in single cases and case-groups. This is best shown in his admirable and almost unrivalled case-vignettes of asthma. These include all well-known forms of allergy and, most strikingly, psychosomatic mechanisms based on the enforced suppression of emotions.[20] However, whatever the catalyst, the morbid essential of the disease does not lie in the individual hypersensitive response to this or that agent, but in the *character asthmaticus* which is the same type-species of disease in all individuals affected. The ontological concept of the disease was thus established with all due recognition of the individual factors which marked its effects and appearances.[21]

If, as with the ancients, disease was the result of humoral imbalance, it had to be an affair of the organism as a whole; it had to be generalised from the start. The humoral theory was not concerned with diseases as "objects", but with disease as the expression of a certain relationship between objects, namely the humours and their qualities. If, as with Van Helmont, each disease was an object in itself, a real thing, it attacked from outside and had to find a locus at which to strike first, and where it could take root. Disease was therefore localised, at least at the outset. It followed that more attention was claimed for the morbid-anatomical changes than ever before. The principle of the local seats and causes of diseases that experienced its climax in Morgagni[22] was pre-formed and conceptually underlaid by Van Helmont. It was connected with his demolition of catarrh, the extreme presentation of disease as a generalised dyscrasia, or error in humoral mixture. To this Van Helmont opposed the local internal fault of the organ attacked by the disease from outside, the error of the lung, for example, in the setting-up of a tuberculous cavity, previously regarded as the product of corrosive mucus "raining down" from the brain. Instead it is from the "idiopathic" affection of each part that diseases arise.[23]

Localising disease involved appreciation of the local anatomical changes, of an image evoked by, and characteristic of, an individual disease and essentially different from that caused by another

---

[20] *Asthma et tussis*, 25, *Opp.* p. 356. Oriatrike, p. 360.
[21] Such recognition also applies to the significance of the "occasional causes" from outside (*species morborum* corresponding to *species causarum*): *De lithiasi*, 123, *Opp.* II, p. 88 and *De febribus*, XIII, 5–6, *Opp.* II, p. 138.
[22] Rudolph Virchow, *Morgagni und der Anatomische Gedanke* (Berlin, 1890).
[23] *Catarrhi deliramenta*, 3, *Opp.* p. 412; ibid., 5, *Opp.* p. 412. Ibid., 61, *Opp.* p. 429.

disease. Indeed, the localist trend illustrates, and follows from, the wider concept of disease as an image. The image represents the blue-print, the ideal plan which is translated into reality and delineated in the diseased organ. The anatomical changes thus depict the character of the disease; the ideal *ens morbi figuratum* has through them received its material garment, it has stepped out into reality.

There is no area in which Van Helmont's inspiration by and dependence upon Paracelsus is as evident as in his ontological theory of disease. First, the prerogative and priority of the spiritual is fundamental for both, and seen as the marrow of all activity or life in the universe. Paracelsus said that "The life of every thing is a thing invisible and incomprehensible and a spirit and spiritual thing".[24] And further, the body suffers, not materially from a material *ens*, but from the spirit. Hence, the cure must aim at the spirit and not the material body – to which there should be administered a spiritual remedy.[25] Qua spiritual, disease is on an equal level with the arcana, the uncreated divine healing powers, that is, which are "volatile like wind and specific". All arcana are thus so that they may accomplish their work without matter and body. For causes of diseases "are not bodies, hence spirit must be used against spirit". The cause does not attack the body directly and materially, but through interaction of one spirit with another spirit or even the enraging of one by the other.[26] Disease, therefore, is the result of a dialogue between spirits, that is, invisible powers with an astral energy far superior to anything within the reach of the merely material humours.

Here we have the first Helmontian principle, the spirituality of disease, its causation in the course of a dialogue between two spirits, two archei, or in Paracelsian parlance the "informing" or "irate" conversation of spirits or astral bodies which takes place by night and in dreams. In the same context Van Helmont quotes the biblical *nox nocti indicet scientiam*,[27] and Paracelsus teaches us that the day belongs to bodies and the night to spirits and that by day it is the bodies and by night the spirits which do their work.[28] By

---

[24] Paracelsus, *De natura rerum neun Bücher*, ed. Sudhoff, xi, 329 (bk IV).

[25] Paracelsus, *Volumen medicinae Paramirum*, IV, 3, ed. Sudhoff, i, 217.

[26] Paracelsus, *Das Buch Paragranum*, II (von der astronomia), ed. Sudhoff, viii, 178; *Volumen medicinae Paramirum*, IV, 3, ed. Sudhoff, i, 217.

[27] Paracelsus, *Philosophiae tractatus quinque*, tract. IV and V, ed. Sudhoff, xiii, 352–4. Van Helmont, *Magnum oportet*, 50, *Opp.* p. 153.

[28] Paracelsus, *Philosophiae tractatus quinque*, tract. IV–V, ed. Sudhoff, xiii, 352–4.

contrast with these, the humours are bare of life, without intrinsic spirit; they are passive, excremental, and not "real". They are without significance in disease and its causation; for to Van Helmont as much as to Paracelsus disease is a real thing, an *ens substantiae*, an individual specific unit in itself. Van Helmont's view of disease as the product of a generative process is also Paracelsian. For him our knowledge is based on all things being possessed of semen or, in his own words: *omnem naturae necessitatem seminibus dicavi*.[29] Diseases, too, must spring from seeds, not elements – they grow just as foliage and grass grow from the earth.[30]

Paracelsus expressed the "thingliness", specificity, and foreignness of the disease by predicating it as "man lying in man"; it attacks a certain organ by sympathy. The morbific semina hail from the time when God repented the creation of man and sowed the earth with thorns and thistles. There is no disturbance in our body other than what is evoked from a seed – the "occult man hidden in man".[31] In this we may find the "thorns and caltrops" which Van Helmont connected with the *Magnum oportet* and the middle-life of invaders in the causation of disease.

The Helmontian *oportet* is derived from Paracelsus. In the latter's view disease derives from the plurality of members united in one body and the consequential discord and ill-will of things and spirits in us. Equally the middle-life is Paracelsian; it stands for the seed in all things endowed with form and figure. Indeed, "figuration" and composition of objects depend upon their middle-natures. Such comprise colour, transparency, and properties accessible to "vulcan", that is to the analytical chemist.[32]

The anatomical changes described and typified by Van Helmont largely conform to Paracelsian tartar, however much he was opposed to their being interpreted simply as deposits of coagulated material, without reference to the all-important setting up of the

[29] Paracelsus, *Astronomia Magna*, I, 7, ed. Sudhoff, xii, 177; Van Helmont, *Imago ferm. impraeg. mass. sem.*, 7, *Opp.* p. 108.
[30] Paracelsus, *Das ander Buch der Grossen Wundarznei*, II, 11, ed. Sudhoff, x, 258; *Labyrinthus medicorum errantium*, XI, ed. Sudhoff, xi, 213; cf. Van Helmont, *De ideis morbosis*, 31, *Opp.* pp. 516–17.
[31] Paracelsus, *Von Blattern, Lähme und Beulen*, II, 10, ed. Sudhoff, vi, 347; *Das ander Buch der Grossen Wundarznei*, II, 1, 10, ed. Sudhoff, x, 255–6.
[32] *Das ander Buch der Grossen Wundarznei*, II, 2, 2, ed. Sudhoff, x, 290. *Opus Paramirum*, I, 3, ed. Sudhoff, ix, 54. Ibid., I, 5–6, 64–7; *De secretis creationis*, in Appendix to *Chirurgische Bücher und Schrifften*, ed. Huser, p. 105, and *Elf Traktat*, III (von farbensuchten), ed. Sudhoff, i, 47.

process by a spiritual ferment. In fact the Paracelsian idea of tartar initiated and strengthened the Helmontian principle of disease location. This is best evidenced by the explanation of the local changes in pulmonary consumption which Van Helmont has in common with Paracelsus: the dry, "caseous", and finally calcifying and ossifying deposits that lead to bronchial obstruction by pulmonary "excrement", and hence to phthisis. All this was seen by Paracelsus as a strictly local and specifically figurated error of the watchman in the "kitchen" or "stomach", the nutritional centre of the lung. Here is the primary seat of the disease, the true *sedes morbi*, as against a secondary involvement as in the catarrh of the ancients.[33]

Nor were image and idea of disease alien to the Paracelsian concept. All things, he said, "stand in images"; it is their anatomy. The anatomy of disease is no exception. Thus, dropsy is "formed in its image"; its anatomy must be known, as if it were a picture painted or carved. Unless we are alive to these anatomies of diseases "nature will not call us physicians". In this light we understand the language of nature, the signature of certain plants that indicates their use in diseases.[34] To Paracelsus, then, as to Van Helmont, disease is image; it is a form, it is a spiritual power. Invisible in itself, it unfolds material effects of a specific type, the body of the disease. All that thus confronts the physician is "in the image inherent in a seed". There is no disease that is not recognisably structured – articulated – like a member, and its remedy ("enemy") "stands in the same image".[35]

Even closer to Van Helmont is the role attributed by Paracelsus to imagination in disease. Qua spiritual, imagination is real and powerful. It is convertible into a physical effect or body such as the cherry-like excrescence conjured up on the body of the foetus by the wilful desire and imagination of the pregnant mother. As it evokes such passions as envy, hatred, and avarice, imagination may touch off the plague, as well as a variety of other diseases. Its penetrating power enables it to induce disease in other people and

---

[33] W. Pagel, "Die Krankheitslehre der Phthise in den Phasen ihrer geschichtlichen Entwicklung", *Beitr. z. Klinik d. Tuberk.*, 66 (1927), 66–98 (at p. 82), and idem, "Zur Geschichte der Lungensteine und der Obstruktionstheorie der Phthise", ibid., 69 (1928), 315–23 (at p. 320). Idem, *Paracelsus*, pp. 170 et seq.

[34] Paracelsus, *Opus Paramirum*, I, 5, ed. Sudhoff, ix, 62, 64.

[35] *De podagricis*, II, Prologue, ed. Sudhoff, i, 327 and 330–1; *Das ander Buch der Grossen Wundarznei*, II, 12, ed. Sudhoff, x, 260.

this again not by physical means, but by calling up images.[36] Equally, it is imagination that is operative in the semina. These are active by virtue of inherent images, the "figures" of the offspring. "Semen lies in speculation." It is human fantasy that attracts the "whole natural character" of the rabid dog – man's speculation poisons itself by imagining dog-nature; both come together like two clouds of smoke.[37]

As we have seen, imagination or fear of having already caught the infection served as an important factor in Van Helmont's concept of the causation of plague. Precisely the same had been stated by Paracelsus: "as if somebody hears of somebody else or sees, now it is attracted into him by virtue of his fantasy"; or, any sharp disease that befalls with fear as if of death is in the same class as plague.[38] In the same way any lust, desire, or will makes a corpus in man; wrath makes a body, and fantasy out of strong imagination makes a will that in its turn creates a corpus, that is to say, it is the seed of the evil.[39] With this we are back to imagination, fantasy, and the idea-image intrinsic in semen (including disease-semen). There is a virus or poison of plague, rabies, and other diseases existing as such and independent of man, but there is no disease, plague, or rabies without sympathetic and magnetic attraction, and joining of the poison-image in man with the same species in the external source, such as the saliva of the dog.

The archeal fury in Van Helmont and its poisonous effect were also anticipated by Paracelsus. Man converts out of fury a latent (*ungemacht*) body into disease, a body that thereby becomes manifest. Disease behaves like a violent man, and paroxysms and recrudescences compare with the wrath of nature.[40] Libido and debauchery

[36] *Weiteres zur Beulenpest,* lib. I (impressio in altum), ed. Sudhoff, ix, 574–5, 579; *De virtute imaginativa fragmentum,* IV, in *Philosophiae magna,* I, 15, ed. Sudhoff, xiv, 310.

[37] *Das Buch von der Gebärung der empfindlichen Dinge,* I, 4, ed. Sudhoff, i, 256. *Erste Buch der Grossen Wundarznei,* I, 3, 1, ed. Sudhoff, x, 169.

[38] *Erste Buch der Grossen Wundarznei,* I, 3, 1, ed. Sudhoff, x, 169. Fear as a propagating agent in plague is not original to Paracelsus or Van Helmont. "De timore pestilentiam propagante" is a commonplace topic in contemporary plague literature, for example in Giovanni Nardi (the correspondent and host of Harvey), *T. Lucretii Cari de rerum natura cum paraphrasibus et animadversionibus* (Florence, 1647), animadv. XXXVIII, p. 545. Paracelsus, *Deutsche Kommentare zu den Aphorismen,* VII, ed. Sudhoff, iv, 510.

[39] *Weiteres zur Beulenpest,* II, 2, 1, ed. Sudhoff, ix, 593–4.

[40] *Ibid.,* ed. Sudhoff, ix, 592; *Deutsche Kommentare zu den Aphorismen,* I, XI, ed. Sudhoff, iv, 513.

(*luxus*) attract specific poisons such as syphilis and gout. The same passions can render gout, or for that matter any other disease, "French", that is, syphilitic. Paracelsus did not regard syphilis as a disease in its own right, but as the result of a specific transmutation of a basic disease as a product of incidental factors and events.[41]

In conclusion, then, it is clear that essential elements of Van Helmont's concept can be found in Paracelsus. These include *Magnum oportet* and middle-life, the dialogue between archei ("astral bodies"), the power of imagination and fantasy, the spiritual generation of a disease-body as an object in itself, and its own specific semen that is actuated by an intrinsic image or idea. It is this image or pre-figuration that determines the character of an individual disease as an *ens morbi* independent of occasional causes and the responsiveness of the patient. Van Helmont rejects the Paracelsian tartar as materialistic, but adopts its underlying localist principle. Disease is thus derived from the local error of an organ and not from humoral displacement or imbalance.

It is interesting to note the attitude to Van Helmont taken in a context of hostility to ontological views, in the middle of the nineteenth century. The parasitic view of the naturalist school was criticised by Jacob Henle, Hermann Lotze, Carl Wunderlich, and others. Attempts were made at saving Van Helmont's respectability. It was implied that he favoured individual response as the universal and distinguishing factor in disease. "Il n'était pas ontologiste" was the verdict.[42] In other words Van Helmont did not mean what he said. This interpretation was based on an arbitrary selection of *obiter dicta* and a drastic omission of the essentials. The ontological concept was then revived in conscious opposition to the critics just mentioned, in Rudolph Virchow's *Cellular Pathology* (1858). Originally also a critic of the concept, Virchow was led to it through his preoccupation with morbid-anatomical disease-localisation and came finally to believe in the principate of the cell as the true *ens morbi*. He regarded it as his personal achievement to have reconciled with a purely scientific body of observations, the old and justified postulate that disease is a living being in itself and has a

---

[41] *Von Blattern, Lähme und Beulen*, IV, 3, ed. Sudhoff, vi, 374. *De podagricis*, II (geomantia), ed. Sudhoff, i, 322–3. J. K. Proksch, *Paracelsus über die venerischen Krankheiten, und die Hydrargyrose* (Vienna, 1882); idem, *Paracelsus als medizinischer Schriftsteller* (Vienna/Leipzig, 1911); idem, *Zur Paracelsus-Forschung* (Vienna/Leipzig, 1912).

[42] W. Rommelaere, *Études sur J. B. Van Helmont* (Brussels, 1868), pp. 90–1.

parasitic existence. For indeed each part that is pathologically changed enters into a parasitic relationship to the body on whose existence it depends.[43]

FEVER, VENESECTION, AND PURGING

Van Helmont tells us that the main body of his work was written "in the full blast of persecutions". He then gave it the title: *Ortus Medicinae: Id est, initia Physica inaudita* – the same title under which it was published four years after his death. This information is to be found in the Preface to the treatise *On the Stone*, following the dedication, which is dated October, 1643. This treatise appeared with the other *Opuscula* in 1644, the year of his death.[44] One of the latter is *On Fevers*, published in its second edition, two years after the first.[45] Van Helmont must have attached particular importance to it. For almost twenty years (as mentioned in Chapter 1) he, on his own account, had published nothing, reduced to silence by persecution. This period occurred during the late 1620s and early 1630s and it would have been then, and particularly during his house-arrest, that the comprehensive presentation of his ideas and researches must have provided the most welcome distraction and retreat.[46] It was from this collection, the *Ortus Medicinae*, that he "tore" *On Fevers*, publishing it separately and as his first statement for two decades, in 1642.[47] It should therefore have been written long before 1642, and yet we find in it a reference to an event that had taken place on 8 November of that very year, namely the post-mortem examination of the "bloodless" body of Cardinal Ferdinand Toletanus, brother of the king of Spain. This incident served as documentary proof of the harm done by frequently

[43] R. Virchow, *Hundert Jahre Allgemeiner Pathologie* (Berlin, 1895); idem, *Einheitsbestrebungen in der wissenschaftlichen Medicin* (Berlin, 1849), pp. 18, 26; idem, *Gesammelte Abhandlungen zur wissenschaftlichen Medicin* (Frankfurt, 1856), p. 50.
[44] *Ortus medicinae* in Van Helmont, *Opuscula medica inaudita* (1644), dedication to Caspar Ulrich Baron de Hoensbroeck, sig.*4v., dated Brussels 6 Kal. Octob. 1643. Ibid., preface philiatro lectori, sig. a3v.
[45] *Febrium doctrina inaudita* (Antwerp, 1642); 2nd edn. with *Accessit tractatus contra quattuor humores scholarum* (Cologne, 1644).
[46] Preface to *Opuscula*, sig. a3v.
[47] *Febrium doctrina inaudita* (1644), p. 3.

repeated and prolonged blood-letting.[48] We must therefore assume that the treatise was revised and supplemented before publication, and that in substance it belonged to an earlier period of Van Helmont's literary activity.

Van Helmont did not deny that a "febrile matter" exists; it can touch-off fever, through providing the occasion for it (*causa occasionalis*). What he does deny is, in the first place, that this matter is putrid, as accepted in Galenic and scholastic tradition. Instead it is a foreign non-vital matter that enters from outside, is retained, and is hostile to the vital principle, the archeus of the organism. In other words it is very much like the tartar of Paracelsus. In order to obtain a perfect cure of the fever it has to be expelled; indeed, fever is the instrument used by the archeus in his endeavour to rid himself of this matter. Van Helmont consequently denies, secondly, that the essence of fever lies in the presence of febrile matter. Nor is its presence the cause of fever. Just as in any other disease, the essence of fever is a morbid idea, image, or semen. This affects a part of the archeus, allowing him to express his indignation at the entry of foreign and hostile matter. Such matter must be vanquished by assault, for its presence maintains a passion – an image of hate (*odiosa imago*) – which prevents the archeus from doing his duty. Therefore what is essential in fever, its *conditio sine qua non*, and what truly causes it, is the vital spirit, the response of the archeus, or rather the partial occupation of the archeus by a foreign – morbid – idea and image (*icone*).[49]

What is true of general body temperature in fever applies to local inflammation. When a thorn penetrates the skin (*spina infixa*) it is not blood that hurries to the site of its own account, as if it had "waited for the thorn", nor is it this blood that "inflames" the site. Rather it is the archeus that commandeers the blood and causes the

---

[48] Ibid., cap. IV, 16, p. 36, *Opp.* II, p. 109. There is also a note concerning a disputation held at Louvain on 21 November 1641 with Vopiscus Fortunatus Plempius in the chair. In this the disputants rejected venesection except in plethora, and advocated hot and roborating (restorative) medicines; thus implicitly admitting that heat or hot "febrile matter" was not the cause of fever, and approximating to Van Helmont's own antitraditional view: *Opp.* II, p. 145; *Aufgang*, p. 352.

[49] *Febrium doctrina inaudita*, XIV, 1, *Opp.* II, p. 139; ibid., XIII, 5, *Opp.* II, p. 138; *Aufgang*, p. 340. *Febrium doctrina inaudita*, I, 27, *Opp.* II, p. 97; *Aufgang*, p. 301, on the archeus as the spirit that "makes *impetus*" in health and sickness, for "what in health performs healthy functions, the same performs faulty actions in disease". The same spirit that warms man naturally, heats him in fever.

site to be overheated. It is the spirit, the total ruler (*cosmocrator*), the initiator of all movement and change in us, who alone is responsible for the rigor that starts, and the heat that maintains, the fever. The "tremulous" rigor is the paramount instrument by means of which the archeus shakes-off excremental matter that adheres to an organ. The first bodily complement to this spiritual action is contraction, a wrinkling of organ surfaces such as that of the heart in particular, rigor being first and foremost noticed in the precordial region. By consensus and cooperation the oblique fibres of the vessels are contracted – hence the rare, hard, small pulse indicating as well as causing chilliness.[50] This is supplemented by muscular contraction. The archeal instruments as a whole – initiating cold that is followed by heat – bear the characteristics of *blas*. The anger of the archeus is expressed in the sweating which also constitutes the expelling effort of the archeus. Hence, sudorific treatment (*diaphoretica*) is the only appropriate and specific therapy in fevers. Here the arcana of Paracelsus must be considered: in the first place, his mercurial preparations such as the red diaphoretic precipitate and his *arcanum corallinum*.[51] Next there are volatile herb-salts from "cephalicks", marjoram, rosemary, sage, and rue; and in the third place certain plasters. The task, then, is to find the universal medicine for fever – to wit, that powder which corrodes, dilutes, dissolves, melts, wipes, and "scratches off" the febrile matter so that it can be discharged via the sweat-pores without causing real sweating.[52]

This briefly gives Van Helmont's ideas on the essence, cause, and therapy of fever. They are spiritualistic, and radically opposed to the materialistic tradition as based on faulty elemental and hu-

---

[50] *Febrium doctrina inaudita*, I, 28, *Opp.* II, p. 97; ibid., IX, 2, *Opp.* II, p. 128; ibid., IX, 7, *Opp.* II, p. 128; *Aufgang*, pp. 301, 331.

[51] *Febrium doctrina inaudita*, XIV, 7–10, *Opp.* II, p. 139; *Aufgang*, p. 342: the mercurial arcana relieve fevers, but also cure cancer, lupus, ulcers (both internal and external), dropsy, and indeed all diseases of prolonged duration. For the composition and preparation of these chemicals see the extensive commentary by Knorr von Rosenroth, *Aufgang*, pp. 342–7.

[52] Van Helmont stipulates that the herb preparations should not be alkaline herb-ashes, but volatile products. He does not specify as to the plasters, but Knorr does (pp. 346–7): these are derived from sympathetic medical folklore, and are composed of turpentine, live spiders, spiders' webs, ground pitch, and white salt armoniack (ammoniac) laid on for nine days and then discarded into running water. Knorr refers to Johannes Stephan Strobelberger, *Remediorum singularium pro curandis febribus introductio* (Nuremberg, 1626): *Wellcome Catalogue*, I, no. 6119, p. 324.

moral balance and putrefaction. In fact it is the closely argued rejection of these traditional terms which occupies the bulk of the treatise *On the Unheard-of Doctrine of Fevers.* Van Helmont's main criticism is directed at the supposed heating effect of decay. Heat that develops in horse-dung ceases before putrefaction. The heat is not due to the rotting, but rather to a specific fermentation caused by the spirits of salts that are pressed together in the dung. Decay implies death of a tissue, organ, or organism; hence it causes cold rather than heat.[53] In other words, febrile matter is neither putrid nor hot in itself. If it were, dead bodies should feel hot. Cooling, at best a palliative for secondary effects of fever, does not go to the root of the matter, which calls for shaking-off of the foreign guest. The thorn infixed is cold in itself, but raises inflammatory heat. There is only one heat and it varies by degree, but there are many fevers and they vary by species.[54]

Just as "rotten" as the theories of the ancients, was their therapy. In this blood-letting was pre-eminent. Galen relied upon it in all fevers with the exception of hectic fever.[55] Van Helmont's response to this is, if venesection cools, why not use it in hectic fever? He himself forbids it absolutely. Its supposed effect of cooling could only be due to a drastic diminution of the blood volume and a complete exhaustion of the vital spirit. This was clearly evident in the post-mortem examination of Cardinal Toletanus, who, at the age of 32, died of a tertian fever unrelieved by frequent and prolonged venesections. There was no blood to be seen, even in the liver, and the heart looked like a shrunken bag. Blood coursing in the vessels is not "bad", and thus to be reduced, as long as there is any life in the body. If it were, venesection would achieve nothing but the addition of further bad blood by regeneration. Blood-letting by "revulsion" (that is, at the opposite side from the affliction) which might be found useful in certain local diseases affecting particular organs, will never help in such generalised conditions as fevers. Pleth-

---

[53] *Febrium doctrina inaudita,* II, 14, *Opp.* II, p. 100. *Aufgang,* p. 304.

[54] *Febrium doctrina inaudita,* II, 12, *Opp.* II, p. 99; ibid., II, 14, *Opp.* II, p. 100; ibid., I, 24, *Opp.* II, p. 98; ibid., I, 28, *Opp.* II, p. 97; ibid., II, 5, *Opp.* II, p. 99.

[55] See P. H. Niebyl, "Galen, Van Helmont and Blood Letting", in *Science, Medicine and Society in the Renaissance, Essays to honor Walter Pagel,* ed. A. G. Debus, 2 vols. (New York, 1972), ii, 13–23.

ora, the only conceivable indication for venesection, is never associated with fever.[56]

Purges and laxatives are similarly criticised and rejected. They are in Van Helmont's view poisons that dissolve organ substance into stinking excrement. There can be no purging of faulty humours, which do not exist. Nor is there an overheated liver in the particular case of the itch (a contagious disease), which might be relieved by purging.[57]

Paracelsus's view was that fever is no disease, although it may be a sign of disease. Fever is abnormal heat and hence cannot stand for any of the many species of disease. These must be distinguished by "matter and cause": a substance, that is, which lends specific properties and cause to a given disease. When the body is overheated in fever this is the effect caused by nitre and incensed sulphur – hence the shivering cold and the intermissions. The term fever is therefore wrong, in that it implies humoral causes which do not exist. The condition should rather bear the designation "nitreous", from its true substantial, or chemical, cause.[58]

Pereira and Campanella were much more explicit than Paracelsus; they were not necessarily influenced by him, although they shared his anti-Galenist attitude. Their detailed arguments strikingly coincide with those of Van Helmont in many respects. Gomez Pereira of Medina del Campo (b. *c.* 1500) published *New and True Medicine* in 1558.[59] At that time Johannes Argenterius (1513–72) and his followers had created a certain, albeit ephemeral, vogue of anti-Galenism. It was Pereira who singled out fever as his main target of attack, in particular the idea that fever formed a disease in its own right and that it was caused by putrefying humours. Against this he argued that febrile and natural heat are identical and differ-

[56] Van Helmont, *Febrium doctrina inaudita*, IV, 16, *Opp.* II, p. 109; ibid., IV, 37, *Opp.* II, p. 112; ibid., IV, 40, *Opp.* II, p. 113; ibid., IV, 4, *Opp.* II, pp. 107–8; *Aufgang*, pp. 311, 313, 316, 317.
[57] *Febrium doctrina inaudita*, V, 12, *Opp.* II, p. 116. See O. Temkin, "Fernel, Joubert, and Erastus on the Specificity of Cathartic Drugs", *Science, Medicine and Society in the Renaissance*, ed. Debus, i, 61–8, reprinted in Temkin, *The Double Face of Janus* (Baltimore and London, 1977), pp. 512–17. Van Helmont also categorically rejected the use of enemas: *Febrium doctrina inaudita*, VII, 8–16, *Opp.* II, p. 124; *Aufgang*, p. 327.
[58] Paracelsus, *Opus Paramirum*, I, 6, ed. Sudhoff, ix, 69.
[59] G. Pereira, *Novae veraeque medicinae experimentis et evidentibus rationibus comprobatae prima pars* (Medina del Campo, 1558). See M. Neuburger, "Gomez Pereira, ein spanischer Arzt des XVI. Jahrhunderts", *Archeion*, 18 (1936), 113–16.

ent only in intensity. Nor could he credit Galen's reasons for the conversion of simple (ephemeral) into putrid fevers or, for that matter, the distinct category of putrid fever as such. In his view it is untrue that the heat of the heart is set alight by a putrid humour; rather, a morbid condition affecting the blood is taken up to the heart whereby this organ is forced to move more strongly and rapidly. All this indicates the true nature of fever, as the war waged by nature in an attempt at getting rid of some morbid cause. Superfluities that affect the body adversely should thus be dissipated, or else be "cooked" and discharged, through openings that are kept widely open by virtue of increased – that is, febrile – heat. Similarly, rigor reveals the struggle between the vital spirits and the harmful cause that has found access to the heart.[60]

The definition of fever as not a disease, but rather an attempt at its natural cure, had thus been clearly established by Pereira long before Van Helmont and his contemporary Campanella. Campanella's earlier work *De sensu rerum et magia* had strongly Helmontian connotations. It was published in 1620 and could have hardly escaped Van Helmont's attention. Campanella there characterised fever as a natural cure rather than a product of humoral corruption, in the course of a discussion of the world as analogous to a mortal animal. Campanella's idea of fever is developed in its own right in his medical work of 1635, *Medicinalia.*[61] Here it is stated that there is no better remedy whereby nature enables man to attain health. All diseases are thus open to healing by fever, and those who fail to develop it are doomed. Fever is not evil, only its cause; it is a symptom, not a disease. There is no "essential" fever, with the exception of fever caused solely by wrath. Nor is there room for a distinction between simple and putrid fever, for no role can be ascribed to putrefaction in the origin of fever. In venereal disease the flesh withers and putrefies and there are ulcers full of pus, yet there is no fever. Conversely, fever may precede putrefaction, which in its turn is due to material causing the obstruction and retention of sooty discharge. Nor does intravascular decay lead to fever. Obstruction and retention of bile is followed by jaundice, but not by fever. In consumption a part may wither

---

[60] Pereira, *Novae veraeque medicinae*, col. 7; ibid., col. 59 and cap. XXVI, cols. 376 et seq.; ibid., col. 415; ibid., col. 110 in cap. VII; ibid., col. 410.

[61] Campanella, *De sensu rerum et magia*: "febrem ego judico utilem", I, 13, p. 46. Idem, *Medicinalium juxta propria principia libri septem* (Lyons, 1635).

away without fever. Hence, it is not the humour, but the kind of lesion, that matters. Nor can different humours account for differences in the duration of fevers, but one humour may be more apt to incite the organism to warfare than another.[62]

The driving force that produces fever and uses it as an instrument of war against disease is the spirit. This is evident from the existence of fever having a purely spiritual cause, such as sadness, fear or, in particular, wrath. Of these, wrath not only causes fever but is essentially a fever in itself. It shares with fever in general the purpose of driving away evil. Hence, its seat, like that of any fever, is in the regulating centre of the organism – *in potestativo*. Here it effects a commotion, using heating and rarefaction of matter as its instruments. *Ira est ipsa febris* just as *febris ipsa est ira*, the only difference being that fever is not outwardly recognisable as wrath, the latter remaining "occult" and "recondite in turbid spirit". Fever develops when the spirit is kindled into wrath by a spectrum of causes ranging from pure emotions (like sadness), annoyance by hot air, hard work, pain, vigil, hunger, and fear via digestive trouble, to tumours. Fever kindled expresses wrath – *accenditur febriliter, quod est irasci*. But simple heating and agitation of the spirit, for example through exposure to the sun or in the hard labour of the blacksmith, is not in itself fever, for what is missing is the hostile cause, the *res odiosa*, which calls for expulsion. External heating of the body (as, for example, by the sun) is therefore not fever, which is, as Hippocrates had known, an internal mechanism.[63]

Not all lesions, then, are productive of fever, but only those that provoke and irritate the spirit. Any lesion, however, is accessible to cure by fever. For fever dissipates such common morbid causes as wind and condensed vapours and also opens up obstructed pathways. Nor is fever primarily brought about by a single governing organ such as the heart, as commonly believed. Any part or particle of the body can agitate the spirit and cause fever, and so can mental activity, including even hard thinking. A part affected with illness may maintain the fever or else come to an armistice with it. A limited influence of the stars should be recognised: to

---

[62] Campanella, *Medicinalium*, lib. VII, cap. 1, art. 2, pp. 598–9; ibid., VII, 2, p. 603; ibid., III, 4, 7, pars. 5–6, p. 98 (misnumb. 80); ibid., VII, 2, 2, par. 1, p. 614; ibid., VII, 2, 1, par. 18, p. 608; ibid., VII, 2, 4, pp. 620–1.

[63] *Medicinalium*, VII, 2, 4, pars. 1–2, pp. 623–4; ibid., VII, 1, 2, pars. 6–8, pp. 599–600.

the extent, that is, of the movement of fluid in the body as a factor in fever and their influence upon such movement. Moreover, an irregular transit of stars, or any conditions that do not normally cause disease, can produce erratic fevers. If any further proof were needed that fever is not a disease, the beneficial effect of crises would provide it. They reveal the energy and confidence that go with the organism into battle and precipitate a confrontation, by contrast with weak and flaccid spirits, which endeavour to postpone it. When several battles have to be fought the intervals will be the shorter, and victory the sooner the stronger the spirits.[64]

The point on which Van Helmont agrees with Campanella is obvious: fever is not a disease, but a symptom that indicates the war waged by nature against disease. What is even more congenial to Van Helmont is the association of fever with wrath, which he developed further, particularly with regard to rigor. This involved the same wrath and ravings of the vital principle which he made responsible for the dramatic clonic and tonic muscular contractions in hysteria and epilepsy. Such arguments are consistent with the thesis common to both savants, that there is not only *sensus*, but also emotion, passion, and even a low-grade knowledge invested in parts of the body, in limbs, and indeed in all tissues.

Compared with these close contacts and parallels, the differences between the two accounts are not so impressive. Though he denied the key role of putrefying humours in fever, humours are still essential to Campanella's *medicinalia*, and have to play a certain albeit subordinate part in feverish conditions. Van Helmont would have none of this. Nor could he have agreed to even the limited influence which Campanella attributed to the stars in fever. Nevertheless, Campanella's *Febris non morbus sed bellum contra morbum* and *Febris ipsa est ira* so distinctly evoke Helmontian principles that they may well be considered as immediate sources of inspiration for the latter. The same may be said of Campanella's monumental pronouncement: not humour and its nature, but the nature of the lesion is responsible for fever – *non pro natura humoris, sed laesionis oritur febris.*

---

[64] Ibid., VII, 1, 2, par. 10, p. 600; VII, 2, 1, par. 5, p. 602; VII, 2, 1, par. 11, p. 606; IV, 1, 1, pars. 4–9, pp. 114–15; VII, 2, 2, pars. 1–4, pp. 614–16; VII, 2, 4, par. 6, p. 622.

"THE MADNESS OF CATARRH"

Catarrh was the key word of traditional medicine for more than two millennia. Its usage implied the application of a sequence of events such as the common cold and coryza to the majority of diseases, if not to all of them. One of the cardinal humours, namely mucus, was assumed to be displaced from its site of origin, thereby acquiring corrosive properties and throwing the humoral balance, which was essential for health, into disarray. The term catarrh implied the downward flux of mucus from the head into lower regions, principally the lungs and joints, with attending obstruction of the pathways of humours, air, and spirits followed by dyspnoea (asthma), haemorrhage, consumption, arthritis, and abnormal growth. It remained to Van Helmont to unmask the ancient doctrine still paramount in his own days and for some time afterwards, as "madness".

Catarrh-fluid and its actions occur in the Hippocratic corpus. Its seven morbid destinations included the chest, with resulting empyema and consumption.[65] Air meeting excess catarrh-fluid was supposed to erode vascular walls with ensuing exudation and conversion of the fluid into pus. Cough, "rawness", and even dropsy were caused in this way, and eyes, ears, nose, and chest are mainly affected.[66] The acid and eroding quality of mucus (phlegm) served to counterbalance a one-sided overrating of humoral qualities such as hot–cold, dry–moist, traditionally regarded as morbific.[67] It is also in Hippocratic treatises that we are informed about the site of origin of catarrh-fluid. "The head is the source and metropolis for the phlegm and the cold and the sticky."[68] Indeed, the fluxes – all seven of them – are "from the head".[69] It is in Aristotle, however, that we find the theory of catarrh lucidly set out in physico-chemical, humoralistic, and physiological terms. This may well have pro-

---

[65] Hippocrates, *De glandulis*, XI, ed. Kühn, i, 497–8; trans. R. Fuchs, *Hippokrates Sämtliche Werke*, 3 vols. (Munich, 1895–1900), i, 171. *De carnibus*, XVI, ed. Kühn, i, 438; trans. Fuchs, i, 162. *De locis in homine*, I, ed. Kühn, ii, 101; trans. Fuchs, ii, 567. Ibid., I, cap. 10, ed. Kühn, ii, 114; trans. Fuchs, ii, 574.

[66] *De flatibus*, X, ed. Kühn, i, 579; trans. Fuchs, i, 447.

[67] *Ancient Medicine (Prisca medicina)*, XV, ed. Kühn, i, 39; ed. Jones, i, 40; trans. Fuchs, i, 31. Ibid., XVII, ed. Kühn, i, 41; ed. Jones, i, 44; trans. Fuchs, i, 32 and ibid., XIX, ed. Kühn, i, 48; ed. Jones, i, 48–52; trans. Fuchs, i, 34.

[68] *De carnibus*, IV, ed. Kühn, i, 427; trans. Fuchs, i, 155.

[69] *De glandulis*, XI, ed. Kühn, i, 497–8; trans. Fuchs, i, 171.

vided the doctrinal pattern for the medical considerations of Hippocratic writers, although much older, pre-Socratic ideas on the hegemony of head and brain may have been instrumental. The central point of the Aristotelian theory is the pre-eminently cold quality of the brain.[70] This organ is normally exposed to steaming evaporations from the food heated in the digesting stomach. If the brain or the adjacent parts have more than a due proportion of coldness, the surplus of vaporised nutriment is cooled and condensed. Flux of phlegm and serum is bound to follow. The process is comparable to the production of rain.[71] The advanced nature of Aristotle's theory is revealed by a comparison with Plato, but the latter's comments at least show the presence of catarrh in the medical syllabus before Aristotle. Indeed, the harmful effect of phlegmatic catarrh was presented by Galen as one of the "opinions shared by Hippocrates and Plato".[72]

The theory of catarrh owed its final shape to the work of Galen. He provided its convincing anatomical basis, enriched its symptomatology, and rationalised much of the Hippocratic and Aristotelian tradition. He accepted its essential framework, though not uncritically. Thus, he inveighs against Aristotle's thesis that the cold brain cools down the hot heart. The latter should rather receive cooling through air from the lung, its immediate neighbour, than from an organ as far distant as the brain.[73] To Galen catarrh was connected with the activity of the brain in forming animal spirit. The by-product of this process was mucoid excrement. This had to be discharged through channels which become evident on a vertical-median section through the brain of, for example, a small domestic animal.[74]

Two kinds of waste were distinguished: the vaporous or smoky, and the watery or muddy. The former was said to evaporate through fine porous openings of the skull-bone including sutures

[70] Aristotle, *De partibus animalium*, II, 7, 652b.
[71] Ibid. Sleep is explained in similar terms: *On sleep and wakefulness, Parva naturalia*, III, 458a, trans. J. I. Beare (Oxford, 1908).
[72] Galen, *De placitis Hippocratis et Platonis*, VIII, 5, ed. Kühn, v, 679–81 (also vol. xviiia, p. 261); Plato, *Timaeus*, 85b. In an epistemological context: *Kratylus*, 440. But compare *Republic*, III, 405, *Opera*, ed. G. Stallbaum (Leipzig, 1850), pp. 315–16, where "catarrh" is pilloried as a stupid and unwise innovation.
[73] Galen, *De usu partium*, VIII, 2, ed. Kühn, iii, 617. May, trans., *On the Usefulness of the Parts of the Body*, i, 388.
[74] See the reproduction of a median section through the brain of a cat after Wilder and Gegenbauer in Pagel, *Van Helmont*, p. 54.

and invisible pores of the covering skin; the latter, the watery, was supposed to be taken down through two conspicuous channels and finally to reach the hard palate, nose, ear, and eye.[75] These two channels fall respectively into an anterior one that goes straight from the bottom of the third ventricle of the brain downwards, and a posterior channel which takes an oblique declining course branching from the aqueduct behind the middle commissure of the ventricle. There the posterior joins the anterior channel whereby a circular basin – a pelvis (*ptyelon*) or *infundibulum* (*choana*) – is formed.[76] This lies on top of the saddle (*sella turcica*) of the sphenoid bone. It was supposed to be perforated, by analogy with the cribriform plate of the ethmoid bone high up in the nose.

Normally but little fluid should be discharged from the brain, lest we should be continually inconvenienced by cough, catarrh, and sputum.[77] Conditions for a surplus to be produced and drained away occur, however, when the stomach is overheated and productive of much vapour; or else the heat of the stomach may contrast with an abnormally cold head. Then, and in the naturally "phlegmatic", catarrh may develop with all its dangerous consequences. Among these, pulmonary consumption – phthisis – is prominent, for it is caused by an ulcer of the lung and the salty and acid flux of catarrh is eminently eligible to set up this condition.[78] The sequence of events would thus be: surplus condensation of vapour and production of acid and corrosive waste that flows down from the brain through the base of the skull in the form of mucinous catarrh; then the setting up of a node (*tuberculum, phyma*) in the lung with subsequent haemorrhage, ulceration, and cavitation (*koilie, vomica*), the immediate source and anatomical basis of consumption.[79]

---

[75] Galen, *De usu partium*, IX, 1, ed. Kühn, iii, 686; May, trans., *Usefulness of Parts*, p. 425. For the Aristotelian exemplar: *Meteorologica*, III, 6, 378a20, ed. and trans. H.D.P. Lee (London, 1952), p. 286.

[76] Galen, *De usu partium*, IX, 3, ed. Kühn, iii, 694; May, trans., *Usefulness of Parts*, p. 429.

[77] This is the argument used by Andreas Laurentius (d. 1609) in vindicating Galen against Argenterius who denied the local origin of cerebral fluid: *Historia anatomica*, X, 12 (Frankfurt, 1602), pp. 906–7.

[78] Galen, *Hippocratis Epidemiorum III et Galeni in illum commentarius*, III, 13, ed. Kühn, xviia, 663. *De locis affectis*, IV, 11, ed. Kühn, viii, 289. W. Pagel, "Humoral Pathology: A Lingering Anachronism in the History of Tuberculosis", *Bull. Hist. Med.*, 29 (1955), 299–308.

[79] Hippocrates, *De morbis*, I, 11, ed. Kühn, ii, 189. Pagel, "Krankheitslehre der Phthise", pp. 66–98 and idem, "Geschichte der Lungensteine", pp. 315–23.

Of the symptoms that indicated lung damage by catarrh Galen emphasised shortage of breath.[80] This he attributed largely to obstruction of the tracheo-bronchial channels. It was confirmed by the discharge of inspissated catarrh-fluid in the form of hail-like pellets with the sputum. Besides their obstructing effect, the corrosive properties of catarrh were given their due in the origin of phthisis. They found expression in the erosion of vascular walls with subsequent pulmonary haemorrhage and haemoptysis. These events were followed by melting of the whole area whereby that ulcer (*helkos*) was set up in the lung which to Galen provided the uniform cause of pulmonary consumption. The bringing-up not only of blood, but also of small fragments of lung tissue with or without blood, provided evidence for the ulcer. The emphasis on ulceration strengthened the view of pulmonary haemorrhage as causing, rather than being caused by, cavitation; a view which was perpetuated until Laennec (1781–1826) disproved it finally in the early nineteenth century.[81]

The obstruction of bronchi by inspissated and calcifying catarrh-fluid as a concomitant of phthisis was stressed by such luminaries of the renaissance as Fernel, Girolamo Fracastoro (1483–1553), and Cardano.[82] However, no turning away from the humoralist catarrh is evident before Paracelsus and Van Helmont. With these writers an interpretation of disease in definite localist terms emerges. Thus, the soft-caseous and hard-stony deposits that were already known to cause phthisis by bronchial obstruction could be understood as local metabolic changes. As such they were primary in character from the beginning, as against those secondary – metastatic – lesions which had been supposed to be due to the displacement of a humour.[83]

[80] Galen, *De locis affectis*, IV, 11, ed. Kühn, viii, 284. Trans. R. E. Siegel, *Galen on the Affected Parts* (Basel, 1976), p. 131. See also Galen, *De difficultate respirationis*, I, 11, ed. Kühn, vii, 781 and Galen, *Hippocr. Epidem.*, I, 18, ed. Kühn, xviia, 61.

[81] Galen, *De locis affectis*, IV, 11, ed. Kühn, viii, 284, 292, 289; trans. Siegel, pp. 131, 134, 133. Galen, ibid., IV, 8, ed. Kühn, viii, 262; Galen, ibid., IV, 6–7, ed. Kühn, viii, 47–52; trans. Siegel, pp. 116 et seq. However, Galen's account may also admit of interpretation in the modern terms of cavity first, haemorrhage second: *Introductio sive medicus*, XIII, ed. Kühn, xiv, 742. Pagel, "Humoral Pathology", pp. 299–308.

[82] Jean Fernel, *De partium morbis*, lib. V, caps. 4 and 10, in *Univ. med.*, pt. II, 82, 105; Girolamo Fracastoro, *De morbis contagiosis* (1546), II, 9, in *Opera Omnia* (Venice, 1555), fol. 122r. and v.; Girolamo Cardano, *Opera* (Lyons, 1663), ix, 89, 107, 81, consil. XVII, XX, XIV.

[83] Pagel, "Geschichte der Lungensteine", pp. 315–23; idem, *Paracelsus*, pp. 170–2.

Lung disease, that is phthisis and asthma in particular, was not the only ailment attributed to catarrh. That the latter was made to serve as the basis of most if not all diseases is evident in Fernel's system, in which differences between individual diseases depend upon the different sites that are reached by the flux "from above". In this way the same fluid in its descent accounts for such various complaints as apoplexy, paralysis, stupor, amaurosis, deafness, ringing in the ears, anosmia, coryza, indigestion, diarrhoea, abdominal venous clotting, and arthritis in all its forms. *Destillatio quam plurimorum est morborum procreatrix* – condensation and flux, catarrh, is indeed the cause of most diseases and "man more than any animal is liable to it because of the size and exalted site of his brain. From there, excremental discharge can easily drop into almost all parts of the body; it can pervade and as it were irrigate them".[84]

Van Helmont made a broad frontal attack on the concept of catarrh. He marshalled a phalanx of unanswerable objections underpinned by closely knit arguments – anatomical, physiological, chemical, and philosophical. Some of these are quite erroneous and misleading by present-day standards, but could not have failed to impress his contemporaries and followers as much as those which have been proved correct. Among the latter his clear formulation of the localist or morbid-anatomical principle in pathology is outstanding. Emphasis is laid on individual seats and causes of a multitude of diseases. Each of these diseases is primary in itself and specifically bound up with one of the many organs that can be its bearer. This, Van Helmont states, should replace the ancient view, which did not recognise a variety of diseases distinguishable from the outset by differences in their seats and causes. Instead, individual organic changes had been regarded as part of a single universal disease, namely catarrh. Each of these was therefore deemed to be metastatic, that is, not primary, and non-specific. According to this view only one organ was primarily affected and had then to act as the source of all changes in distant organs. This was the "head" or brain.

Van Helmont's statement of localist principle is given at the beginning of his treatise on "the madness of catarrh" and is conspicuously repeated at its end. He says: "not from one single source,

[84] Fernel, *Univ. Med.*, pt. II, 83.

the human head (from which the imagination of the scholastics makes catarrh rain down) do diseases spring, but from an idiopathy proper to each individual part, that is to say an indisposition inflicted upon it by specific local forces".[85] He concludes on the same localist note. Here he singles out the two central events in two of the diseases that had been prominently and tenaciously attributed to catarrh, namely phthisis and arthritis. Of the former Van Helmont asserts:

I deny that the cavity is catarrh or that death is due to the latter. Even more sharply I reject that the cavity is from vapour ascending from the stomach. Thus I do not call consumption a flux down into the lung – I know however that it springs from an error that is internal to the lung. I agree that podagra can present with the sensation of an intensely hot drop flowing down, but I do not admit that it is the product of catarrh by matter, essence, means and end.[86]

What, then, remains of the anatomical data on which the ancient idea of catarrh was based? First of all, vapour from the stomach would have to pass via the oesophagus. This, however, is normally closed and like the bladder devoid of contents. It does not contain air for, if it did, air should be pressed down into the stomach by each bite of food, to be followed by persistent eructation. Vapour could not escape from the stomach without a similar noise, nor forcefully open the oesophagus without first being condensed to drops of water. Hence, it could only be air, "wild spirit", or *gas* that was responsible for eructation. It follows that no vapour can be carried from the stomach to the head. If it were, a healthy (warm) stomach should produce more catarrh than a diseased (cold) stomach. All healthy men should of necessity be afflicted by catarrh and like a grunting hog ceaselessly belch.[87]

Before being able to reach the brain the vapour should have been breathed out by mouth or nose and the breath have a flavour of the food. There is no empty space either in the throat or at the base of the brain into which the vapour could penetrate and which could act as a distilling helmet, since the canals at the base of the brain, on the scholastics' own showing, are permanently full of mucoid discharge. Above all the latter in itself ought to be more

---

[85] Van Helmont, *Catarrhi deliramenta*, 3, *Opp.* p. 412.
[86] Ibid., 61, *Opp.* p. 429.
[87] Ibid., 19, *Opp.* p. 415; ibid., 20, *Opp.* p. 415.

harmful than a few droplets of fluid distilled at a time from ascend-ing vapour. No salty, acid, or sharp catarrh-fluid is obtainable by distilling mucus or saliva, only a thin insipid fluid. Were the brain really colder than other parts, what force would there be to drive the vapour to it? Perhaps a wise choice made by the vapour itself? Moreover, what gives the vapour the impetus to penetrate through the sutures of the skull-bone and lift up the skin closely adherent to it, and how could it flow down between bone and skin into the face?[88] Would not the skin, being more porous than the bone, immediately reconvert any fluid reaching it to vapour, and then discharge it by perspiration? Moreover, what is the driving force by means of which the skin is lifted from the ribs in order to give access to catarrh-fluid and thereby to cause pleurisy? How could such fluid reach the teeth via their nervous pulp in view of the lack of any space between the exit of the nerves and the skull-bone?

But what about the fluid of exudate and oedema? This is blood serum (*latex*). It is a fluid in its own right. It serves to dilute and, not unlike sweat, to dissolve salts. It reduces acid in the blood. Like a detergent, it washes-off residues of nutriment attracted by the organs from the blood. It is called upon to assist in this very capacity the "watchman" (*custos*) in the "kitchen" – the nutritive centre – of the organ in disease. Though deriving from the blood, its distribution and appearance is conditioned by factors that are specific to, and operative in, a certain locus. It is secreted by the lung as it were by a gland, and discharged with the breath.[89]

All this leaves no place for catarrh. Fluid does not "rain down" from a remote source, but is drawn locally out of the blood supply to an area in which error of the parochial watchman initiates dis-ease. Nor could any examination of sputum be justified as a pro-cedure in diagnosis of a lung disease if it were not produced by the lung, but was merely catarrh-fluid that came to it from outside. Even allowing to the watchman of the brain a role in the produc-tion and quality of mucus collecting in the ethmoid region in coryza, not a single drop of this could reach the lung without provoking suffocation. Were the sputum due to catarrh, its re-moval would be favoured by placing the patient in a horizontal or

---

[88] Ibid., 20–3, *Opp.* pp. 416–17.
[89] Ibid., 25–6, *Opp.* pp. 417–18. *Latex humor neglectus*, passim, *Opp.* pp. 358–65. *Custos errans, Opp.* pp. 245–53: this treatise epitomises the *Catarrhi deliramenta* in a general physiopathological context.

reclining position; but it is just such situations which increase rather than relieve his difficulties and make him try to sit up.[90] As the irritated eye sheds tears, the lung when irritated, damaged, pierced by cold sharp air or a harmful *gas*, betrays its displeasure by reacting locally. Why, then, should the schools define coryza as a disease in its own right but refuse the diseases of the lung this very privilege? There is no place for a therapy that "dries-out". Drinks of China and Zarza or infusion of Guayak, as employed by the schools, cannot achieve what is required, which is the total removal of material produced locally in an organ. Starvation or sweating cannot dry-out anything, nor, most importantly, can such treatment pacify the "fury" of the "workmaster". This is the vital and nutritive centre of the organ, its resident archeus. For it is he who transmutes blood into phthisical sputum when irritated. The origin of the sputum is an ulcer of the lung; only the strong chemical remedies of Paracelsus which heal cancer and gangrene can influence it.[91]

What, then, is the alternative which Van Helmont proposes in place of catarrh? His solution presupposes a function of the lung that stood in patent opposition to traditional Galenic physiology. Van Helmont regards the pleural surface of the lung as porous, and hence as permeable to air. Before reaching the thoracic and abdominal cavities the air had to be purified in the lung. The result of the local formation and retention of mucus would be obstruction of the pleural pores and thus of the free circulation of air. Dyspnoea, cavitation, erosion of vessels, haemoptysis, ulceration, phthisis, and death would follow. It is this closure of pores that explains why curing lung disease is so difficult, rather than the constant movement of the lungs traditionally regarded as the cause.

Van Helmont manages to collect no less than twenty-one "cogent reasons", eight "arguments", and seven "conclusions" reject-

---

[90] *Catarrhi deliramenta*, 32–3, *Opp.* p. 419; ibid., 36, *Opp.* p. 420; ibid., 37, *Opp.* pp. 420–1.

[91] Ibid., 38, *Opp.* p. 421; ibid., 40, *Opp.* p. 421; ibid., 42, *Opp.* p. 421. For Van Helmont on Paracelsian chemical medicines see *Potestas medicaminum*, 39, *Opp.* p. 456 and ibid., 44, *Opp.* p. 457. On Paracelsian universal medicines: *Arcana Paracelsi, Opp.* p. 742. See also Knorr von Rosenroth's commentaries in *Aufgang*, on *In verbis, herbis, et lapidibus*, 10–11 and 14 at pp. 1083–6, preceded by his metrical translation of Augurellus at pp. 1079–82; on *Potestas medicaminum*, 1–3, Dutch addition, notes to 39–45, pp. 1137–9; on *Arcana Paracelsi* ("Vom langen Leben"), 24–5, pp. 1253–9.

ing the (correct) Galenic description of respiration as a rhythmic expansion and compression of the lung in obedience to the up-and-down movement of the chest. Moreover, Van Helmont denied not only any movement of the lung but also any role of the diaphragm in respiration. In this he drew confirmation from the porous, permeable, and fixed lung of birds – an argument adopted by contemporaries.[92] The epiglottic watchman saw that no fluid could reach the lung directly. None of the cruel experiments on dogs had disproved this. Even drinking while standing on one's head does not bring any fluid to the windpipe and the lung. Obviously, then, none of the syrups and electuaries usually prescribed can reach the obstructed pores: if they did they would only make matters worse. Extracts from the lungs of such renowned sprinters as foxes or colts, as traditionally prescribed in electuaries, could not help either. Nor could anything be expected from inhaling coriander-infusion, or combing, or massage. No wonder that Rome was healthier in its first five hundred years before Greek medicine was introduced, than thereafter.[93]

Not all changes are necessarily primary. Secondary or meta-static lesions, however, are not caused by catarrh, nor are they due to salty, sour, sharp, mucinous, or bilious humours that flow down. The fluid that can set up secondary lesions is blood serum, when charged with impulses that act like contagia. These are meant to wash-off harmful invaders and are sent to the organ affected by the archeus of either an individual organ or the organism as a whole. The archeus thus infects the serum; its movement is directed towards a single place and aim. Hence, it does not obey mechanical principles such as gravity, let alone those that govern descent of a fluid as applied to catarrh. Mucus can "go down", but only mucus swallowed normally by healthy people and formed by the watchman in the upper parts of the nose. This has nothing to do with catarrh; nor is it really a secondary or morbific event. On the contrary, it proves the localist principle and incidentally shows Van Helmont's awareness of the local production of mucus, by one mucous membrane at least.[94] In conclusion, then, the existence of secondary lesions cannot detract from recognition of the local seats and causes of diseases, an insight gained by the demolition of

---

[92] *Catarrhi deliramenta*, 45 (C), *Opp.* p.422.
[93] Ibid., 55, *Opp.* p. 427; ibid., 51, *Opp.* p. 425.
[94] Ibid., 59–60, *Opp.* pp. 428–9; ibid., 23–5, *Opp.* pp. 417–18 and 32–3, p. 419.

the concept of the madness of catarrh and closely connected with the reform of disease concepts as a whole.

ASTHMA AND PLEURISY

Any breathing difficulty, especially if experienced in a horizontal position, was called asthma (*anhelitus, orthopnoea*) by classical authors.[95] Cold and moist air and thick humours collecting in the tracheo-bronchial tree were held responsible. Women appeared to be more susceptible to it than men because of their cold and moist humoral complexion. Building workers, miners, and blacksmiths were known to suffer from it. Associated symptoms were heaviness in the chest, inability to climb, loss of voice, hoarseness, and red cheeks contrasting with general pallor. *Pnix* or *catochos* indicated a sudden attack of asthma with loss of voice. Uterine asthma, the *pnix hysterike*, was distinguished as a special category. Following a Platonic tradition it was attributed to an independent, upward movement of the uterus with subsequent oppression of the liver and epigastric region. Moving like a being in its own right, the uterus was able to cause strangulation and suffocation. It was supposed to deal a sudden blow, not unlike an epileptic fit, to liver, diaphragm, lungs, and heart.[96]

In his detailed discussion Galen saw asthma as the result of bronchial obstruction either by thick mucus inside, or by the pressure of crude nodes (*tubercles, phymata*) from outside the bronchial tubes. He also regarded uterine suffocation as indicating a specific

---

[95] Hippocrates, *Aphorisms*, VI, 46, trans. Jones, p. 189; ibid., III, 22, trans. Jones, p. 130. Aretaeus, *On the Causes and Symptoms of Chronic Diseases*, I, II, *peri asthmatos*, ed. and trans. F. Adams, Sydenham Society (London, 1856), p. 73 and trans. p. 316.

[96] Plato, *Timaeus*, 91C; trans. in Cornford, *Plato's Cosmology. The Timaeus*, p. 357. Aretaeus, *On the Causes and Symptoms of Acute Diseases*, II, 11, *peri hysterikes pnigos*, ed. Adams, p. 44, trans. "On Hysterical Suffocation", p. 285. For the Hippocratic exemplar: *De morbis mulierum*, II, 14 and 16; trans. Fuchs, *Hippokrates, Sämtliche Werke*, ii, 519. On the epileptoid symptoms: *De morbis mulierum*, ed. Kühn, ii, 825 – explained by Heinrich Fasbender, "Suffokationserscheinungen durch Beeinträchtigung der Abdominalrespiration bei Wanderung der Gebärmutter", *Entwickelungslehre, Geburtshülfe und Gynäkologie in den Hippokratischen Schriften* (Stuttgart, 1897), pp. 246–8. On therapy see: *De natura muliebri*, cap. 32, trans. Fuchs, iii, 351 and passim. Aulus Cornelius Celsus (*c.* A.D.30, encyclopaedist), *De re medica* (Paris, 1529), IV, 20, fol. 53r. and v.; trans. in E. Scheller, *Celsus über die Arzneiwissenschaft*, ed. W. Frieboes and R. Kobert, 2nd edn. (Braunschweig, 1906), IV, 27, p. 203.

relationship between lung and womb.[97] This concept showed its perennial appeal in the speculations of Sennert on asthma as caused by thick vapour and smoke which he believed to emanate from the uterus. In the same discussion asthma in miners and metalworkers is ascribed to an abnormal dryness of the lung caused by thick metallic vapour.[98]

Asthma, then, had been well known since antiquity. "Uterine" or hysterical asthma in particular had engaged the attention and curiosity of physicians. The alleged tendency of the uterus to behave erratically and independently, like an animal within an animal, was taken up again by Paracelsus. He viewed the uterus as a "cosmos within a cosmos". All properties of the greater world and the lesser world come together in the womb. The womb carries the lesser world.[99] It is as traditionally described, *matrix* – an arable field comparable to the earth.[100] Contemporary woodcuts show a cosmos-woman with the uterus as bearer of the earth.[101] Hysterical asthma for Paracelsus was also an outstanding example of the special afflictions suffered by women in addition to all those experienced by men.[102] Here again, asthma is seen as a form of epilepsy, which may well have prompted Van Helmont's identification of asthma with epilepsy of the lung.

Subsumed under the "funeral dirge" of catarrh, the true nature of asthma had remained unknown, and as a result it was hardly ever cured. Van Helmont therefore felt called upon to devote a special treatise to it. Much of this is based on what he had to say on the madness of catarrh. Strangely enough, in the *Ortus* of 1648, the *Opera* of 1682, and Chandler's translation of 1662, as well as all later editions of these three works, the treatises on asthma and on pleurisy precede, and are separated from "The madness of catarrh"

[97] Galen, *De difficultate respirationis*, I, 11, ed. Kühn, vii, 781; idem, *In Hippocratis praedictionum*, 74, ed. Kühn, xvi, 662; idem, *In Hippocratis Aphorismos*, 22, ed. Kühn, xviib, 623. Idem, *De locis affectis*, VI, 5, ed. Kühn, viii, 425; trans. Siegel, p. 187, with ref. to Plato, *Timaeus*.

[98] Daniel Sennert, *Institutionum medicinae*, II, 3, 2, cap. 2, in *Opera*, ii, 408; idem, *Practicae medicinae*, II, 2, cap. 2, in *Opera*, iii, 335–6.

[99] Paracelsus, *Astronomia Magna*, I, 2, ed. Sudhoff, xii, 49; *De caduco matris*, par. V, ed. Sudhoff, viii, 346; ibid., par. II, ed. Sudhoff, viii, 327.

[100] *Opus Paramirum*, IV: de matrice, ed. Sudhoff, ix, 183.

[101] Title page to Albertus Magnus, *Philosophia pauperum* (Brescia, 1493), as reproduced in Pagel, *Paracelsus*, p. 239. See also Jung, *Psychologie und Alchemie*, p. 438.

[102] Paracelsus, *De caduco matris*, par. VI, ed. Sudhoff, viii, 356. *Opus Paramirum*, IV, ed. Sudhoff, ix, 184.

by a number of unrelated pieces; it is only in the *Aufgang* of 1683 that the treatise on asthma immediately follows that on catarrh, on which it perceptibly depends. Thus, the former treatise reiterates the localist view of disease: what is ejected by cough is locally formed in the lung-tubes, by fault of the organ proper. The lung itself is the authority that gives and executes the order, that acts and receives. It is also repeated in the treatise on asthma that the lung is porous; the pores which allow the air to penetrate into the chest become invisible after death.[103]

According to Van Helmont, catarrh, cough, and asthma had hitherto been confused. In spite of this failure, asthma itself, and two large groups of asthma-cases are eminently recognisable. One of the latter concerns the female sex alone, the other both sexes. Just as, in the case of catarrh, vapour ascending from the stomach had been incriminated, so asthma in women was attributed to harmful exhalations of the uterus. These were supposed to reach the lungs and to be amenable to enema, venesection, and cauterization. However, the uterus does not exercise its power of dominion over the whole organism through such material means as vapours and exhalations. It is rather through its passions, its wrath, sadness, or terror that it is able to shut down the pores of the lung, as if by a mere "nod". Just as the moon dominates the sea simply by looking upon it, so the uterus forges the female characteristics, the form of intellect, chin, muscle, hair, or blood that distinguish the female from the male.[104] The uterus lives its own life; psychic trouble may induce it to fury. This may be directed toward viscera as well as bones; it may throw into utter confusion heart and head, sense and intellect. Tendons curved and contracted as if by torture, strange cramps of the muscles, serious dislocations of bone, apoplectic and epileptic fits, paralyses, jaundice, dropsy, stomachache and headache – all these "disease-tyrants" Van Helmont had observed to spring from the uterus. They were not recognised by the schools, who merely ascribed asthma to this cause, as if it were the throat alone that obeys the uterus. How much, then, Van Helmont remarked, do women deserve our sympathy at having to suffer a double set of diseases, those that they have in common

---

[103] Van Helmont, *Asthma et tussis*, 2, *Opp.* p. 343. Invisibility after death had been claimed for the pores of the interventricular septum of the heart since Galen. Van Helmont still believed in their existence: *Blas humanum*, 21, *Opp.* p. 174.

[104] Van Helmont, *Catarrhi deliramenta*, 9–15, *Opp.* pp. 344–5.

with man and those that are reserved for them alone: a double punishment for sin, though a blessing, too, because of their patience in suffering which brings them closer to the Son of God. [105]

The asthma that is common to both sexes falls into two categories according to its product, namely, dry and moist. The latter is continuous in its manifestations, the former sudden. The picture becomes clear when a series of characteristic cases is considered. With these case-reports, Van Helmont created a clinico-pathological masterpiece in which for the first time asthma was presented as due to specific hypersensitivity of some kind. There are six such reports. [106] In these not only the type of hypersensitivity is specifically and sharply defined; the dramatic symptoms are detailed more incisively than ever before.

In case (1), there is first of all trauma, which after an interval is followed by asthma attacks in a strong middle-aged man who liked his drink. During the night preceding the attack he is sleepless and disturbed with a dry mouth, much diuresis, and especially by three motions of the bowels. In the morning breath is suddenly cut off; he lifts his shoulders like wings, seeking support with both hands to do so more effectively, his face glowing, his eyes protruding. This lasts a few days and nights. When it is over he is perfectly normal, walks, climbs, hunts, rides on horseback, travels. He has completely forgotten what happened.

In case (2), a young nobleman, a good hunter and proficient sprinter, is suddenly attacked after changing his place of sojourn, and suffers every third day from fear of suffocation and the sweating of the dying. Soon restored, he returns to his home where for two years he does not dare to lie down, but spends his nights sitting next to the hearth. For as soon as he lies down his latent asthma becomes manifest. It troubles him more or less in accordance with weather and the seasons. Certain phases of the moon make it worse and so do thunderstorms, which he was able to predict on the basis of his own sensations. It is worse in summer than in winter, and in mountainous regions than in the flat country. A few hours before the attack he has salty saliva, contracting gums, much audible peristalsis, three to four thin motions, and much diuresis, passing watery urine in large quantities. Then,

[105] *Asthma et tussis*, 9–10, *Opp.* p. 344. Women as subject to a double set of diseases is an aspect of Paracelsian medical thought.

[106] *Asthma et tussis*, 21–6, *Opp.* pp. 345–7.

finally, asthma grips him as if a rope is strangling him and threatens death by suffocation. After bringing up foamy sputum four or five times, he is liberated as if the rope had been removed.

In case (3), an elderly canon is asthmatic for most of the time in summer, but free in winter. As soon as he is attacked his whole body itches and becomes scaly as if he were a leper. His mother and one sister used to suffer from the same disorder, the former having been killed by it, the latter losing it spontaneously after the birth of a second child.

In case (4), a Franciscan lay-brother had to help with demolition work in a building. Ever since, any scattering of dust lays him immediately prostrate, as if suffocated. Though conscious, he lies there like a corpse devoid of breath. He can sleep only in a sitting posture. Eating fish fried in oil as ordained and to his taste causes him immediate collapse with suffocation. He believes he is able to predict an attack even when it is not one provoked by dust or food.

In case (5), a wise, prudent, and "hearty" citizen, "being by a Peer or great man openly *disgraced and injured* unto whom he might not answer a word without the fear of his utmost ruine, in silence *dissembled* and bears the reproach: but straightway after an Asthma ariseth, the which did daily more increase on him (otherwise in good health) for two whole years space. At length a little before his end a moderate Dropsie killed him in few dayes."

In case (6), a sexagenarian remembers having been particularly breathless when running in young adulthood. At the age of fifty he is observed to suffer from real asthma, increasing until in his sixtieth year, when climbing even a low gradient, he is immediately breathless, saliva starts flowing, the heart palpitates, the pulse loses its rhythm, the tongue dries up, foam collects around the teeth, his knees weaken. And yet he has no difficulty in walking in the open, or sitting, standing, or walking about the house. A rich meal in the evening will render him breathless during the night, when his chest contracts and his throat gives out a constant rattling and gurgling noise. Sitting up he is free again after spitting some mucus. After a moderate meal, there is "repose in the stomach and peace in the lung". The patient locates his asthma in the region between the cardia of the stomach and the umbilicus.

Where, then, is the "nest" of dry asthma? It is, for Van Helmont, the vital principle of an individual organ where a specific disease-

semen has planted its root; in the present case, a semen that closes
the peripheral pores through which air passes from the lung into
the chest cavity. It is a semen with the property of causing contraction of members and parts. This is evident from the phenomena
associated with asthma, notably diuresis, diarrhoea, gurgling of
the gut, palpitation, and contraction around the gums. The lung
contracts, not unlike the scrotum in the pangs of defaecation (*te-
nesmus*). It is an "epilepsy of the lung" in that it is latent for long
periods, only to provoke on special occasions attacks of contraction that chiefly concern one organ: in this case the lungs, in real
epilepsy the nervous system. Basically, however, neither of these
is a localised ailment, but one conditioned by the influent archeus,
the vital principle of the organism as a whole. This is shown by
the associated symptoms outside the lungs. But the anatomical
changes must be looked for in the lung, where the poison attacks
directly, and where they are produced as at a specific seat. To that
extent asthma (as indeed every other disease) is a local and localised
affair. Its poison irritates in the same way as cantharides do, and is
essentially identical with the poison of epilepsy, but not strong
enough to produce the latter. Isolated uterine (hysterical) contraction of the throat was observed by Van Helmont in a countess
who for three months could not swallow anything. Starved and
emaciated, she was subject to continuous falling-sickness with
intractable constipation.[107]

The significance of the local anatomical changes is evident from
two sets of evidence: first the post-mortem findings in the case of a
priest, well-to-do and of impeccable life, who had symptoms of
sudden loss of voice, hoarseness, and breathlessness of a year's
standing. The left lower lobe of his lung was hard as pumice-stone
and appeared inside as if swollen and thickened by an obstructing
mass. "Caseous" masses of a consistency between cartilage and
pumice were observed at the bifurcation of the trachea and several
small stones at odd places in the lungs. His asthma had been
continuous rather than occurring in distinct attacks. Hence, it may
be interpreted as a mixed form of dry and moist asthma.[108]

---

[107] *Asthma et tussis*, 29, *Opp.* p. 347; ibid., 30, *Opp.* p. 347; ibid., 31, *Opp.* p. 347.
[108] *Asthma et tussis*, 43, *Opp.* p. 349. The coincidence of "old-*caseous*", calcifying-
gypseous and stony nodes distributed in the lung in asthma was presented by
Fernel as typical. This was obviously not unknown to Van Helmont who employed the significant term caseous (*grumi caseosi*) for the inspissated material that
had caused bronchial obstruction and thereby asthma in his observation. "Case-

Secondly, local effects were obviously important in "occupational" asthma. This is due to a *gas* that enters with the air, and affects by contact bronchi and lung tissue in miners, smelters, separators, coiners, gilders, chemists, and artificers in nitric acid (*chrysulca*), ceruse, red lead, verdigris, and vermilion.[109] All these workers are soon the victims of asthma. In local, anatomical terms it affects the proper metabolic ("digestive") ability of the lung tissue to absorb and assimilate its nutritive material from the blood.[110] Instead, a "wrong" ferment causes the lung to produce excreta that are retained and which thus obstruct the canal-system of the lung. Such excreta are continually forming, render the person breathless, and if not removed by cough, lead to death by suffocation. Exhalations of some mineral dust can even kill immediately, just as a dog was killed when entering a certain grotto in Sicily: it is mercurial exhalation that instantaneously closes the throat by contraction.

In both forms of asthma – the dry[111] as well as the moist variety – it is the local change in the organ that lends the disease its specific characteristics.[112] In the moist form such change is reflected in the production of sputum; in the dry form it lies in the closure of the pleuro-pulmonary pores. At any rate it is the error of the local custodian, the vital centre of the organ, that touches off the chain of events. This is clearly seen in the chemist, the miner, the metalworker, and those affected with a lung ulcer. This ulcer appears as the cavity (*vomica*), the immediate precursor of consumption. Like asthma, ulcer is a local product in which bronchial obstruction caused by inspissated mucoid material is conspicuous.

ous" was thereafter used as the technical term indicating a tuberculous lesion and deriving from its dry appearance resembling, in Virchow's parlance, "reindeer-cheese" (*Renntierkäse*). In other respects Van Helmont's account differed from Fernel's: Fernel, *Consilia medica*, XXV, *Universa medicina*, pt. II, 345 and *Pathologia*, V, 10, *Universa medicina*, pt. II, 106. On the significance of "dryness" in the lung, see also Fracastoro, *De morbis contagiosis* in *Opera*, fol. 122v, lib. II, cap. 9, "de phthisi contagiosa".

[109] Van Helmont, *Asthma et tussis*, 44, *Opp.* p. 349.

[110] *Sextuplex digestio alimenti humani*, *Opp.* pp. 198–214. In terms of Helmontian physiology it is the last of six "digestions" that is concerned with nutritive assimilation by an individual organ.

[111] *Asthma et tussis*, 46, *Opp.* p. 349 and 54, p. 351, with implied ref. to "dry-smoky" and "moist-watery" exhalation in Aristotle, *Meteorologia*, III, 6, 378a, ed. Lee, p. 286.

[112] *Asthma et tussis*, 60, *Opp.* p. 353.

Not infrequently, mixed forms of dry and moist asthma can be observed, and a weak lung is liable to be susceptible to the characteristic air of certain places, that is, to *endemica*, which may imply the presence of potentially harmful agents suspended in the air.[113] None of these affections, however, occurs or persists without action and reaction on the part of the influent archeus at the centre of the organism.

Obviously, then, the traditional practices of treating asthma with "soups", electuaries, blood-letting, sweating, cauterization, or physiotherapy are absurd. Only the strong chemical arcana of Paracelsus, mostly mercurial, can here bring help and cure. In one case, however, it was sufficient to abandon a rich diet that had been prescribed in fear of a supposedly threatening consumption. As asthma is a local product and has nothing to do with flux from the head or any other place, "exsiccating" therapy, as for example with laxatives, is also senseless. An "issue" (*fontanelle*) may sometimes seem to help, but not because it cures catarrh; it rather diminishes the quantity of *latex* or blood. It has no effect whatever on the seat of the disease, the organ that is the destructive villain in the house. It would, indeed, be necessary to bring the electuaries into direct contact with the lung by inhalation, supposing there were any useful ingredient in them. This is surely not the case even when fox-lung (the fox being a fast runner), or colt-foot (*tussilago*) is added. Instead, intake of sulphur-vapour with a drink should be considered. The medicament can thus penetrate the whole body with the blood and remove decay as it does in wine vats.[114]

In ancient and traditional medical theory asthma was seen to develop in two stages: the initial catarrh followed by bronchial obstruction. The material required for obstruction was provided by catarrh-fluid, viscous either from the outset or becoming so through inspissation when retained. Van Helmont's destructive criticism was directed against the initial stage, catarrh, and the essentials on which this view was based: gastric vapours, their

[113] Ibid., 63, *Opp.* p. 354; ibid., 65, *Opp.* p. 354.
[114] Ibid., 69, *Opp.* p. 356 and 71, p. 356; ibid., 74, *Opp.* p. 357; ibid., 77, *Opp.* p. 358.

condensation to acid mucus in the brain, and its flowing down through the base of the skull. Similarly, he inveighed against the analogous vapours and smokes from the uterus which were supposed to account for hysterical asthma.

The position was different with regard to bronchial obstruction and the significance that had been attached to it since ancient times in asthma and consumption. Neither Paracelsus nor Van Helmont had any quarrel with this. However, Fernel still presented bronchial obstruction within the strait-jacket of catarrh. This being the very target of their attack, the former two thereby achieved the emancipation of obstruction from catarrh and with this turned away from ancient humoralism towards the localist orientation of pathology.

The localist view which Paracelsus had to set against the generalising humoralist interpretation hinged around his idea of *tartarus*. Tartar in organs was comparable to the deposit that occurs in wine-vats. It was just as much a local formation as the latter. Tartar of the lung was thus interpreted by Paracelsus in terms of a local metabolic error of the lung's nutritive centre. The canals in the lung, he said, are its stomach, for here the pure is separated from the impure. What is found inappropriate is discarded: such are the excreta that are specifically and chemically produced in the lung by distillation. They must be coughed out. If they are not, they stick as tartar to the bronchial walls in the form of slaty plates or granules. It follows that the lung can no longer perform its normal rising up and coming down whereby it receives the air. Hence, a number of diseases supervene, variously named asthma, cough, phthisis, and hectic fever; and yet they are all simply owing to tartar and therefore are tartar-disease.[115]

The key word, then, is still obstruction. However, in Paracelsus, it is obstruction divested of mucus and vapours. It is obstruction emancipated from catarrh, and consisting of a local metabolic change. It is presented in chemical and anatomical terms as a primary lesion of the lung itself. The lung's nutritive centre, its stomach, has committed an error. Instead of digesting and assimilating its

[115] Paracelsus, *Opus Paramirum*, III, "de morbis ex tartaro", tract. 4, ed. Sudhoff, ix, 149–51.

organ-specific nourishment from the blood, it has produced material that should have been discharged. Retained, this has coagulated, become more and more inspissated, and thus caused asthma. It finally brings about the destructive changes that are responsible for phthisis.

This is essentially Van Helmont's view. He accepted and elaborated the Paracelsian "tartar of the lung", however much he may have modified and spiritualized the idea of tartar in general. Like Paracelsus, he emphasized the local metabolic character of lung obstruction as a primary affection of its nutritive and vital centre. This he associated with a spiritual ("fermental") impetus. It was not simply due to a deposition of crude tartar-material, but in the final issue to an "imperial nod" of the central regulating authority, the influent archeus, of the organism as a whole. In obedience to this the pleuro-pulmonary pores close, and thus touch off the error that brings about obstruction and tartar. This account tallies with Van Helmont's general spiritualist and dynamist leanings in natural philosophy, which are also reflected in his comparison of asthma with epilepsy. However, his reference is to epilepsy of the lungs, indicating the local change in a single organ, rather than to a generalised disease such as epilepsy proper. The specific is related to the general form, but the underlying irritant was only strong enough to cause local obstruction in the lung.

In Van Helmont's presentation the point which strikes the present-day observer lies in the original and broadly based recognition of specific hypersensitivities which touch off the condition of asthma. The six case reports in which this view is developed seem to the modern reader to be of singular value and incisiveness. The influence of heredity, conditioning by weather and season, itching and scaling of skin, intestinal spasm, salivation, diuresis, and prodromal *aurae* were all noticed by Van Helmont in this context. Equally outstanding (and only paralleled by a closely similar and coeval observation of William Harvey) is Van Helmont's insight into the significance of passion and its suppression in causing asthma.[116]

Of course, idiosyncrasies expressing sympathy and antipathy as prevailing in all realms of nature had engaged the close attention of ancient, mediaeval, and especially renaissance writers. They had

---

[116] Harvey's report is almost identical with Van Helmont's: *Exercitationes duae de circulatione sanguinis* (Rotterdam, 1649), pp. 100–1. Pagel, *New Light on Harvey*, pp. 45–6.

been almost codified in books on natural magic such as, notably, Agrippa von Nettesheim's *Occult Philosophy* and Martin del Rio's *Disquisitiones magicae*. This was a tradition taken up by Goclenius, and in the second half of the seventeenth century by Pomarius and others.[117] Van Helmont himself is full of such topical stories, which he seems to have avidly collected, gladly accepted, and integrated with his general ideas in natural philosophy. As against this his observations on specific hypersensitivities as the basis of asthma are original and sound, but Van Helmont's role in the history of the recognition of such factors seems to have been forgotten by historians. Also notable, in the history of occupational diseases, are the comments in his treatise on asthma about the danger from specific poison-gas to which miners, smelters, metal and mintworkers, chemists, gilders, and other artificers are exposed. It is not unlikely that Paracelsus's famous work on *Miners' Disease* influenced him specifically and decisively.[118] In Paracelsus's discussion, "asthma" symptoms – that is, chronic dyspnoea – had formed the focus of clinical observation and toxicological assessment. However, Paracelsus was concerned with mines and miners. Van Helmont advanced beyond this. He connected the occupational aspect with three elements transcending it: his new typology of asthma, the recognition of specific hypersensitivities, and his novel interpretation of bronchial obstruction in dynamic as well as anatomical and chemical terms.

Pleurisy had to have its share in "mucinous madness". What Van Helmont called a welter of inept speculations had been added to the original errors. Such was to incriminate the azygos vein simply because of its topographical proximity to the pleura.[119] It was supposed to cause a phlegmon therein by allowing thin bilious blood to flow towards the pleura and the chest-wall that covers it.[120] Additionally, there was catarrh-fluid that in flowing downwards was to tear-off the pleural membrane as if it had the

---

[117] Goclenius, *Mirabilium naturae liber* (Frankfurt, 1643); Pomarius (Samuel Baumgarten), *Tractatus de consensu et dissensu corporum naturalium*, ed. alt. (Wittenberg, 1669). For a collective account: L. Thorndike, *A History of Magic and Experimental Science*, Vol. VII (New York, 1958), pp. 272–371.

[118] Paracelsus, *Von der Bergsucht und anderen Bergkrankheiten* (Dillingen, 1567); ed. Sudhoff, ix, 463–544 (at p. 522).

[119] Van Helmont, *Pleura furens*, 6, *Opp.* p. 378.

[120] Fernel, *Pathologia*, V, 11, in *Universa medicina*, pt. II, 112–12; Sennert, *Practicae medicinae in Opera*, iii, 311.

force of a hundredweight behind it. Obviously pleurisy had never been well defined. In the event, it meant lateral chest-pain in general. Still more confusion was created by Paracelsus.[121]

In accordance with his own view Van Helmont introduces his paradigm of the "thorn infixed" (*spina infixa*), which immediately helps to clarify cause and effect. The thorn provokes pain, pulsation, afflux of blood, swelling, fever, and suppuration. What matters in pleurisy, therefore, is not the tearing-off of the pleural membrane with effusion. Its cause, which alone matters, is abnormal acid, which is due to an abnormal "information" of the local blood-supply by the local vital principle, the archeus of the organ. Instead of executing its normal (sixth) digestion, the archeus reverts to the first digestion, which is the task of the stomach proper and which operates by means of acid. The action of the archeus on the local blood-supply produces an acid that leads to ulceration and destruction. It provokes contraction and thereby the tearing-off of the membrane. Cruor when acidified coagulates, and is deposited – with which we return to the tartar of Paracelsus.

Here as elsewhere humoralist therapy had been directed against the effect rather than the cause. Treatment should aim at the removal of the thorn infixed, the washing-off of the acid, through influencing the erring local archeus. Traditional venesection will never do this; it will do nothing but diminish our vital fluid. This procedure may appear to be improving the condition when performed early, but it brings phthisis or a return of the pleurisy when administered at a later stage. In any case, venesection will not alter the basic condition, either by "derivation" when made on the same side as the lesion, or by "revulsion" when made on the opposite side. What is needed is to prevent the local archeus from producing acid under the influence of a harmful agent either from outside or formed inside. He must be prevented from poisoning the local blood supply by rendering it acid. Removal of the acid thorn must be attempted as early as possible, for if it is not removed, a fully developed pleurisy may act as a second thorn; it may thus persist, it may "live" of itself. This self-perpetuation explains why the typical sequel of pleurisy, the phthisical ulcer, is intractable.

Van Helmont's suggested therapy derives from folklore. He recommends powder of the genital of a stag or bull, blood of a

[121] Paracelsus, *Autographisches zu De Tartaro*, ed. Sudhoff, v, 141; *Kollegienhefte aus der Tartarus-vorlesung*, ed. Sudhoff, v, 165.

he-goat, or juice of wild chicory or wild poppy-flower. Blood of the he-goat must be specially prepared and taken from the castration wound of the live animal; it must be dark black and of such hardness as to resist pounding with a pestle, by contrast with the ready-made and commercial product from sheep which is easy to pound and of a red colour. Van Helmont reports how speedily he relieved pain at the side of the chest and haemoptysis in himself at the age of sixty-three with a stag's genital and goat-blood. This pleurisy was supposedly caused by a splenic ailment which was then aggravated by the successful suppression of the pleuritic pain.[122]

Van Helmont's demolition of catarrh has not received the recognition it deserves. There are two main reasons for this. First, traditional humoralist medicine lingered on into the eighteenth and even early nineteenth centuries and with it one of its buttresses, the concept of catarrh. This was modified by gradually being divested of its obvious "incongruities, impossibilities and absurdities"; but it retained some identity. For example, by 1690 the cerebro-spinal fluid could still be said to assume "acerbity" by stagnation and to cause catarrh in remote parts of the body if allowed to spread.[123] Catarrh of the brain was supposed to be due to obstruction of its glandular framework. If severe, this caused apoplexy, paralysis, or sopor; or else its product, a thin or viscous fluid, might be distributed by the blood followed by "catarrhal" disease elsewhere in the body. It was, then, still the brain which was basically at fault and still a mucoid fluid that was transmitted. However, transmission was by means of the blood and no longer directly through the skull. This would imply a certain advance, since by the middle of Van Helmont's century the whole of the traditional interpretation had become embodied in academic teaching. The new and highly influential iatrochemical orientation introduced by Sylvius not only failed to reject, but perpetuated

---

[122] Van Helmont, *Pleura furens*, 32, *Opp.* p. 382 and 35, p. 383, and *Sex. dig. alim. hum.*, 76, *Opp.* p. 213. Extreme hardness was traditionally claimed for bull's as well as goat's blood, but bull's blood was also thought to be toxic. Van Helmont ascribed this to a "sealing" of the bull's fury into its blood when killed: *De magnetica vulnerum curatione*, 120, *Opp.* p. 724; notum est vulgo: *Natura contrariorum nescia*, 48, *Opp.* p. 170. See P. Brain, "Bull's Blood: a Mystery of Antiquity", *South Austr. Med. Jour.*, 50 (1976), 22–4; E. O. von Lippmann, *Beiträge zur Geschichte der Naturwissenschaften und der Technik*, Vol. I (Berlin, 1923), p. 213. Pagel, *Helmont*, p. 122.

[123] B. M. Franck, *De catarrho* (Dissert. Altdorf, 1690) as quoted in Pagel, *Van Helmont*, p. 127.

catarrh as one of its own chief supports, however much it may have promoted localist pathology in other respects. [124] On the other hand, definite opposition to the concept of catarrh is demonstrable in academic pronouncements and, as early as 1660, was stiffened by the influence of Thomas Willis's *Anatomy of the Brain*. [125] Willis's work has no truck with the brain as producer of mucus or the impossible ways in which it had been made to flow down, nor with the possibility of fluid reaching the lungs or trachea directly. Instead it is the local production of mucus as connected with local changes in the blood supply, which accounts for bronchial and lung disease. [126]

What most obscured Van Helmont's merit and priority in the rejection of catarrh was the counter-claim of Conrad Victor Schneider (1614–80) of Wittenberg. [127] This claim has been supported in our own time and Van Helmont given recognition only exceptionally. [128] It is true that Schneider deserves a position of dignity in medical history: as the discoverer, that is, of the mucous membranes. He described them in detail and accurately, and had full insight into their anatomical and pathological significance. In this respect his work represented a definite advance on Van Helmont. Schneider also collected literature to show that traditional points in connection with catarrh had been contested before Van Helmont. He even cited Hippocrates, who knew that the oesophagus was not normally patent whereas the larynx was; hence the comparative frequency of hoarseness as against catarrh of the stomach. Of

---

[124] Pagel, "Humoral Pathology", p. 301.

[125] Lysthenius, *Dissertatio medica de catarrho narium ad normam recentiorum dogmatum* (Jena, 1660) (praes. Werner Rolfinck). Thomas Willis, *Cerebri anatome* (1664), cap. XII, in *Opera*, pp. 301–5. Willis favoured intra- and trans-parenchymatous diffusion of superfluities. He does not mention Van Helmont and Schneider.

[126] Thomas Willis, *Pharmaceutice rationalis*, pt. 2 (London, 1679), sect. I, cap. 2, p. 21. Compare ibid. (Oxford, 1675), p. 57 with ibid. (1679), cap. 3, p. 23.

[127] Conrad Victor Schneider, *De catarrhis* (Wittenberg, 1660–4), lib. II, cap. 7, p. 463. Ibid., II, 6, p. 390. Here he castigates Van Helmont who, he said, was ignorant of the true movements of mucus and still believed in a role of the brain in its production and flow. What he probably had in mind was Van Helmont's exceptional admission of irritation and "error" of the "watchman" of the brain caused by air at the ethmoid region. This hardly justified Schneider in presenting him as an adherent of those ancient concepts which he had so thoroughly rejected.

[128] F. Klinge, "Der Rheumatismus", in *Ergebnisse der Allgemeinen Pathologie*, ed. O. Lubarsch and R. Ostertag, 22 vols. (Wiesbaden, 1896–1928), xxvii, 1–351. Cf. E. S. Clarke, "Brain Anatomy before Steno", in G. Scherz, ed., *Steno and Brain Research in the 17th Century* (Oxford, 1968), pp. 27–35 (at p. 32).

later authors, Botallus had adduced that the closure of the oesophagus tells against catarrh; Falloppio denied the patency of the
sutures of the skull. Schneider could have added Vesalius and
Ingrassia; these, as did others, found the sphenoid bone solid at the
site of the "pelvis" at the base of the brain. There was therefore no
possibility of a downflow of fluid cerebral excreta through the
"gland" at this place, as Galen had stipulated. However, ample
provision was still made for this very catarrh from the brain,
especially by Ingrassia. Substituting the passages carrying nerves
and vessels through the skull-bone near the sphenoid, for its non-
perforated saddle, Ingrassia felt himself capable of "consoling"
Galen, rather than having recourse to philological emendation of
his clear text.[129] Other references adduced by Schneider against Van
Helmont's priority were concerned with humoralist quibbles. None
of this can really detract from Van Helmont's pre-eminence. It
was he and not Schneider who first mounted a concerted attack on
the traditional catarrh-doctrine and thereby on the theoretical structure dominant at the time.

An additional point which may well have contributed to depreci-
ate Van Helmont's merit in this respect was his error concerning
the anatomy and physiology of respiration. His desire to embellish
the lung with "pores" probably misled him into assuming that air
passes through the pores into the chest and abdominal cavity, that
the lung does not move, and that inspiration and expiration are
regulated by the abdominal muscles. This is the price which Van
Helmont had to pay for his elegant version of "obstruction", which
he emancipated from catarrh by locating it at the site of the pores.
However, this deviation from the correct view of respiration Van
Helmont shared with the luminaries of his age. It had been taught
by Galen that the lung moves like a pair of bellows; it expands with
the chest in inspiration owing to the negative pressure in the pleural
cavity and is compressed in expiration. It was not until a century
after Van Helmont that the Galenic view was proved correct and
reinstated in the physiological syllabus through the experimental
work of Haller and his pupils, in the context of his famous controversy with Hamberger about the role of the intercostal muscles.[130]

[129] Giovanni Filippo Ingrassia (1510–80), *In Galeni librum de ossibus* (Panormi, 1603),
p. 106, with reference to Vesalius, *Fabrica*, I, 6 i.f., I, 12 and VII, 11.
[130] Albrecht Haller, *De respiratione experimenta anatomica* (Gottingen, 1746). *Cum
continuatione Trendelenburgii* (1749).

One of Van Helmont's points of reference was the action of the lung in birds, which "refuses any dilatation and compression of its cells because it is adherent to the chest-wall – and yet serves the same function as our lungs". The same analogy was exploited by Harvey. In his early Lumleian Lectures on the *Whole of Anatomy* (1616) – unpublished until 1886 – he mentions the lung pores as being closed in expiration when the lung is stretched. Consistent with this is the proper attention he gives the matter in his work on generation (1651).[131] Here he speaks of the small perforations of the lung – a discovery of his own. They are neither obscure nor doubtful, but fairly conspicuous, especially in birds. A probe passed down the trachea makes its way out of the lungs and is discovered lying naked in the abdominal cavities. Harvey queries whether in man during life there is not also a passage from openings of the same kind into the cavity of the chest. For how else should the pus poured out in empyema, and the blood extravasated in pleurisy, make their escape? In penetrating wounds of the chest, the lungs themselves being uninjured, air often escapes from the wound; or, liquids injected into the cavity of the thorax are discharged with the spit.

Admitting the existence of pores did not necessarily mean revision or rejection of the Galenic thesis that the lungs are moved like a pair of bellows following the movement of the chest. In fact, the porosity of the visceral pleural membrane of the lung was generally accepted, as can be seen from Bartholinus's *Anatomical Institutions* of 1641 and the *Anatomia reformata* of 1655.[132] Yet, in both texts the lung is made to move passively with the lifting of the chest because of the "flight from the vacuum", just as water is lifted up in pipes. Contradictory views are met with in Jean Riolan the younger (1577–1657), the well-known Galenist adversary of Harvey. He found against Galen that the fine visceral pleural membrane is studded with small holes; they serve for the absorption of fluids collecting in the pleural space so that this matter may be

[131] Van Helmont, *Catarrhi deliramenta*, 45 (C), *Opp.* p. 422; Harvey, *Praelectiones*, fol. 83v. See *The Anatomical Lectures of William Harvey*, ed. G. Whitteridge (Edinburgh and London, 1964), pp. 282–4; Harvey, *De generatione* (Amsterdam, 1662), cap. III, p. 6.

[132] Caspar Bartholinus et Thomas, Caspari filius, *Institutiones anatomicae* (Leyden, 1641), II, 9, p. 220; Thomas Bartholinus, *Anatomia reformata* (The Hague, 1655), II, 9, pp. 279–80. See also Vopiscus Fortunatus Plempius, *Fundamenta medicinae* (Louvain, 1644), II, 7, pp. 119–20.

discharged by the lung. Riolan also rejected the traditional Galenic view of suction as the force causing the lung to inflate following expansion of the chest; this mode of action he restricted to forced breathing when there is "fear of the vacuum". The pleural pores also provide an outlet when the lung is pressed and overloaded in suffocation.[133] He concluded that the lung is moved passively through being filled like a bag. Thus, Riolan relied on a mixture of half-admissions and half-denials in the anatomy and physiology of the lung, a position reminiscent of his attitude towards the newly discovered circulation of the blood.

It can be said, then, that lung pores had been admitted to the syllabus before Van Helmont, although the consequential passage of air into the pleural cavity had not been generally accepted. It was, however, maintained by many authorities, chiefly on account of the experience of air and effusions escaping through wounds in the chest-wall.[134]

In conclusion, then, Van Helmont remains the first to have de-molished the concept of catarrh. It is also to his merit to have based on this platform the reform of medical theory: the concept, that is, of localist and aetiological pathology. What Van Helmont had initiated was complemented in its anatomical aspects through the description of the mucous membranes by Conrad Victor Schnei-der. This concession takes nothing away from Van Helmont's stature as a key figure in the history of such principal diseases as rheumatism, asthma, and tuberculosis.

THE ANATOMY OF URINE AND URINARY CALCULUS

Urine examination had provided the central diagnostic aid in an-cient and traditional medicine. It had grown into a system of divination based on distinctions of colour and their dependence upon the supposed admixture of bile. Van Helmont eloquently rejected this, asserting that colour is accidental, and that there is no bile in urine, not even in the jaundiced. This is easily learnt from the absence of any bitter taste, which a few drops of bile will give if added to any specimen of urine. The error of the traditionalists

---

[133] Jean Riolan, *Anthropographia* (Paris, 1618), III, 11, pp. 383–4, 381; idem, *Encheiridion anatomicum* (Paris, 1648), III, 6, p. 282.
[134] For a good summary of opinion see Charles-Louis Dumas, *Principes de physiologie*, 2nd edn., 4 vols. (Paris, 1806), iii, 40–5.

in this matter followed from their omitting to taste urine and their false appraisal of bile as a noxious excrement that meanders in the body inflicting damage in both expected and unexpected places. That the yellow colour of urine really derives from the gut is shown by its faecal smell on distillation.[135] *Nubecula*, the small "cloud" that occasionally does appear in urine, is a product of coagulation, caused by the gastric acid and passed on by the liver to the kidneys. This appearance merely indicates digestive activity or its restoration after a fever which may have impaired it for some time.[136]

Van Helmont can have had as little patience with the urinary fancies of Leonhard Thurneisser von Thurm (1530–95), the notorious chemiatric adventurer and Paracelsian naturalist. Thurneisser had constructed a tall still representing the human figure in which he distilled urine specimens from the sick, noting the regions to which the vapours ascended: this to him indicated the seat of the disease and even details of morbid changes. To Van Helmont this was mere divination, suggestive of evil and magic delusions, and thus an utterly impious and useless addition to medicine.[137] However, Thurneisser had based his "anatomy of urine" on two sound principles. First, there was Paracelsus's critique of traditional uroscopy. Mere inspection of urine achieved nothing; chemical methods must be employed instead to discover tartar and morbid species that are hidden in urine just as silver is hidden in acid solution. It should be noted in connection with this collation of the urine with the anatomy of man that the idea of the whole microcosm being

---

[135] Van Helmont, *Scholar. humorist. pass. deceptio*, IV, *Opp.* II, pp. 188–94. On the misconception concerning bile: ibid., IV, 18, *Opp.* II, p. 192. Apart from his vindication of bile, Van Helmont regarded urine as a specific product of the kidney which had nothing to do with the secretion or excretion of bile. Equally dropsy was in his opinion due to kidney failure and not to the bile-secreting liver as traditionally believed: *Ignotus hydrops*, 3, *Opp.* p. 484.

[136] Paracelsus had previously connected the appearances of urine with gastric digestion: *Deutsches zur Harnlehre*, tract. I, ed. Sudhoff, iv, 625.

[137] Leonhard Thurneisser, *Prokatalepsis...gemachter Harm Proben* (Frankfurt Oder, 1571), and idem, *Bebaiosis agonismou...Confirmatio...der...Kunst dess Harn probirens* (Berlin, 1576): see J.C.W. Moehsen, *Beiträge zur Geschichte der Wissenschaften in der Mark Brandenburg* (Berlin, 1783), p. 189, no. III, and no. IX, pp. 191–2. Pagel, *Paracelsus*, pp. 190–200. Idem, *Das medizinische Weltbild des Paracelsus*, pp. 19–20. J. Bleker, *Geschichte der Nierenkrankheiten* (Mannheim, 1972), pp. 41–6 and idem, "Chemiatrische Vorstellungen und Analogiedenken in der Harndiagnostik Leonhart Thurneissers (1571 und 1576)", *Sudhoffs Archiv*, 60 (1976), 66–75. Van Helmont, *De lithiasi*, III, 20, *Opp.* II, p. 16; *Aufgang*, p. 434.

pre-formed in the urine had also derived from Paracelsus.[138] Second and more important, Thurneisser had insisted on the careful comparative weighing and measuring of each specimen before it was subjected to distillation. His vagaries had thus included, albeit in a confused way, a suggestion of the significance of specific weight. He tried to "read" from his measurement of weight the proportional distribution of the Paracelsian "three firsts" – salt, sulphur, and mercury – in any given specimen of urine.

Van Helmont adopted the specific gravity of a urine specimen as an essential part of its true chemical analysis. Cusanus is likely to have been his source of inspiration here, as in other areas. Cusanus had stated that weight and colour of blood and urine gave better information than the traditional inspection of colour alone. He suggested that standards should be prepared for the normal specific weights in all age groups and races, to provide a basis for judging the condition of the sick. Van Helmont also recommended this, as the "safe method of examining urine". He proposed a quantity of rain water as the standard weight. He filled a glass vessel weighing 1,354 grains with rain water, the weight of the filled vessel being 4,670 grains. When the vessel was filled with the urine of an old man the weight came to 4,720 grains, that is, 50 grains more than rain water; when filled with the urine of a healthy woman aged 55, to 4,745. The total for a healthy adolescent of 19 was 4,766; a sample from the same youth during an attack of tertian ague weighed 4,848, more than the urine of a similar subject when thirsty (4,800). Van Helmont was aware that the temperature of the specimen makes a slight difference in weight; he therefore advised using a short-necked and sharply pointed vessel. The ease of operation of this method made it preferable to the weighing of the whole person as prescribed in the "Aphorisms" of Sanctorius. Van Helmont concludes with a warning against indulgence in prognostication. He himself had always given his whole attention to the essentials of the disease and its cure, rather than to the ambiguous prognoses that earn a popular reputation.[139]

---

[138] Paracelsus, *Deutsches zur Harnlehre*, ed. Sudhoff, iv, 636, 624 et seq.; *Opus Paramirum*, III, 5, 164.

[139] Nicolaus Cusanus, *De staticis experimentis*, in *Opera*, fols. 94v and 95r; Van Helmont, *Scholar. humorist. pass. deceptio*, IV, 31, *Opp.* II, pp. 193–4. See also Pagel, *Paracelsus*, p. 199.

In all provinces of his research Van Helmont felt the first priority to lie with the rejection of traditional, especially materialist, doctrine. According to the traditional view, stone was a product of mucus that under the influence of heat dries up and petrifies. But nothing like mucus can be found in urine, let alone in urinary calculus. Material as such, or the agglomeration of materials, cannot explain any pathological process or formation, nor can the interplay of elemental contraries such as hot and cold or moist and dry. Paracelsus's radical reformation of medicine had involved deprecation of the humours as pathogenic agents. He had, however, introduced another materialist interpretation of the stone, in regarding it simply as the product of a deposit of indigestible food material, comparable with tartar in wine-vats. His analogy was weak, since there was an obvious chemical difference between the latter and the stone. Tartar is water-soluble whereas the stone is not.[140]

To Van Helmont formation of the stone is a vital process. It is an event de novo, and as such requires a fermental "semen" or "idea" of its own. Indeed stone is from non-stone; it is primarily form and not matter, that is, form disposing matter and thus creating the possibility for stone to develop.[141] In chemical terms Van Helmont concentrates on the salts which he had identified in urine. He distinguished three such salts: (a) common sea-salt, (b) a "fixed" salt proper to urine, and (c) a "volatile" salt. From the outset Van Helmont insists that ordinary salt has no part in stone formation. On the contrary, sufferers from stone find it most beneficial; it also prevents stone, and is not found in the actual stone-specimen. All this belies the traditional idea that salty mucus, inspissated, is the basic material of stone. For salt dissolves mucus and drives out sand. This makes it desirable both for itself and as a promoter of acid (*spiritus*), as notably in gastric digestion and its indirect prevention of stone.[142] Nor has alkali a part in stone-formation: it never appears in urine, not even after long-standing intake of

---

[140] Van Helmont, *De lithiasi*, II (causae Duelech veterum), 2–4, *Opp.* II, p. 7 and VII, 19, *Opp.* II, p. 48. *De lithiasi*, IV (processus Duelech), 4, *Opp.* II, p. 23; *Aufgang*, p. 443.

[141] *De lithiasi*, V, 5, *Opp.* II, p. 30 and III, 17–18, *Opp.* II, p. 15.

[142] Ibid., III, 31, *Opp.* II, p. 18. This passage and ibid., VII, 28, *Opp.* II, p. 52 are significant for their near-identification of the digesting "spirit" (acid) in the stomach with hydrochloric acid. See Pagel, "Van Helmont's Ideas on Gastric Digestion", p. 532.

alkali-salt such as vegetable potash from lime or the cure of wounds. Hence, nothing can be expected from alkaline medicines in the stone. Alkali does not reach the urine, or what produces it.[143]

Van Helmont sees stone as the result of coagulation. Its formation requires not one, but two, agents and rightly deserves the Paracelsian term *duelech*.[144] One of these two is the volatile urine-salt, an "earth" that causes and is subject to coagulation. If it were rendered incapable of coagulation by "fixing", no stone could develop. The second agent is fermental, a seminal spirit which prepares and disposes the "earth" to stone-formation, that is in a specific direction. The seminal ferment comes to the urine from outside. It is a "foreign accessory", a stercoral agent from the gut that may lodge in the kidney.[145] Here like a *Gorgo* it may petrify the volatile "earthy" salt of urine, uniting with it and producing a solid body by coagulation. The process is comparable to stony deposits forming more readily in an old smelly vessel than in a new and freshly cleaned container.[146] Indeed, the stercoral agent belongs to the "odorific ferments": it is a *spiritus putrefactus* that unites with the volatile urine-salt as the *spiritus coagulativus*. These are the two agents required for the stone. However, to complete the process there must be an intermediary, a "pander" (*leno*). This Van Helmont believed to be alcohol (*aqua vitae*). For on mixing the volatile salt of urine with alcohol he immediately obtained a white clot (*offa*, i.e., morsel or cake), a subtle and fugitive *coagulum*. The stone is the product of a true chemical combination; the components are not merely juxtaposed but made inseparable.[147]

To prevent and to cure the stone in the human subject is a highly specialised task, in view of its different nature compared with ordinary minerals, and calculi found in animals. Such differences correspond to those between the composition of urine in man and in brutes, such as the absence of "spirit coagulating and fermenting" as well as of *aqua vitae* in the urine of the horse.[148] Van

---

[143] *De lithiasi*, III, 25–8, *Opp*. II, pp. 16–17.

[144] Ibid., III, 35, *Opp*. II, p. 21.

[145] The ferment is not indigenous to urine. Urine may be retained in the bladder for a whole day without showing any trace of deposit when finally voided, but will develop deposits very soon when left exposed to the ferments of air: *De lithiasi*, V, 6, *Opp*. II, p. 30 and ibid., II, 13, *Opp*. II, p. 10. Pagel, *Paracelsus*, pp. 164–5.

[146] *De lithiasi*, V, 5, *Opp*. II, p. 30. The *Gorgo* seduces the resident archeus of the kidney, subordinating him to the orders of a foreign archeus.

[147] *De lithiasi*, III, 2–5, *Opp*. II, pp. 12–13; *Aufgang*, pp. 430–1.

[148] *De lithiasi*, III, 43, *Opp*. II, p. 22; *Aufgang*, p. 442 (III, 42).

Helmont experienced much disappointment in his empirical search for a cure. He tried, in vain, material obtained from ordinary stones, from alkali, or from saltpetre derived from decaying bricks.[149] Nor was any more benefit gained from extracts of gastric mucosa, which preferably included that of birds (pigeons). This was a procedure based on Van Helmont's insight into the production of acid by the gastric wall, and the Paracelsian statement that acid mineral waters prevented and had healing effects in the stone.[150] Thus, in spite of the disappointing results with gastric mucosal extracts, the virtues of salt and salt-spirit remained a guiding light in Van Helmont's attempt at preventing stone. He set great store by the antiseptic properties of salty-acid products, expecting from them inhibition of the odorific (putrid) stone-ferments and thereby of the coagulation responsible for the stone. Indeed "spirit of salt is the most acid of all and a remedy without its equal". In his own observation a man deemed susceptible to stone had benefited from it, remaining free of the condition for sixteen years, and so did many others.[151] The spirit of Spanish sea-salt, strongly fired and with clay added, not only heals strangury in the old but also reduces large stones to small granules which are amenable to discharge with the urine.[152]

In a single observation Van Helmont succeeded in isolating a substance through re-distillation of a urine deposit recalcitrant to removal from the vessel-wall; this eventually dissolved the deposit, so he concluded that urine can contain a stone-preventive.[153] He also considered the various Paracelsian arcana against the stone. First there is the "aroph" (an abbreviation of *aroma philosophorum*), chosen for its golden colour; it is neither mineral nor flesh, but a herb fermenting when bread is steeped with wine.[154] Paracelsus failed to indicate its true nature. According to one tradition it was

---

[149] *De lithiasi*, III, 28, *Opp.* II, p. 17, and VII, 28, *Opp.* II, p. 52. Ibid., III, 28, *Opp.* II, p. 17. Ibid., VII, 28, *Opp.* II, p. 52; *Aufgang*, pp. 435, 480, 481.

[150] Paracelsus, *Das Buch von den Tartarischen Krankheiten*, XVI, ed. Sudhoff, xi, 99.

[151] *De lithiasi*, III, 31, *Opp.* II, p. 18: *Aufgang*, p. 437. *De lithiasi*, III, 30, *Opp.* II, p. 17. *Aufgang*, p. 436. The single case concerned a male aged 60.

[152] *De lithiasi*, VII, 28, *Opp.* II, p. 52; or, more briefly, ibid., III, 31, *Opp.* II, p. 18. Salt thus dissolved deposits, rather than consolidating them as traditionally thought. Ibid., II, 3–4, p. 7.

[153] *De lithiasi*, III, 33, i.f., *Opp.* II, p. 20.

[154] Paracelsus, *De viribus membrorum*, II, 5, ed. Sudhoff, iii, 21. Ibid., III, 8, ed. Sudhoff, iii, 26. *Aufgang*, VII, 14, p. 470.

made from blood-stone and salt ammoniac; it was supposed to be ferric ammonium borate and to be found near Antwerp.[155]

Next there was the *ludus Paracelsi*, a mysterious "stone against stone". This was said to be to the earth what the stone is to the body, that is, the earthly equivalent to lithiasis in man. It grows from earthy tartar, being consolidated in the terrestrial fluid through something akin to the "spirit of urine".[156] Van Helmont explains that it derives its name from its cubic form, which likens it to a "play-stone" (*ludus*). He gives a lengthy description of its preparation which defies understanding, involving as it does the mysterious liquor alkahest, the universal solvent. Moreover, he warns that to produce it requires a special, personal skill.[157] Other such nostrums included juice of birch-bark, wild carrot-seed broiled in beer from Malines, brook-lime seed, and "nephritick wood" or santalum blue, a diuretic from India.[158]

Van Helmont gives us to understand that he is convinced of the stone-preventing virtues of salt and salty acids as well as of the stone-dissolving power of the *ludus*, a "stony-antistone". However, he is very secretive about the latter and its proper preparation. In his own words, he does not feel entitled to indicate more than "brother can communicate to brother". Admittedly pity for the sufferer should call for promulgation of the cure "by trumpet". However, for reasons known to God alone it must remain among

---

[155] Castelli, *Lexicon*, 78, 378. H. Haeser, *Geschichte der Medizin*, 2 vols. (Jena, 1875–81), ii, 358, 361: *aroph* as *Eisensalmiak*. Partington, *History of Chemistry*, ii, 226 with ref. to Boyle, *Works*, 5 vols. (1747), ii, 74. Alchemical tradition connects *aroph* with mandragora.

[156] Van Helmont, *De lithiasi*, VII, 22, *Opp.* II, p. 49; *Aufgang*, p. 476. With ref. to Paracelsus, *Das sechste, siebente, und neunte Buch in der Arznei*, tract. II, 1, ed. Sudhoff, ii, 385–6. Other names for *ludus: cevill*, ibid., tract. I, 4, p. 381, and *fel terrae altholizoi*, *Buch von den Tartarischen Krankheiten*, XX, ed. Sudhoff, xi, 113–14; "altholizoi" is according to Van Helmont "al-tho-oli-gesotten", i.e., "all broiled until converted into an oil"; emended in Sudhoff to "alkalisati". Ruland, *Lexicon Alchemiae*, p. 307, identifies *ludus* with an actual stone removed from the bladder which would cure any other stone on homeopathic principles. Traditionally regarded as a *Pyrites* of cubic shape with copper and iron predominant (communication to the present author by Prof. G. S. Rousseau with ref. to J. B. de Secondat, *Observations de Physique* [1750], pp. 43–9); according to Partington, *History of Chemistry*, ii, 226, possibly boracite or magnesium.

[157] *De lithiasi*, VIII, 23, *Opp.* II, p. 50.

[158] *De lithiasi*, VIII, 24, *Opp.* II, p. 59. Brook-lime seed is beccabunga; birchbark is "berckenboom" in S. Blancard, *Lexicon medicum Graeco-Latinum* (1777), p. 171. The efficacy of nephritic wood (other than as a diuretic) was doubted by Helmont and Blancard; ibid., p. 844.

the secrets, the arcana, which God himself has reserved to reveal to those few elect. Nevertheless, Van Helmont tells us where to find the material for the *ludus*, namely on the shores of the river Schelde where bricks are fired, and also that it should be converted into a volatile salt and then into an oily salt with a flavour reminiscent of urine. It should be taken daily with drink, perhaps white wine, in the same way as he prescribed for Spanish sea-salt as a prophylactic against stone.[159]

Van Helmont regarded his work on stone as a legacy of his declining years.[160] It is distinguished by a number of remarkable chemical observations, analyses, and experiments.[161] Here it is that he comes close to the identification of gastric acid with hydrochloric acid, that he realises the specific chemical properties of the stone in man, rejects the supposed role of mucus in its formation, and emphasises the dissolving rather than solidifying effects of salt. Again in accordance with his first principles the whole process is seen from a spiritualistic perspective in which specific "ferments" and "odours" replace any primary interaction of matter with matter. On the practical side, his firm advice to replace the metal catheter by one of leather should not be overlooked. I invented, he said, a new catheter because of the pain and frequent haemorrhages inflicted by the curved silver instruments of the barber-surgeon. He had tried many substitutes, and finally found those to be most suitable which were made of leather treated with cerussa (white-lead) and linseed oil and sewn round a copper-wire. The tube so obtained should be broad enough to admit the nozzle of a syringe for injecting or withdrawing fluid. Before use the copper-wire is replaced by a flexible equivalent such as a fishbone.[162] It is true that replacement of the metal catheter by one of less rigid material did not entirely originate with Van Helmont, but non-metal types were apparently used only rarely and his version employing leather carefully sewn and adapted would seem to have been distinctly progressive.[163] There are, on the other hand, not a few points in the treatise which are unrealistic, such as the cooper-

[159] *De lithiasi*, VIII, 23, *Opp.* II, p. 50; ibid., VII, 22, *Opp.* II, p. 49.
[160] Ibid., III, 34, *Opp.* II, p. 21. *Oriatrike*, p. 848. *Aufgang*, p. 440.
[161] These undoubtedly entailed progressive views for medical therapy as well as in physiology and pathology. See E. J. Gurlt, *Geschichte der Chirurgie und ihrer Ausübung*, 3 vols. (Berlin, 1898), iii, 338.
[162] *De lithiasi*, VII, 34, *Opp.* II, pp. 53–4.
[163] See Gurlt, *Geschichte der Chirurgie*, iii, 770; ibid., ii, 358 and i, 890.

ation of a "spirit of urine" – the odorific ferment – with alcohol in the formation of stone, the number of internal medicines which he praised, and the vague, unconvincing, and sometimes fantastic cases he has to report.

PRINCIPLES OF MEDICINAL ACTION

We have seen that for Van Helmont disease is not determined by any material, such as, in particular, humours or vapours. Its nature is spiritual: the vital spirit, the archeus, is seduced from his normal schedule by a morbid idea, a foreign guest, the product of his imagination or his desire for an outside agent whose schedule is thus superimposed upon his own. Disease, therefore, does not call for fresh material to counteract a material culprit. The remedy must be as spiritual as the disease itself. In other words it must be a better idea – one that is capable of inducing the archeus to think again, of persuading him to find his way back out of his entanglement with a seducer. To "superimpose another idea" (*superinducere ideam*) is therefore the rationale of all medicinal action. This excludes direct action through the "qualities" or "grades" of a substance, as envisaged by the ancients. On the contrary, it should be indirect, a therapy by diversion. Idea must stand against idea – and there is a ternary of them: the normal, healthy idea of the archeus of the patient, the hostile morbific idea, and the idea embodied in the remedy.[164]

This, however, can be no excuse for the welter of superstitious practices which followed on disappointment at the inefficacy of ancient prescriptions worked out from pseudo-scientific "mathematical" tables of qualities and grades. All the nonsense of astrology, "word-salads" inscribed on "virgin" vellum or purified metal with letters arranged according to constellations at certain hours, seals, talismans, gems to attract astral power into sublunary bodies, fumigations, had been given their chance.[165]

By contrast, words, herbs, and stones are endowed with real and great virtue. Their magic must be strictly distinguished from

---

[164] *Tractatus novus posthumus...de virtute magna verborum ac rerum, Opp.* pp. 754, 753; *Aufgang,* 8, 1–4, pp. 1063, 1061 (a treatise first published posthumously in the *Opera* of 1682).

[165] *Tractatus novus posthumus,* p. 756 and *Aufgang,* 14–15, p. 1065. *Tumulus pestis* (Zenexton), *Opp.* II, p. 261; *Aufgang,* XVIII, 7–9, p. 642.

the rank superstition mentioned above. Though indefinable and little understood, this medicinal virtue is a great gift; it is at the same time divine and quite natural. Through words of power, counter-ideas are induced that should unhook the archeus from the morbid idea that has kept him prisoner; it should normalise his relationship with the archei of the objects with whom he "converses".[166] What Van Helmont seems to have in mind is a kind of suggestive shock therapy, a counterblast comparable to the "cure" of hydrophobia sometimes achieved by throwing the patient into water.[167] Unfortunately he does not specify what kind of "words" qualify; he contents himself with assuring us that such formulae are not superstitious, and excuses their failure in some cases as being due to the shortcomings of all medicinal cures. Indeed, there is no difference between the curative word and ordinary *pharmaka*. Both are to restrain and correct the excited archeus. There is something of sorcery in all diseases and medicinal action, just as there is in the exemplar that forms the basis of all natural philosophy, namely, the mutual conversion of idea (image) and material change. Herbs, verbs, and stones act like the hand of the pregnant mother "signing" the foetus at a place corresponding to that she touched on her own body; this is a perfectly natural event. The royal cure by touch is not through the personal virtue of any of the many kings who are capable of it, but through the power of the word, that is, of imagination and of desire for an effect firmly believed in as in a part of revelation.[168] The same applies to all occult cures unknown by cause, but natural, such as the magnetic cure of wounds with the weapon-salve, and the averting (*apotropaeic*) power of the turquoise which saves the life of persons falling from great heights by "transferring the [fear and] blow to itself" and breaking in place of the bones of the fallen.[169]

There is a deep difference between digestion and the action of medicines. The former leads to transmutation and assimilation of

---

[166] "Confabulantur cum archeo": *Opp.* p. 757; *Aufgang*, 20, p. 1066.

[167] *Opp.* p. 764; *Aufgang*, 45, p. 1075.

[168] *Opp.* p. 764; *Aufgang*, 45, p. 1076.

[169] *Opp.* p. 763; *Aufgang*, 41, p. 1074. For the long tradition of the turquoise story see Vincent of Beauvais, *Speculum naturale*, IX, 106; Albertus Magnus, *De mineralibus*, II, 2, cap. 18 in *Lulli de secretis naturae...*, ed. W. H. Ryff (Strassburg, 1541), fol. 115r. Volmar, *Steinbuch*, ed. H. Lambel (Heilbronn, 1877), p. 19, 1.551. For the sceptical reaction of Erasmus, see P. Krivatsky, "Erasmus' Medical Milieu", *Bull. Hist. Med.*, 47 (1973), 113–54 (at p. 134).

food. Medicines, and in particular mineral and metal medicines, are effective without any substantial change to themselves. They absolutely refuse to enter into chemical combination with any part of the body.[170] They achieve their purpose by confrontation, merely "looking" at their objects. Mercury destroys lice on cloth without loss of substance and even prevents their recurrence; it can change acid spirit of vitriol into aluminous salt "by mere touch and without any mixing".[171] The process may be repeated a thousand times without costing the mercury any of its substance. One ounce of mercury "infecting" a thousand measures of water enables this to kill worms, simply by sealing it. In the same way medicinal action is "by ray and look" at an object foreign to the remedy; it acts freely, that is, without any reaction, assimilation, diminution, admixture, or penetration. In this lies its magic and arcanum, its infinite and miraculous effectiveness as displayed in the arcana Paracelsi and the Stone of the vagrant Irishman Butler at the Court of King James.[172] For the unilateral action of the true arcanum to occur, which is "all at once" and "all or nothing", the substance is required in its full integrity and simplicity, by contrast with the practice of the ancients who relied on mixtures worked out from the proportions of qualities and grades of components. In this way the virtues of many herbs are lost. This also happens during digestion; the herbs being then denatured, they fall short of reaching the vital centre.[173] It remains to select the few herbs which can resist this loss and which are not resistant because they are also poisonous. Consequently, Van Helmont favours mineral medicine as against words and herbs.

Our understanding of the "healing word" has much to gain from a consideration of the Paracelsian iatrochemist Croll.[174] In his view

[170] That minerals cannot be digested and assimilated, and were therefore alien to man, had been the strongest argument proffered by Thomas Erastus (1523–83) against Paracelsus: *Disputationum de medicina nova Philippi Paracelsi*, pt. IV (Basel, 1573), pp. 308–9. Idem, *Disputatio de auro potabili...* (text dated 1576; Basel, 1584), pp. 66 et seq., 76, 79.

[171] *Opp.* p. 544; *Aufgang*, 5, p. 1078. Ibid., *Opp.* p. 545 and *Aufgang*, 8–9, p. 1078.

[172] Van Helmont himself witnessed Butler's "Stone" operate without any quantitative loss, lag of time, or "confermentation" with any bodily parts. Minimal touch, oscillation, aiming, or mere radiation of light enabled it to reach the vital centre: *Opp.* p. 545; *Aufgang*, 9, p. 1078.

[173] *Opp.* p. 546; *Aufgang*, 13–17, pp. 1084–6. See also *Opp.* p. 546; *Aufgang*, 14, p. 1084.

[174] On Croll, see D. Goltz, "Vis und Virtus im Paracelsistenstreit", *Medizin-historisches Journal*, 5 (1970), 169–200; eadem, "Naturmystik und Naturwissenschaft", pp. 45–65; Hannaway, *The Chemists and the Word*.

it is not through its material substance that a drug is effective. The drug as such is merely a dead shell. What makes it active is its spiritual kernel – its internal seal, whereby it acquires its specific therapeutic power. This seal or signature is the signet of the "sealed word" (*signum signati verbi*).[175] It is the verbal fiat of the creator which has allocated to each creature its specific task. It is the divine word that is transferred to the earth and its fruit.

The close kinship between the Crollian and the Helmontian principles of medicinal action is difficult to overlook, but it is not surprising in view of their common source, Paracelsus. The first principle on which they agree lies in the rejection of any material interaction of medicine and body, in favour of its spiritual nature. It is not the herb that is the medicine, but rather its invisible virtue, the intrinsic command, the creative word whereby it can exercise its power. To Croll the word is a panacea; there is no cure without it. Van Helmont, too, sets great store by the "word of power". To him this meant in the first place "word" in the literal sense – the spoken word that is addressed to the archeus of the patient in a psycho-therapeutic effort. "Word" also stood for the command of the divine creator as revealed in the specific virtues of each mineral and herb qua objects of divine creation – God's fiat. In this latter, Crollian sense, "word" was in Van Helmont's view tantamount to the non-material nature of medicinal action. It was to this sense rather than the spoken word that his reflections on therapy were devoted. On the other hand, he rejected the classic Paracelsian idea of "signatures" to which Croll subscribed; for example, that celandine (*cheledonium*) with its yellow colour was signed with the sealed word of its creator as the remedy for jaundice. In the same vein he attacked fraudulent amulets and astrological connotations proffered by believers in signatures.[176] God, he says, gives the knowledge of medicines (simples) to whom he pleases, but not through signs of nature.[177] He himself would rather pray for the divine gift of knowledge (*scientia*), enabling him to find explanations of magical effects in naturalistic terms, than to accept them as mystical signs that defy understanding.

[175] Croll, *Basilica chymica*, praef. admonit., p. 44, 1.12. On later versions of the concept of "signatures" see C. H. Schubert, *Symbolik des Traums* (Bamberg, 1814), pp. 36, 45, 55, 83.
[176] Van Helmont, *Tumulus pestis*, Opp. II, pp. 262 et seq; *Aufgang*, XVIII, 14, p. 643 and 7–8, p. 642. See also Paracelsus, *Liber de imaginibus*, X, ed. Sudhoff, viii, 379.
[177] Van Helmont, *Pharmacopolium et dispensatorium modernum*, 5–6, *Opp.* p. 437.

6

Final assessment

Van Helmont's work touched off a landslide reaction on the literary, scientific, and medical scene in Puritan and Restoration England. Paracelsianism had emerged in the 1570s on the continent and culminated in England in the admission of Paracelsian medicines to the *London Pharmacopoeia* of 1618.[1] Paracelsian loyalties shared by partisans on both sides before, during, and after the Commonwealth were easily though not unanimously transferred to Helmontianism.[2] This transition gave evidence of strong religious overtones and motives; Helmont, the "chemical evangelist", was to "worke more upon the Papists than many books of learned Divines.[3] Practical considerations, including the ineffectiveness of traditional medicine in the relief of human misery, its bookish intolerance and remoteness from nature, weighed here more than theories. The investigation and application of mineral, that is, "specific" medicines traditionally condemned as poisonous, remained the principal issue. A College of Helmontians, the Society of Chymical

---

[1] G. Urdang, "How Chemicals Entered the Official Pharmacopoeias", *Arch. internat. d'Hist. Sci.*, 7 (1934), 303–14. Idem, "The Mystery about the First English (London) Pharmacopoeia, 1618", *Bull. Hist. Med.*, 12 (1942), 304–13.

[2] C. Webster, *The Great Instauration: Science, Medicine and Reform, 1626–1660* (London, 1975), pp. 273–88. For certain theoretical positions adopted by Helmontians see P. H. Niebyl, "The Helmontian Thorn", *Bull. Hist. Med.*, 45 (1971), 570–95, and idem, "Science and Metaphor in the Medicine of Restoration England", *Bull. Hist. Med.*, 47 (1973), 356–74.

[3] George Starkey in *Pyrotechny Asserted* (London, 1658), p. III. Idem, *Nature's Explication and Helmont's Vindication* (London, 1657); the translation used here is *Chymie oder Vertheidigung Helmonts samt e. Beschreibung des Liquor Alkahests* (Nürnberg, 1722), pp. 52–4. Letter from Appelius to Hartlib, 5 Feb. 1645, quoted from Webster, *The Great Instauration*, p. 277 and note 89. See also P. Rattansi, "The Helmontian-Galenist Controversy in Restoration England", *Ambix*, 12 (1964), 1–23, which emphasises religious and antischolastic motives, in preference to socioeconomic pressures.

Physitians, established itself as a shadow cabinet in opposition to the College of Physicians; not only minor Puritan chemists and controversialists but also respectable authorities such as Walter Charleton (1619–1707) and George Thomson (fl. 1648–79) were Helmontian sympathisers, the former at least being for some time a conspicuous adherent.[4] It was the Helmontians who braved the plague from which their learned colleagues fled in 1665. Iatrochemistry, which under Thomas Willis and Sylvius became the ruling trend in the second half of the century, was Helmontianism diluted and mechanised in a characteristic way. At the other extreme of influence lay the "animist medicine" of Georg Ernst Stahl (1660–1734). Stahl was just as one-sided a Helmontian as the iatrochemists; wedded to dualism, he ignored the dynamic, that is, "energetic" nature of the living substance, the fundamental principle which Van Helmont had put in the place of impetus ("soul" and motion) super-added from without. The vitalists of Montpellier overruled Stahl on this very issue and found their way back to Van Helmont by way of Haller's experiments on tissue irritability.[5] Secular Helmontian controversies concerned venesection, the fermental (acid) or mechanical nature of gastric digestion, and the consensus of organs under direction from the stomach.[6] Boyle not

---

[4] Walter Charleton, *Spiritus Gorgonicus...de causis, signis et sanatione lithiaseos* (Leyden, 1650). C. Webster, "The Helmontian George Thomson and William Harvey: The Revival and Application of Splenectomy to Physiological Research", *Med. Hist.*, 15 (1971), 154–67.

[5] Theophile de Bordeu (1722–76), "Sur l'histoire de la médicine", in *Oeuvres*, ed. A. B. de Richerand, 2 vols. (Paris, 1818), cap. VII, 3, p. 671.

[6] For a defence of Van Helmont's rejection of venesection see J. G. Wolstein, *Anmerkungen über das Aderlassen* (Vienna, 1791). D. M. von Sallaba, *Galen vom Aderlassen gegen den Erasistrat* (Vienna, 1791), pp. 112–40 defends Galen and venesection. For a Puritan endorsement of Van Helmont see Noah Biggs, *Mataeotechnia...the Vanity of...Purges, Bloodletting...* (London, 1651). On acid-gastric digestion see Jean Pascal, *La nouvelle découverte et les admirables effets des fermens* (Paris, 1681); M. F. Geuder, *Diatriba de fermentis variarum corporis animalis partium specificis et particularibus* (Amsterdam, 1689), pp. 8, 64. As a reaction against acid fermentation in favour of mechanical breaking-up of food see Philippe Hecquet, *De la digestion...de la trituration ou du broyement* (Paris, 1712); Archibald Pitcairne, *Elementa medicinae physico-mathematica* (London, 1717). For an opponent of Hecquet see Jean Astruc, *Traité de la cause de la digestion où l'on prouve véritable fermentation* (Toulouse, 1714). On consensus of organs and the principate of the stomach see Hendrick Joseph Rega, *Tractatus medicus de sympathia et consensu partium...ac potissimum ventriculi in statu morboso* (1713; Frankfurt and Leipzig, 1762), pp. 237–42 and passim. An Helmontian encyclopaedia with ecclesiastic approval is Franz Oswald Grembs, *Arbor integra et ruinosa hominis...ex Archeis spiritibus innatis...de remediis Paracelsicis juxta consensum et dissensum Hippocratis, Galeni et Helmontii* (Frankfurt, 1657).

only praised Van Helmont as an outstanding chemist in general terms but also repeated his experiment with the willow-tree, adopted his water-theory, and was prepared to recommend such Helmontian – specific – cures as stroking with a dead-man's hand, which he had seen practised on tumours by "as rigid a naturalist" as Dr Harvey.[7] Boyle shared Van Helmont's religious motives, and his rejection of elements and principles; both believed in transmutation, neither being dismissible as an alchemist on this account.[8] Van Helmont's archei as created individual units determined by spiritual directives bear a close kinship to Leibniz's monads.[9] Schopenhauer (1788–1860) ascribes the origin of this term to Van Helmont in his essay on the will in nature.[10]

Having wound our way in Van Helmont's company through a welter of strange ideas and concepts we now take leave of the reader with the question: was this exercise really necessary? No

[7] On Boyle, and religious motives in naturalism see his *Some Considerations touching the Usefulnesse of Experimental Naturall Philosophy*, 2nd edn. (Oxford, 1664), pp. 29, 113. On "thingliness" and specificity of natural bodies see idem, *The Origine of Formes and Qualities* (Oxford, 1666), pp. 66–7; on specificity in medicine, idem, *Of the Reconcileableness of Specifick Medicines to the Corpuscular Philosophy* (London, 1685), passim; on semina and seminal principles, idem, *The Sceptical Chymist*, 2nd edn. (Oxford, 1680), p. 380; on Helmontian water-theory, *The Sceptical Chymist*, p. 355. On liquor alkahest, *The Sceptical Chymist*, pp. 226, 431; *Usefulnesse*, III, 7, p. 70. On weapon-salve and sympathetic powder see *Usefulnesse*, V, 1, p. 111 and V, 11, pp. 224–5. For the poisonous effect of fury, see *Usefulnesse*, II, 14, pp. 48–9. For Harvey and cure by stroking, *Usefulnesse*, II, p. 230, and *Reconcileableness*, pp. 122 et seq. At all these loci Boyle found support for Van Helmont. There was, however, also Boyle's preoccupation with air. Owing to this the Helmontian concept of *gas* as object-specific exhalation foreign to air was blurred. Designated as "factitious air" by Boyle it was ignored for some long time.

[8] Partington, *History of Chemistry*, ii, 499. R.E.W. Maddison, *The Life of the Honourable Robert Boyle* (London, 1969), p. 176. K. Figala, "Zwei Londoner Alchemisten um 1700, Sir Isaac Newton und Cleidophorus Mystagogus", *Deut. Museum, Veröff. Forsch. Inst. Gesch. Natwiss. Tech.*, no. 206 (1977), 245–73 (at p. 249). For the religious motives of Boyle's naturalist research see Pagel, "Religious Motives in Medical Biology", pp. 305–9.

[9] Leibniz, *Monadologie*, 6, in G. W. *Leibnitii Opera philosophica*, ed. J. E. Erdmann, 2 vols. (Berlin, 1839–40), ii, 705. *Système nouveau*, 11, in *Opera*, i, 126. On individualised matter and the omnipresence of monads and life, *Principes de la nature et de la grâce*, 1, in *Opera*, ii, 714. On central monad, see *Epist. ad Rev. Patrem Des Bosses*, in *Opera*, ii, 713a. On consensus by virtue of small perceptions, *Epist. ad Rev. Patrem Des Bosses*, III, in *Opera*, ii, 438; *Principes de la nature*, 2, in *Opera*, ii, 714.

[10] Arthur Schopenhauer, *Über den Willen in der Natur* in *Sämtliche Werke*, 6 vols. (Leipzig, n.d.), iii, 181–350, p. 322 et seq. on will and imagination.

doubt a strange fascination has been experienced by those who have come to terms with the difficulties inherent in his style, language, and "dark side". Readers who have felt the urge to continue studying his bulky literary remains have not been lacking through the two-and-a-half centuries that have elapsed since his death. Historians of science and medicine have no difficulty in accounting for this. Van Helmont has enjoyed a place of high dignity in the development of chemistry and medicine. He expressed vital phenomena in biochemical terms. His employment of the balance in planned observations led him to conclude that matter was indestructible, as shown, for example, in the quantitative recovery of metal from acid solution. It was through his experiments that the precipitation of a metal from a salt solution on addition of another metal was correctly interpreted in terms of mutual substitution, rather than of the contemporary concept asserting transmutation of one into the other. He is rightly celebrated today as the discoverer of gas, the volatile representative of an individual object as distinct from such general media as air and water vapour of which all objects partake indiscriminately. He recognised acid as the agent responsible for gastric digestion and came close to its identification with hydrochloric acid. He vindicated bile as a noble and vital part, reversing its traditional role as excremental. He deliberately rejected the cornerstones of the traditional syllabus such as the humours, innate heat, and radical moisture, and the cooling of the last by respiration and pulse. Instead he argued that it was the pulse that produced and distributed heat, and not heat that produced the pulse. He visualised respiration as a gas exchange in the lung whereby the blood combines with a "ferment" from the air whilst disposing of a certain residue conveyed with the venous blood. He described the rhythmic movements of the pylorus by which digestion is regulated and controlled, and observed and analysed peristalsis in situ.

Van Helmont integrated such phenomena with his view of irritability and natural perception as inherent in tissues, which described this in terms of a certain "knowledge" possessed by the living substance. "Soul" and energetic impulse were thus regarded as immanent in, rather than superadded to, body – a monist solution of the perennial problem of the relationship between body and soul. His new concept of diseases as entities that existed and were classifiable as such initiated a radical departure from traditional humoralism. This innovation directed attention to local and primary changes accessible to anatomical and chemical analysis, and to external morbific agents. It ultimately implied a complete transformation of medicine with all the consequences of this for diagnosis and therapy. Treatment needed no longer to be dependent on the suppositious elemental qualities of herbs, but on chemicals curative by substance. Specific gravity of fluids, in particular urine, was available as a diagnostic tool, and venesection, the universal expedient of humoralism, could be rejected. Allergy and immunity were carefully observed and interpreted in descriptive terms hardly superseded today. Spontaneous or natural healing was reinstated in its proper place of dignity and responsibility. The priority in refuting unanswerably the "madness of catarrh" is entirely Van Helmont's. Catarrh – the down-flow of corrosive mucus, produced by hot vapours from the stomach ascending to and condensed in the cool brain (*rhume de cerveau*) – had to serve as the universal cause of disease for two millennia. In Van Helmont's period it still formed one of the principal articles of the medical syllabus. In its place as the culprit in inflammation and pus-formation Van Helmont postulated a *local* action of acid; he associated oedema and dropsy with an affection of the kidney in which salts played an important part. Among the instruments which he devised were a new thermometer and a new catheter. His proposal to use a pendulum for measuring time more correctly than before was contained in an extensive critique of the ruling conception of time, which he replaced with an original theory in biological terms. In this, individual and species reactivity were to serve as yardsticks of true time – *duratio* – in preference to conventional clock-time.

Examples of observations, experiments, concepts, and arguments original to Van Helmont which have prepared or directly contributed to modern standards in science and medicine could easily be increased. The list already given suggests a neat, simple, and straightforward conclusion: that Van Helmont belongs to the group of illustrious pioneers and brilliant innovators of the early seventeenth century, that he has a share in the *peripeteia* which brought about the turning-away from the ancient masters, from unreal philosophy and imagination towards reality and true knowledge.

However, Van Helmont's case reveals more profoundly than any other that this transition was far from smooth and simple, if it took place at all. First, there are the misrepresentations that have been inflicted upon him, in our own time and before. On the one hand, his original discoveries and innovations have simply been ignored; it is alleged either that they could not have been made, or that those which were could not have had any real value. Thus, his work was rejected by some because as a whole as well as in detail his writings betray a belief in alchemical transmutation by virtue of the philosophers' stone, the "powder of projection" which changes base metal into silver or gold. There is no doubt that Van Helmont did indeed cherish the idea of transmutation as a general principle underlying natural action at large, and that he consequently confirmed its working in the alembic of the alchemist on the basis of observations by himself and other savants. He was and professed to be *philosophus per ignem*, the fire that is which burns day and night in the oven, the *athanor* of the artisan who imitates, nay, overtakes, nature. But the conclusion that this in itself disqualifies and deprives Van Helmont of his high place in the history of science and medicine is simply absurd; it is due to cross ignorance of this very history, the development of these branches of learning and artful practice. Attention to this history should have taught us that in Van Helmont's life time it was the alchemists, the believers in transmutation, who alone practised and possessed knowledge of chemistry and chemistry-based medicine. It should suffice to recall the real founder of chemistry as a scientific and academic subject, Andreas Libavius (*c.* 1560–1616), a firm believer in transmutation.

On the other hand, Van Helmont has been forcibly made into a "modern" through misinterpretation of some of his views and concepts which were really foreign to any modern trend. This is pre-eminently due to the selection and presentation of detail out of context. *Gas*, for example, meant to Van Helmont much more than an individual chemical. It was rather a cosmosophic concept, in which the recognition of a special category and grouping of volatile substances emerged as a by-product. Its wider conceptual meaning encompassed that spiritual nucleus which is the object in its true spiritual form divested of its solid husks; that is, the "energetic substance" that makes the object operational. It is true that Van Helmont, through the rejection of an unrealistic, ancient, but still-prevailing view of disease in general, arrived at a new design in which diseases became classifiable. Thereby he provided a solid basis for the modern definitions of diseases that – as it were – gain possession of and consume the body, as do parasites – the parasitistic and ontological concept of disease. Van Helmont gave due consideration to individual reactivity, again foreshadowing modern trends. The bulk of his deliberations, however, centred around ideas that are remote from anything modern. He interpreted disease spiritualistically in terms of pre-formed morbid ideas and semina, of morbid imagination and dialogues between the vital principles (the archei), of aggressors (the outside objects that inflict disease), and the aggressed (the sufferers from it, the patients).

Viewed in context, then, what seems progressive, scientific, and modern regains a complexion that is utterly different. When intimately interlarded with crass superstitious beliefs, such thinking may impress us as being mediaeval. This is not quite correct, however; Van Helmont's credulousness springs from the conviction that the power of nature is unlimited. For everything that is reported, a natural explanation must be sought by legitimate probing or argument, however circuitous and far-fetched. Nothing should be discarded out of hand as impossible or as deceit inflicted on mankind by the devil; Satan is not an authority to be invoked in matters natural. Nevertheless, the admission Van Helmont granted to stories taller than are imaginable today detracts not a little from what otherwise might have looked like sound naturalism. In fact, this cast of mind is neither mediaeval nor modern, but simply Helmontian. The same applies to his deeply felt religious sentiments, which are far from reflecting a mediaeval theology of reason, being as they are of a reflective, visionary, and ecstatic nature, coming to him in dreams by day and night. Van Helmont himself saw them as the immediate sources of his scientific, cosmological, and medical ideas, prefiguring and inspiring his *inventio*. From them as forging direct communication with God he derived his claim to express a truth which was not man-made and thus at the same time both real and divine, by contrast with the *entia rationis* of ancient tradition as stubbornly adhered to by contemporary scholastics.

Considered as a whole, then, Van Helmont's image as a key figure in scientific and medical history is decidedly complex and difficult to accommodate in a simple formula. The historian intent on presenting a figure as he "really was" cannot connive at any selective or restrictive practices whereby he is measured against present-day standards instead of those of his own period and cultural climate. He must be considered as in a world of his own – idiocentrically – rather than as a figure that is fitted into our world – nostricentrically – through consigning to the lumber-room of human error what seems irrelevant or wrong today. On the contrary, that which is not admissible in modern science and medicine or which did not help or even hindered the development of these areas to the present climax, must be examined for its historical coherence with the progressive and "legitimate" part of a work. The historian must analyse what was really meant by certain terms which have found access to modern technical nomenclature and syllabuses. Insight into their original wider (non-technical, but rather cosmosophic) meaning should inevitably uncover how such terms and concepts could have emerged from a religious and philosophical background that is foreign to the modern reader, and yet retain their relevance today, albeit in a greatly reduced key and compass. In other words, there can be no historical assessment of a figure like Van Helmont without an understanding and integration of all facets of his compound image. This presents the historian with the challenge of making himself contemporary to his subject. This effort of empathy should not obscure a figure's originality, the *simul et semel* that distinguishes his work from contemporary or older philosophies. For it will soon be seen in what respect he presents a world peculiar to himself, a synthesis in which there are no real predecessors or followers, however incisive his influence on posterity.

On the other hand, even Van Helmont did not arise in empty space. His great forerunner in rejecting all that had gone before and forging instead the basis of something new, however fanciful and ephemeral it might be in certain details, was Paracelsus. Van Helmont may even be called the outstanding Paracelsian of the second generation of Paracelsists and indeed the most successful in perpetuating the main Paracelsian principles and concepts. However, Van Helmont had distinct reservations, and felt himself to be quite independent of the master, while admitting that it was Paracelsus who had awakened him from the "dogmatic slumber" induced by traditional academic doctrines. He objected vociferously to much of Paracelsian symbolism, particularly the microcosmic analogies with the cosmos at large. These had been overriding, but Van Helmont recognised that they had no basis in reality, being admissible at best as allegory. His rejection was partly motivated by his religious mysticism: nothing should come between him and his creator, no directing authority other than God Himself, with whom he felt his immortal mind to be in immediate communication. Constituents of the greater world, especially the stars and their somewhat mechanical courses, should not enjoy any privilege of themselves or by divine commission as delegates. Any such activity would constrain the liberty of man and his creator. By and large Van Helmont finds fault with Paracelsus for not having given enough prerogative to the spiritual. He takes over the concept of tartar from Paracelsus de facto, but emphasises the difference from his own concept in that Paracelsus had in mind a merely chemical and metabolic deposition of solid material, without regard to the spiritual "ferment" that Van Helmont thought was indispensable to the very initiation of the process. In other words, he finds in Paracelsus still too many fragments, materialistic "eggshells", too great a tendency to replace the humours of the ancients by different substances which to an equal degree derive from matter alone. Most of Van Helmont's concept of disease, even its terminology, is Paracelsian, but here again his own modification consists in its further spiritualisation.

What, then, are Van Helmont's chief and original trends and tendencies? They seem to lie in his consequential and sustained effort to overcome the dualist separation of matter and spirit. He achieves this by reducing matter to an inert and "empty" medium, namely water – the water, that is, on which God "hovered" in the days of creation, planting into it the forms and ferments that are responsible for the existence of all created objects. To "become flesh" these roots combine with water; the object-specific combines with the non-specific empty medium to produce something new. This is the individual object as represented by its largely spiritual nucleus. It is the latter, its archeus or *gas*, that accounts for its activity and its direction to certain ends. In other words the object is neither matter nor spirit, but a unit with a spiritual and material root. The individual offers two sides to the observer, the psychic and the somatic. These are interchangeable since they are but aspects of the same individual unit. The unit thus remains essentially constant even when body is made volatile in the form of *gas* or when spirit is clad with material husks and made solid. Generally speaking, what engages Van Helmont's overriding interest is the quest for "thingliness", for things as they were meant to exist by the creator and which therefore do so exist in reality and truth. For him this search for object-specificity in nature constitutes the departure from ancient natural philosophy, which was concerned not with discrete individual units, not with things, but with relationships between them. Thus, he saw ancient humoralism, this being the search for "complexion" and "temperament", as the result of a proportional combination of non-specific components. Here all depended upon multiples as against units; things were not themselves, real and true, but mixtures of humours or elements in certain arithmetical proportions put together in accordance with their qualities. What really existed were therefore not things in themselves, but the mathematical patterns which made their appearance possible. It is for this reason that Van Helmont inveighs against the introduction of mathematical considerations into natural philosophy. It may well be found difficult to reconcile with his persistent use of the balance and quantification to which he owed not a few of his innovations. However, applying quantification as a tool is one thing; to regard it as the key to deciphering the hieroglyphic script of nature is another. What Van Helmont really aimed at in his criticism was the dominant role granted to complacent human reason in general – an un-Christian heathenish heresy that had led mankind away from God.

All this points to the highly complex character of Van Helmont's work, the intricate interaction of disparate motives, in particular the inclination to religious-mystical meditation and legitimate scientific research. To examine, not either of these, but both in a coherence which must have existed between them in his mind, must claim priority in any account which sets out to present a true portrait of the man. This complexity, however, only reflects the complexity of the *Zeitgeist*, the intellectual climate in which Van Helmont worked, and indeed of the seventeenth century which gave birth to modern science. As in the case of Van Helmont himself, the achievements of this period cannot be represented as a forceful drive in a single direction, but as the result of complicated and apparently contradictory tendencies. At all events, what seems contradictory to the mind of the modern observer should challenge him to seek for an explanation. Returning then to our initial question, why study Van Helmont? – the answer should be: to obtain and to enjoy insight into the true character of the cradle of modern science.

BIBLIOGRAPHY OF VAN HELMONT

The Ortus *and the* Opera

There are four quarto and three folio editions.
A. First Edition. *Ortus Medicinae. Id est, initia physicae inaudita. Progressus medicinae novus, in morborum ultionem, ad vitam longam . . . Edente authoris filio, Francisco Mercurio Van Helmont, Cum ejus praefatione ex Belgico translatâ.* Amsterdam, apud Ludovicum Elzevirium, 1648. 4°.

Followed by: *Opuscula medica inaudita. I. De lithiasi. II. De febribus. III. De humoribus Galeni. IV. De peste. Editio secunda.* Amsterdam, apud Ludovicum Elzevirium, 1648.

The first edition of the *Ortus* has been cited herein unless otherwise stated.
B. Second Edition. *Ortus Medicinae. Id est, initia physicae inaudita . . . Nostra autem haec editio, emendatius multo, & auctius cum indice . . . Ad clarissimum, & excellentissimum virum Antonium Serrati . . . Venetum.* Venice, apud Juntas & Joannem Jacobum Hertz, 1651. F°.

Followed by: *Doctrina inaudita, de causis, modo fiendi, contentis, radice et resolutione lithiasis itemque De sensu, sensatione, dolore, insensibilitate, stupore, motu, immobilitate, prout de morbis huius classis, lepra, caduco, apoplexia, paralysi, spasmo, comate, etc. Nova et paradoxa hactenus omnia. Tractatus tam physico, et medico, quam spagyro utilis: miseris autem utilissimus.* Venice, 1651.

The second edition is distinguished by its excellent printing and its ornateness, and by the first appearance of the invaluable index, which was hardly improved on in subsequent editions, in spite of claims to the contrary. The index was prepared by Otho Tachenius (fl. 1650–post 1699; M. D. Padua 1652), known for his advances in chemistry in the Helmontian and Sylvian tradition: See Partington, *History of Chemistry*, ii, 291–6. The recommendation of the *Opuscula* on the title-page as 'Spagyro utilis: miseris utilissimus' is significant.

C. Third Edition. As (A)....*Editio nova, cumque indice, pro illa Venetiis nuper excusa adauctior reddita & exornatior.* Amsterdam, Elzevir, 1652. 4°.

Followed by *Opuscula.*

D. Fourth Edition. *Ortus Medicinae...Editio quarta. In qua praeter quaedam auth. fragmenta adiecti fuerunt indices*.... Lyons, sumptibus Joannis Baptistae Devenet, 1655. F°. Index as in previous editions.

Followed by *Opuscula.*

E. Fifth Edition. As (D). Lyons, 1667. F°.

F. Sixth Edition. *Opera omnia. Additis his de novo tractatibus aliquot posthumis...antehac non in lucem editis; una cum indicibus.* Frankfurt, sumptibus Johannis Justi Erythropili, typis Johannis Philippi Andreae, 1682. 4°.

Followed by *Opuscula.*

This edition (abbrev. *Opp.*) is that quoted herein, unless otherwise stated.

G. Seventh (and Last) Edition. *Opera omnia, Novissima hac editione ab innumeris mendis repurgata, et indice...instructa, una cum introductione atque clavi Michaelis Bernhardi Valentini, Haereditarii in Dirshrot, Phil. et Med. Prof. P. Gisseni, Archiatri Hasso-Darmstatini.* Frankfurt, ex bibliopolio Hafniensi. Hieronymi Christiano Paulli, 1707. 4°.

Followed by *Opuscula.*

This is a reprint of the 1682 edition with identical pagination; it includes a short introductory vindication of Van Helmont and a useful glossary of Helmontian terms, also a fair number of printer's errors. Valentini (1657–1729) is the author of *Museum museorum* (1704–14). See J. Pagel, in Hirsch (ed.), *Biog. Lex. hervorr. Ärzte*, vi, 57.

Translations of the Ortus

1. *Aufgang der Artzney-Kunst, das ist: Noch nie erhörte Grund-Lehren von der Natur, zu einer neuen Beförderung der Artzney-Sachen, sowol die Kranckheiten zu vertreiben als ein langes Leben zu erlangen. Geschrieben von Johann Baptista von Helmont, auf Merode, Royenborch, Oorschot, Pellines etc. Erbherrn. Anitzo auf Beyrahten*

dessen Herrn Sohnes, Herrn H. Francisci Mercurii Freyherrn von Helmont, In die Hochteutsche Sprache übersetzt, in seine rechte Ordnung gebracht, mit Beyfügung dessen, was in der Ersten auf Niederländisch gedruckten Edition, genannt Die Morgen Röhte. . .auch einem vollständigen Register. Sultzbach, Johann Andreae Endters Sel. Söhne, 1683. Reprinted, and edited by W. Pagel and F. Kemp, 2 vols., Munich, Kösel, 1971.

On the editor of the *Aufgang*, see 1971 repr. pp. xxi–xxxviii. The *Aufgang* is an exemplary work, indispensable for its correct and apt translation, the much improved arrangement of the treatises, the commentaries, especially those on chemical and alchemical subjects, and for the insertion of supplementary passages translated from the *Dageraad*. It is obvious that, through his close cooperation with the younger Van Helmont, Knorr had access to material previously unknown: See p. 93, note 168, this volume.

2. *Oriatrike, Or, Physick Refined. The Common Errors therein Refuted, And the whole Art Reformed & Rectified: Being a New Rise and Progress of Phylosophy and Medicine, for the Destruction of Diseases and Prolongation of Life. . .now faithfully rendred into English, in tendency to a common good, and the increase of true Science; by J. C. Sometime of M. H. Oxon* [John Chandler of Magdalen Hall, Oxford]. London, Printed for Lodowick Loyd, 1662. Second edition, London, 1664, as *Van Helmont's Works*.

The English translation is both useful and akin to the original, although sometimes quite incorrect.

3. *Les Oeuvres de Jean Baptiste Van Helmont, traittant des principes de médecine et physique, pour la guérison assurée des maladies: De la traduction de M. Jean Leconte, docteur médecin.* Lyons, I. A. Huguetan, 1670.

An unsatisfactory selection of pieces.

Juvenilia

These were first edited by Broeckx:
C. Broeckx, *Commentaire de J. B. Van Helmont sur le premier livre du Régime d'Hippocrate: peri diaites* (Antwerp, 1849); idem, 'Commentaire de J. B. Van Helmont sur un livre d'Hippocrate intitulé: peri trophes', *Annales de l'Académie archéol. belg.*, 8(1851), 399–433, reprinted separately Antwerp, 1851; idem, 'Le pre-

mier ouvrage (Eisagoge in artem medicam a Paracelso restitutam, 1607) de J. B. Van Helmont', ibid., 10(1853), 327–92, and 11(1854), 119–91, reprinted separately Antwerp, 1854.

The Dageraad

Dageraad, oft nieuwe opkomst der geneeskonst, in verborgen grondt-regulen der Natuere...Noit in't licht gesien, en van den Autheur selve in't Nederduits beschreven. Amsterdam, Jan Jacob Schipper, 1659. Also Rotterdam, Joannes Naeranus, 1660; facsimile reprint of 1660 edition by Flemish Academy of Medicine, Antwerp, 1944. See also p. 14, this volume.

Editions and translations of treatises

1. *Disputatio de magnetica vulnerum naturali et legitima curatione, contra R. P. Joannem Roberti.* Paris, Victor Leroy, 1621. Also Liège, 1634. See pp. 8–13, this volume.
2. *Supplementum de Spadanis fontibus.* Liège, apud Strael, 1624.
3. *Febrium doctrina inaudita.* Antwerp, apud viduam Joan. Cnobbari, 1642. Second edition, see (4):...*Editio secunda, Accessit Tractatus contra quatuor humores Scholarum.* Cologne, apud Jodocum Kalcoven, 1664. Followed by *Scholarum humoristarum passiva deceptio atque ignorantia* and *Appendix ad tractatum de febribus sive Caput XVI.*
4. *Opuscula medica inaudita. I. De lithiasi. II. De febribus.* [i.e., second edition; see (3)] *III. De humoribus Galeni. IV. De peste.* Cologne, apud Jodocum Kalcoven, 1644.
5. *A Ternary of Paradoxes. The Magnetick Cure of Wounds. Nativity of Tartar in Wine. Image of God in Man...Translated, Illustrated and Ampliated by Walter Charleton.* London, by James Flesher for William Lee, 1650. Also 'Second impression, more reformed', etc., London, 1650.
6. *Deliramenta Catarrhi: or, the Incongruities, Impossibilities, and Absurdities Couched under the Vulgar Opinion of Defluxions...The Translator and Paraphrast Dr Charleton.* London, by E.G. for William Lee, 1650.
7. *Tumulus Pestis; Das ist, Gründlicher Ursprung der Pest Dero Wesen Art und Eigenschafft; als auch deroselben zuverlässig-und beständiger Genesung. Nebenst Beyfügung der wahren Ursach und Grund*

allerhand Fieber; und worinnen bis zu dato in Curirung derselben ist geirret worden. Durch Jo. Baptistam von Helmont. . .in Nieder-Teutsch; und folgend auch Lateinisch beschrieben. Anjetzo aber bey obschwebenden gefährlichen Läuffen und grassirenden Seuchen männiglich zum besten, aus dem Niederländischen ubersetzt. Durch Johannem Henricum Seyfrid. Sultzbach, Druckts Abraham Liechtenthaler, 1681.

Interesting bibliographical points are the priority given to the *Dageraad* and its use as an original text, the proximity in time and place of printing to Knorr's *Aufgang*, and the choice of Lichtenthaler, the publisher of Franciscus Mercurius's *Alphabeti vere naturalis Hebraici brevissima delineatio* (1667).

8. *Die Morgenröthe. Das ist fünff herrliche und geheimnissvolle Receptbücher zum leiblichen wohl der Menscheit.* . . .Sultzbach, J. A. Endter, 1683.

This is a revised anthology of parts of *In verbis, herbis et lapidibus* and *De vita longa*, taken from *Aufgang*, pp. 1061 et seq., 1077 et seq., 1093 et seq., 1247 et seq., and 1261 et seq., respectively.

9. *Irrwitz der Katarrhlehre. Asthma und Husten. Tobende Pleura.* All in W. Pagel, *Jo. Bapt. Van Helmont. Einführung in die philosophische Medizin des Barock* (Berlin, 1930), pp. 144–219.

New German translations.

10. *De tempore.* Par. 1–46 in W. Pagel, 'J. B. Van Helmont, De tempore and Biological Time', *Osiris*, 8(1948), 356–76.

A new English translation.

Letters

These are published in P. Tannery and C. de Waard (eds.), *Correspondence du P. Marin Mersenne*, Vols. I–III (Paris, 1932–46). The fourteen extant items (three appear in Vol. II, eleven in Vol. III) were written between 1630 and 1631. For a detailed discussion see p. 93, this volume.

Portraits

The only authentic portrait forms part of the double vignette of the Helmonts, father and son, which occurs as the frontispiece to all editions of the *Ortus* and *Opera* except the second Venetian folio edition of 1651. The large portrait adorning the *Aufgang* of 1683 is obviously based on the frontispiece to the *Ortus* of 1648. The large oil painting by Sir Peter Lely (1618–1680) in the National Portrait Gallery, London (see M. Davies, *National Gallery Catalogues. The British School*, 2nd edn., London, 1959, p. 75, No. 3583), represents Franciscus Mercurius, not Joan Baptista Van Helmont. It has misled several authors. Its date is about 1671, that is, some thirty years after the father's death. The son stayed for a considerable time in England with Lady Conway, to whom Henry More wrote in 1671: 'Mr Lilly told me he had drawn Mr V Helmonts picture which yett I had not the happinesse to see': M. H. Nicolson, *Conway Letters* (London, 1930), p. 322 et seq.

De Waele (1947) reproduces the portrait bust in the Palais des Académies (Académie Royale de Belgique) of 1814 and rightly derives it from the frontispiece vignette of 1648.

INDEX